The Arkana Dictionary
of New Perspectives

Stuart Holroyd was born in Yorkshire in 1933 and is a graduate of the universities of London and Sussex. Now a full-time author, he has written nearly twenty books covering a wide range of topics. His more recent titles include *Psi and the Consciousness Explosion, Alien Intelligence* and *The Quest of the Quiet Mind.*

D1227900

THE ARKANA DICTIONARY OF
NEW PERSPECTIVES

———

STUART HOLROYD

ARKANA

ARKANA

Published by the Penguin Group
27 Wrights Lane, London w8 5tz, England
Viking Penguin Inc., 40 West 23rd Street, New York, New York 10010, USA
Penguin Books Australia Ltd, Ringwood, Victoria, Australia
Penguin Books Canada Ltd, 2801 John Street, Markham, Ontario, Canada l3r 1b4
Penguin Books (NZ) Ltd, 182–190 Wairau Road, Auckland 10, New Zealand

Penguin Books Ltd, Registered Offices: Harmondsworth, Middlesex, England

First published 1989
10 9 8 7 6 5 4 3 2 1

Copyright © Stuart Holroyd, 1989
All rights reserved

Made and printed in Great Britain by
Richard Clay Ltd, Bungay, Suffolk

Filmset in 9 on 10 pt Monophoto Baskerville

Except in the United States of America, this book is sold subject
to the condition that it shall not, by way of trade or otherwise, be lent,
re-sold, hired out, or otherwise circulated without the
publisher's prior consent in any form of binding or cover other than
that in which it is published and without a similar condition
including this condition being imposed on the subsequent purchaser

Contents

PREFACE

Deference to the Chinese classic, the I CHING[3], forbade my calling this 'A Book of Changes', but if the title had been available it would have been apt. There are on the one hand events that change the world, and on the other hand there are fundamental changes that may or may not manifest in specific events, and while the former are the staple of orthodox historical study, the latter are often too indeterminate and fugitive for the historian's attention. It is with such changes that the present book is primarily concerned. They are more often changes in our perceptual, mental or experiential perspectives upon the world than in the world itself. Such changes are not always equatable with or determined by the advent of something new, or by progress in science or technology. They may consist as much in rediscovery as in discovery, in shifts in human priorities and purposes as much as in increments in knowledge or power, in image change as much as in material change. Change is of its nature a time-related concept, and we are accustomed to thinking of it in terms of progress, of the future coming into our world and our lives and requiring us to accommodate to it; but it may equally come from the past, from the wealth of knowledge that has accrued from man's experience of and endeavours in the world. New perspectives open up in both time directions.

This preamble is by way of explaining what some will consider the incoherence of this book, the incompatibility of some of its subjects, the juxtaposition of science with so-called pseudo-science, of approved orthodox ideas and subjects with speculative cultic alternative ones. The idea that science should consort with ESOTERICISM[3], psychology with parapsychology, orthodox medicine with alternative medicine, the established culture with the counterculture that seeks to subvert it, is still for many people heresy or sheer humbug. Oddly, though, it is not so heretical to propose that significant changes are often engendered by such seemingly mismatched couplings. To look at something from a different perspective, to throw light upon it from an unusual angle, is known as LATERAL THINKING[1], and is respectable. For orthodoxy, heterodox perspectives are all right as vantage points, or goads to creative thought, but not to be taken seriously as subjects in their own right. That some of them are so taken in the present book will no doubt give offence and draw predictable criticism. Parapsychology, for instance, is still widely regarded as a crank science, and the phenomena it deals with as either illusory or the subject of unscrupulous charlatanry. That it is given an independent section here will be rightly construed as authorial bias.

But then any dictionary or encylopaedia of modern thought that you care to consult will have a bias. One of the things that gave rise to the present work was the author's dissatisfaction, sometimes irritation, with the tendentious treatment of many subjects, and the omission of many others, in a certain compendious volume which purports to be an authoritative guide to modern thought.

A consensus of assumptions as to what is real and what is relevant underlies human thought and endeavours in any society or historical period, and when great achievements issue from this consensus they serve to consolidate it. But any consensus is by definition a tacit agreement to settle belief and opinion upon a bedrock of metaphysical premisses, which are, for all the authority they may accrue, human intellectual constructs. Even bedrock shifts, as the tectonic plates of the earth's crust shift, maybe slowly and imperceptibly, but ultimately to bring about tremendous changes. The metaphysical assumptions of the scientific-rational-materialistic worldview that have determined the consensus reality of Western societies over the last three centuries have been subjected to some seismic tremors of late, and some cracks have appeared in the impressive superstructure that have cast doubt upon the soundness of its foundations. A purpose of the present book is to expose some of the cracks and probe some of the foundational fractures.

I have written 'of late', 'new' and 'modern', and perhaps some clarification of these imprecise terms is called for. Some of the alleged new perspectives, for instance RELATIVITY THEORY [2] and FREUDIAN PSYCHOLOGY [4], were opened up in the early years of the present century, but they are included here because they precipitated a momentum of fundamental change, both in and beyond their specific subject areas, that can only be comprehended by reference to them. The mental and material world that the educated person will inhabit around the year 2000 will be very different from the one his counterpart in the year 1900 inhabited and, roughly speaking, 'new' in the present context refers to the changes that will constitute this difference. To propose to be comprehensive in such an enterprise of analysis and prescience would be presumptuous even for an interdisciplinary committee of august authorities, and I am well aware of the partiality, in both senses of the term, of the present book. But if it throws light on some of the changes we have gone through and are still going through, if it opens up some new perspectives upon the world and the future, and if it contributes a little to the understanding of how arbitrary are some assumptions widely considered to be axiomatic, it will serve its purpose and its time.

The Arkana Dictionary of New Perspectives is intended both as a reader and as a reference book, and the treatment of subject entries accordingly ranges from the short essay to the brief definition. In the interests of coherence, and for the convenience of the reader as distinct from the referer, entries have been subdivided into seven sections. The first, 'Worldview', deals with philosophical terms and modern movements, and with ideas of general relevance to the new perspectives viewpoint. Many such ideas derive from science, or base their authority on it, and there is a certain area of overlap with the second section, which deals with specific developments in twentieth-century science, in particular physics, and both orthodox and unorthodox ideas that have evolved from these developments. The jump to the third section, 'Spirituality and Esoteric Thought', may seem abrupt in view of the traditional antagonism between science and religion, but one of the major changes that have been taking place recently has been the dissolution of this antagonism, with the erosion of the MATERIALIST[1] and POSITIVIST[1] basis of science and the dogmatic sectarianism of religion, and even the acknowledgement of some common ground. 'Psychology', the subject of the fourth section, has seen twentieth-century revolutions as radical, and as prodigal with new ideas, as the revolutions in science, and the development of new criteria of mental health and human potentials together with innovative therapies and trainings designed to fulfil them. There remains, however, a whole area of human experience and capability that both science and psychology have tended to ignore, although (or because) it carries implications in respect of the physical world and of human nature that are difficult to reconcile with prevailing ideas in these disciplines, and this is the subject of the fifth section, 'The Paranormal'. The sixth, 'Medicine and Health', surveys another area where demonstrable effects are often irreconcilable with the causes that orthodoxy acknowledges and the conceptual and methodological approaches that it sanctions. The final section, 'Society, Environment and Technology', deals with contemporary and planetary situations and problems and ideas and movements relevant to them, and hazards some peeps into the future but leaves to the reader so disposed the task of inferring from facts as to how the world is a prognosis as to how it may become.

There are inevitably omissions, and some no doubt will be accounted grievous. I can only say I regret them and apologize, but hope that what is included will compensate and prove usefully informative.

Note

CAPITALIZED terms cross-refer to other entries in the dictionary, and when these are in a different section a figure above the term indicates which one (e.g. ANDROGYNY* refers the reader to the entry on androgyny in the fourth section, 'Psychology'). An asterisk * above a name indicates that further biographical and/or bibliographical information will be found in the Names index and/or the Bibliography. Numbers in square brackets at the end of entries refer to the Bibliography and identify source material and recommended further reading.

I

WORLDVIEW

Anthropic principle

Nineteenth-century theologians were fond of the 'argument from design'. If a watch implied the existence of a watchmaker, William Paley argued, the wondrous design of the universe and of man implied the existence of the Creator. Since then physical science and cosmology have ascertained facts that make the evidence for design even more cogent than the mechanical watch analogy did. The existence and continuance of life in general and human life in particular depends on the co-incidence of thousands of felicitous conditions which it is inconceivable could pertain by blind chance. A slight variation in any of the physical constants that constitute the 'laws' of the universal order would have resulted in conditions inhospitable to life. From the 'BIG BANG²' onwards, everything seems to have been designed and orchestrated to favour human life. This fact is known as the anthropic principle. It is not necessarily taken as evidence for the divine governance of life and the universe, or even for the existence of an inherent intelligent ordering and purposive principle. Sceptics tend to decry 'anthropic reasoning' as *a posteriori* thinking, although the facts that constitute the anthropic principle are beyond dispute, and the alternative 'blind chance' explanation of them would appear to rest upon a faith no less naïve even if ostensibly more scientific. [136]

Aquarian conspiracy

A term coined by Marilyn Ferguson* to designate a loose-knit group, or network, of people, engaged in a wide range of professions and activities, whose work is intelligently future-oriented and consistent with the several PARADIGM shifts that are taking place at the present time. These people constitute a 'conspiracy' not in the manner of ideologues and terrorists; they are concerned not so much with overthrowing the old as with creating the new. Typical shifts in emphasis brought about by 'conspirators' are: in politics and business, from competition and exploitation to co-operation and consensus; in education, from performance and achievement to developing capacities for intelligent evaluation and encouraging ongoing learning; in health care, from deferment to specialists and institutions to self- and mutual-help; in industry, from a growth and profit-maximizing orientation to a resource-conserving and ecologically responsible one. [88]

Cartesian

Belonging to the philosophy of René Descartes*.

Catastrophe theory

The theory that in the geological evolution of the earth there were episodes of cataclysmic change which separated land masses, threw up mountain ranges, and possibly exterminated life. The alternative, and more widely held and orthodox view, known as uniformitarianism, holds that geological changes occurred gradually over aeons of time. When the two alternative views were debated in the nineteenth century, catastrophe theory suffered from association with biblical fundamentalism, and the more rational uniformitarian view prevailed. But catastrophe theory has steadily gained ground in the present century, with the accumulation of palaeontological, climatic and archaeological evidence to support it. Its main advocate has been Immanuel Velikovsky*, who in a number of books presented a wealth of evidence and argument that challenged the orthodox view. The fact that the alleged evidence was drawn from disparate sources, including ancient literatures and folklore, discredited Velikovsky in the eyes of many scholars, but some were influenced to look at the evidence afresh and to take catastrophe theory more seriously.

Possibly more influential has been the general acceptance by geologists of the theory of continental drift, which holds that originally all the continents constituted a single land mass, which broke into pieces and drifted apart. Continental drift is said to be occurring all the time, through the relative movements of the plates that constitute the earth's crust, and the phenomenon is not inconsistent with uniformitarianism, but until quite recently it was considered as outlandish as catastrophe theory in general. Because catastrophe theory is invoked by believers in lost or submerged continents and civilizations (Atlantis, Lemuria), or in imminent cataclysms that will fulfil prophecy or give an errant human race its just deserts, it is understandably regarded with some

scepticism, but the evidence for it purely as a geological theory is substantial and difficult to reconcile with the conservative uniformitarian and gradualist view. [334, 335, 336]

Causality

The fact that events or situations have antecedent events or situations that bring them about is fundamental to our experience and to our sense of living in a coherent and manageable world. But when we say that an event or situation is caused by another or a convergence of others, we generally mean that there exists a relation between them specifiable in terms of physical laws, and modern physics has shown this to be not always or necessarily the case. Whether this is because there are no such laws, or because we cannot fully comprehend them, has been the vexed question, and the great intellectual problem for philosophical physicists in the present century has been to decide whether the universe is fundamentally incoherent or merely incomprehensible. The concept of causality has been at the root of this problem, and for instance the ERP EXPERIMENT[2] appeared to imply a fundamental incoherence that Einstein* and others found distressing and unacceptable. The idea that events or situations might be coherently related without there being any material or physical connection between them has emerged from modern QUANTUM PHYSICS[2] as an alternative to the concept of physically deterministic causality. The same idea was proposed by

Carl Jung* in this essay on SYN-CHRONICITY, which he called a 'non-causal connecting principle'. Jung sought to specify a principle that would explain certain psychic events and experiences and also esoteric methods of divination such as the I CHING[3], which the ideas of physical causality and of a chain of causes and effects could not explain. Instead of the metaphor of a chain, modern theoretical physicists prefer that of a web, an intricately connected whole in which any event has repercussions throughout the whole system. Although we may usefully isolate chains of physical causes and effects, for instance in medical science, we cannot assume on the basis of results so achieved that causality is necessarily chain-like and physical. Even in such isolated chains, coherence and predictability are rarely total. Indeed, they are only ever so in simple mechanical systems. In living systems, and in life and the world generally, there is such a complex of interactivity and interdependence that the concept of local or proximate causes is quite inadequate. Rather, it seems that everything affects everything else, and specific effects can only be predicted on a basis of statistical probability. [161]

Cognitive dissonance

The incompatibility of fact or theory with an established belief system gives rise to cognitive dissonance. The term was coined by the psychologist L. Festinger*. The corresponding term 'cognitive consonance' designates the consistency and coherence of knowledge and ideas comprising a belief system. Festinger demonstrated that when cognitive dissonance arises people seek to diminish it, generally by denying the truth or reality of the ideas or facts that cannot be coherently assimilated to the established belief system. Orthodox science comprises such a belief system, and Thomas Kuhn's* analysis of how scientists reject anomalies and novelties that are not consistent with the prevailing PARADIGM may be cited in support of Festinger's theory. [89]

Coincidence

'Puns of destiny', Arthur Koestler* called them. Everyone has experiences of unusual and highly improbable convergences of events, sometimes seemingly providential, often quite trivial, which appear to occur by chance but are perceived as meaningful, whether highly significantly or fugitively. 'Mere coincidence' is often invoked as an explanation of PARA-NORMAL PHENOMENA[5], with the implication that such rogue events are of the nature of things, sports quite consistent with PROB-ABILITY[2] theory, and their meaning is not intrinsic but projected upon them by the mind. However, in some cultures and by some philosophers chance and coincidence and their implications have been more profoundly considered (see SYNCHRONICITY, I CHING[3]). [168]

Continental drift

See CATASTROPHE THEORY.

Demythologize

To render the spiritual meanings of scripture more accessible by distinguishing them from the myths and legends in which they are enshrined. The theologian Rudolf Bultmann* argued that the imagery and symbolism appropriate to the propagation of the Christian message in the first century AD was not appropriate to its propagation in the twentieth century, although the underlying message is as relevant now as it was then, and that it was the function of a modern theology to translate the message into terms compatible with modern philosophy and science. The principle that scripture can and should be demythologized, and that belief in its literal truth is not incumbent upon Christians, is now widely accepted, but there is no consensus among Christian thinkers as to precisely what needs to be demythologized, and how. [199]

Determinism

In philosophy, the theory that every event or condition in the world is the inevitable outcome of antecedent causes. The theory has implications for moral philosophy, for scientific thought, and for psychology. In respect of morality, if it is true, choice and free will are illusory and human beings may not be held responsible or accountable for their actions. In science, determinism allied with MECHANISM remained the dominant orthodoxy until QUANTUM PHYSICS[2] drew attention to the fundamental indeterminacy of events at the subatomic level. In psychology, determinism is the philosophical cornerstone of both the FREUDIAN[4] and the BEHAVIOURIST[4] theories and practices. While nobody could seriously argue that events and conditions are not determined by antecedents, or dispute the value, in science and psychology, of studying and comprehending causal relations between events, it does seem that a thoroughgoing deterministic theory and approach is both scientifically insupportable and practically too restrictive. [45, 273]

Dialectic

In philosophy, a method of arriving at truth by rationally resolving an interplay of opinions, in the manner exemplified in the Socratic dialogues of Plato. Whereas the analytical method applies logic to the data established by observation or experience of the world, the dialectical method applies it to beliefs or opinions about the world. In nineteenth-century IDEALISM, in particular in Hegel*, the dialectical process became not only a method of reasoning about the world but also a dynamic of development in the world itself, through the conflicts of antitheses being resolved in achieved syntheses. In MARXISM, the principle was applied to history, and the development of human societies was construed as the product of conflict between different classes and social systems.

Dogma

A belief or teaching, the truth of which is deemed by its adherents to be so self-evident or authoritative as to be beyond dispute or private judgement. Originally confined to religious beliefs and having a merely descriptive meaning, use of the term has in the present century spread to other fields, notably to politics and science, and its meaning has become pejorative.

Dualism

The theory that to comprehend life or the universe a distinction must be made between two irreducibly different kinds of thing. In philosophy, the Platonic distinction between eternal forms, or ideas, and temporal objects, or phenomena, produced a conceptual dualism to do with appearance and reality, to which most philosophers in the western tradition have subscribed (see IDEALISM). Descartes'* mind-body dualism proved a distinction of more than academic implication (see MIND-BODY PROBLEM). Although in practice too rigid a demarcation between the physical and the mental, for instance in clinically treating one aspect irrespective of the other, is incompatible with HOLISTIC thinking and approaches, the fact that the brain and the mind, or the body and the soul, are entities of different natures and potentially independent although generally interactive, is suggested by both modern neurophysiological and PSI[5] research.

Empiricism

In philosophy, the view that the only sound basis for knowledge is experience, and that the only relevant modalities of experience are sensory. Empiricism denies the existence of any innate ideas in the human mind and regards it as originally a *tabula rasa*, or blank slate, upon which sense-experience impinges a multiplicity of impressions which the mind then proceeds to co-ordinate into laws. It follows that there can be no *a priori* (i.e. prior to experience) laws or concepts, and that inferences from experience (for instance that the sun will rise tomorrow) do not imply the existence or operation of any such law. Some empiricists admit a limited range of data derived from introspection as experiential, but all would deny the validity of any proposition as to knowledge or truth based on intuition or the idea of an innate property of the mind or the world. Empiricism specifically repudiates propositions in the realm of METAPHYSICS. As a school of philosophy, it is chiefly associated with the British tradition consolidated by David Hume*, John Locke* and Bishop Berkeley*, and its authority was reinforced by its close links with the development of the classical SCIENTIFIC METHOD[2].

Evolution

The process of the emergence of progressively more complex forms of life or organization from simpler forms. The fact that over the millennia biological life on earth has evolved, producing both a greater diversity of species and an improvement within some species, is almost universally accepted (dissent being limited, by and large, to certain Christian fundamentalists). But questions about what initiated evolution, what principle governs the process, whether evolution occurs gradually or in spurts, and whether it is still going on, are highly controversial. LAMARCK-ISM[2], which holds that acquired characteristics can be inherited, is generally discredited, but it still has adherents and some scientific evidence that apparently supports it. DARWINISM[2] and neo-Darwinism, which hold that evolution occurs through random mutation, represent the orthodox viewpoint in evolution theory. Recently, however, serious flaws in Darwinian theory have been uncovered and some alternative theories have been proposed. As the orthodox theory supports the related philosophical concepts of MATERIALISM, MECHANISM and POSITIVISM, and as the alternative theories repudiate these concepts, evolution theory is a chief focus of discussion about the 'PARADIGM shift'.

Arguments against the idea that blind chance determines evolution have gained strength from recent discoveries about the complexity of genetic material and the amino acids that constitute organic life. Orthodox theory sees the origin of life (see LIFE: ORIGIN OF[2]) as a coming together of amino acids in a primeval chemical broth until a level of complexity is attained which endows the aggregate with the properties of life. However, as Fred Hoyle* and others have demonstrated, when this hypothesis is examined in the light of mathematical probability, its plausibility is considerably diminished. Similarly, mathematics shows the Darwinian principle of evolution through natural selection of random genetic mutations to be extremely unlikely, as any significant evolutionary change would require a large number of simultaneous, co-ordinated mutations.

The alternative explanation is that evolution is governed by a principle of selection that is intelligent, i.e. capable of discrimination in order to ensure the appearance and survival of increasingly complex life forms. Whether this principle is an immanent property of life or transcends it, and whether the evolutionary process is fulfilling a predesigned plan, are metaphysical questions that cannot at present be resolved scientifically. Theories have been proposed to support both views.

The idea that an inherent property of life is an inexorable drive towards greater complexity and order is proposed by GENERAL SYSTEMS THEORY. According to this theory, the stability of a living system is always liable to be disrupted by the pressures of internal fluctuations. When such disruption occurs, a principle of SELF-ORGANIZATION within the system enables it to transform itself into a new system with a higher degree of complexity and order. The theory does not posit the existence of a predetermined evolutionary plan. It does, however, imply that evolution is purposive, although its purposes are not preordained and referential to an ultimate target state, but rather are specified variously and progressively by the living systems themselves as an essential component of the dynamic of self-transcendence that characterizes them.

Theories that postulate a transcendent cause and governance for evolution have clear correspondences to the traditional religious views that Darwin refuted, but in their modern formulations they are not a return to pre-Darwinian naïve fundamentalism. One major theory is that of Pierre Teilhard de Chardin*, who proposed that as biological evolution progressed, new properties emerged, in particular CONSCIOUSNESS[4] and spirituality. He further proposed that these properties exist not only in human beings but also in larger organized systems (see NOOSPHERE[3]), that their appearance is ordained and overseen by God, and that evolution is working to fulfil a divine plan.

The existence of the higher human faculties of creativity, artistic and mathematical genius, the moral sense, and the religious impulse, cannot easily be explained in terms of Darwinism. According to orthodox evolution theory, each adaptation occurs to fulfil a need; yet such higher faculties confer no advantage in the struggle for existence. Indeed, as Nietzsche and other philosophers have pointed out, they can be positively disadvantageous. This fact has led some theorists to postulate a special status for human beings in the evolutionary scheme. Some suggest a return to the traditional view of man as the lord or steward of creation. Others regard life and evolution as cosmic, rather than purely terrestrial, phenomena, and see the higher faculties of man as means of participating in the functioning of a cosmic intelligence. Hoyle, for

instance, postulates an 'information-rich' universe, and suggests that the information that controls the processes of life and evolution comes from a cosmic mind that embraces all space and time.

As for the precise mechanism that governs evolution, the evidence of the fossil record does not support the orthodox theory of step-by-step gradualism. It appears to support, rather, the theory of PUNCTUATED EQUILIBRIUM[2], which maintains that evolution takes place in 'jumps' (or *per saltum* as Darwin expressed it when he considered the possibility and rejected it as irreconcilable with his own theory). The credibility of punctuated equilibrium, as developed by palaeontologist Stephen Jay Gould*, is enhanced by its consistency with general systems theory. That it carries the implication that a major evolutionary leap can take place in a short time, and thus could in the present time, is a fact which leads some of its critics to reject it as wishful thinking and some of its supporters to embrace it as a hopeful portent. [51, 61, 62, 111, 136]

Existentialism

A European philosophical movement which originated as a revolt against Hegelian IDEALISM by the Danish philosopher Søren Kierkegaard*. Its fundamental principle is that for human beings 'existence precedes essence', i.e. man finds himself in existence in the world compelled to act and to choose, and through his acts and choices he makes and defines his essential self. Kierkegaard rejected not only the abstract totalizing philosophy of Hegel*, but also orthodox Christian doctrine concerning the relations of man to God. He insisted on the inscrutability of divine purposes, the separateness of God and man, and the importance of the subjective pursuit of truth, particularly in situations of ethical choice.

Twentieth-century existentialism took up Kierkegaard's concern with the metaphysical and ethical implications of the human situation in a world not governed by divine purposes and sanctions. It stressed the human need to discover and establish a personal 'authentic existence'. For Martin Heidegger*, the prerequisite of this was the individual's recognition of his mortality, of death and nothingness as his ultimate state. Jean-Paul Sartre* took from Heidegger the concept of two distinct modes of being, being-in-itself (*être-en-soi*) and being-for-itself (*être-pour-soi*). The former is the mode of being of things, the latter should be the mode of human beings, although it rarely is because human beings allow themselves to be determined in their existence and their choices by others, by conforming with expectations or roles. They relinquish the freedom that is fundamental and unique to the human condition, and thus live inauthentically, or in 'bad faith' (*mauvais foi*). Authentic existence may be bleak, may offer no solace for the despair and anguish that arises from consciousness of the contingency, finiteness and absurdity of the individual human life, but it is noble in its stoicism and in its acceptance of the existential consequences of human freedom.

Although Sartre stressed this noble aspect of existentialism, and even claimed that it was a form of HUMANISM, and although Heidegger stressed that in the realization of authentic existence there arose care for others (*Sorge*), the philosophy's implicit nihilism and antinomianism, and its tendency to invest anguish and alienation with a romantic *élan*, have sometimes, both in the arts and in conduct, been superficially construed as justifications for an irresponsible licence. [125, 164, 283, 284, 362]

Games theory

The development of military, economic, political and business strategies has been influenced by modern games theory, originally developed by the mathematician John von Neumann*. It is a theory of the rational behaviour of two or more people in circumstances of conflict or competition. In what von Neumann called 'zero-sum' games, there are two persons involved and a gain for one results in a corresponding loss for the other. Strategies to minimize the loss that one can impose on the other produce a situation of equilibrium, known as the 'minimax solution', which depends upon a player being able to choose at random from a variety of strategies available to him. In further developments of the theory, concepts relevant to games involving a number of participants were proposed, which might involve co-operation and the formation of coalitions. The best-known example of games theory, because it emphasizes the paradoxicality of conflict situations, is the so-called 'prisoner's dilemma', in which, given the strategy available to the other, neither player would wish to change his own move, although the resultant situation is worse for both players than any alternative. [235, 335]

General semantics

A proposed 'non-Aristotelian' system of science and philosophy developed by Alfred Korzybski*, which mysteriously relates linguistic behaviours with physiological processes and maintains that both psychic and somatic pathology are 'neurosemantic' in origin. Korzybski's system and terminology are abstruse to the point of being virtually impenetrable except to the dedicated student, and eccentric to a degree that renders dedication to them a dubious undertaking. But there is one principle enshrined in general semantics which has had a profound and wide influence, and it is expressed in one of Korzybski's few coherent utterances, i.e.: 'the map is not the territory'. In other words, we shouldn't confuse language with reality. And further, we must recognize the extent to which our language determines our perception of reality. In particular, the Indo-European languages, with their subject-predicate structure, make us conceptualize reality in terms of fragmentation and cause-effect sequentiality, and positively inhibit our perception of processes, relationships, simultaneity and multi-causality. In respect of its understanding of the limits and pitfalls of language, general se-

mantics has affinities with the LINGUISTIC PHILOSOPHY of Wittgenstein*, and in drawing attention to the specific bias of our language it helped liberate scientific comprehension, for instance in QUANTUM THEORY[2], from conceptual constraints. It is the more ironical that its own language should be so obscure, as evidenced in the following description: 'General semantics is ... a body of co-ordinated assumptions, doctrines, principles, etc., and the methodological procedures and techniques for changing the structure of ... neurosymbolic reactions to fit an assumptive world of dynamic processes.' [171]

General systems theory

What is known as a systems approach has become increasingly common and influential in contemporary thought. It is arguable that the concept of 'system' constitutes an alternative model or PARADIGM to that of MECHANISM, and similarly carries implications for theoretical approaches in a wide range of areas, from physics and biology to sociology, ethics, medicine, economics and ecology.

Whereas mechanism looked at phenomena as parts constituting a whole and sought to determine how the parts 'add up' to a whole, the systems approach takes the whole as its primary datum and recognizes that it has properties or characteristics that cannot be construed in terms of the sum of its parts. The systems approach focuses attention upon structures of interrelationship and interdependence between the constituent parts, and seeks to comprehend the dynamics of a system in terms of these structures rather than in terms of quantifiable forces exerted upon each other by the parts, as mechanism did. The question it puts to nature is not how things work, but how they are organized or organize themselves.

General systems theory was developed in the 1930s and 1940s by the philosopher Ludwig van Bertalanffy*, who defined it as 'the scientific exploration of "wholes" and "wholeness" which, not so long ago, were considered metaphysical notions transcending the boundaries of science'. Bertalanffy was primarily concerned with specifying in general terms properties manifested by systems of all kinds with a view to facilitating and encouraging interdisciplinary thinking and cross-fertilization and combating the errors and excesses that narrow specialization tends to produce. In specifying such properties as hierarchic structure, goal-directedness, approach to and maintenance of steady states, organization, and transaction, Bertalanffy helped create a scientific metalanguage which enabled correspondences between systems of different kinds to be perceived which the specialist languages of classical science had obscured.

The systems view construes the universe in terms of systems within systems within systems, a hierarchy of lower and higher order systems that are all interrelated and interdependent. In living systems the single cell is a low-order system, an organ such as the brain is a higher-order system, an individual animal or human being a still higher one. Each system is at once a whole and a part. As a whole, it has a degree of autonomy, it has its own teleology or goal-orientation, and, correlated with its degree of complexity, a range of alternative ways of attaining its goal, i.e. of attaining and maintaining its steady state. But this degree of autonomy is limited and conditioned by the needs of the greater whole of which it constitutes a part. In living or natural systems this conditioning or limitation is determined and controlled by complex processes, and it is rare for the part to exercise its autonomy in ways inimical to the integrity or health of the whole, though this does sometimes happen, for instance in the case of a mutant gene or a cancerous cell. As systems become more complex, however, and correspondingly possessed of higher degrees of autonomy, the possibilities of individual behaviour being discordant with and disruptive of the needs of the whole are increased. In the systems view the individual human being, although a highly developed and complex living system, is still a part in relation to other systems, for instance of social and natural order. Individual behaviour which is self-regarding and unconcerned with the needs and integrity of the environmental systems of social and natural order can perturb such systems, possibly to the extent of utterly destroying them. Likewise, systems of social and economic order can perturb and destroy systems of natural order, for instance

ECOSYSTEMS[7], if they conduct their affairs in ignorance of or indifference to the needs of such systems.

General systems theory developed in tandem with and under influence from developments in modern physics. It has clear analogies with FIELD THEORY[2], but is at once a more radical and more comprehensive concept, completely irreconcilable with mechanism and totally compatible with QUANTUM THEORY[2] and BOOTSTRAP THEORY[2]. It at once endorses and is endorsed by the recent developments in biomedical thought and practice which have made HOLISTIC MEDICINE[6] increasingly respectable and popular. The great development in ecological awareness in recent times is also evidence of the pervasiveness and relevance of the systems view. The power of the systems view resides in the fact that it is at once descriptive and prescriptive. Its descriptions of how natural systems are established and maintained are clear and demonstrable, and at the same time they imply prescriptions as to how individuals and societies should conduct themselves and their affairs.

See also HOLON, HIERARCHY, SELF-ORGANIZATION, DISSIPATIVE STRUCTURE[2], IMPLICATE ORDER[2]. [26, 45, 169, 181]

Hermeneutics

Derived from the Greek *hermeneus*, an interpreter, the term refers to the art or theory of interpretation. Hermeneutics involves probing beyond ostensible or surface significances and deploying skills to understand more profoundly and fully, for instance human actions and utterances, institutions, rituals and cult objects and products.

Hierarchy

In GENERAL SYSTEMS THEORY the metaphor of a hierarchy is often used to describe the multi-levelled structure of natural systems or organisms. It is in some ways a misleading metaphor, because in hierarchies of human social organization the lower orders are subject or subservient to the higher, and the governance of the whole structure and its component parts is determined and controlled from above. In natural systems a principle of SELF-ORGANIZATION operates on all levels, lower orders manifest a greater degree of autonomy, and between higher and lower there is a greater degree of reciprocity, than is implied by the metaphor of a hierarchy. For this reason some systems theorists have preferred to speak of 'stratified order', although generally the term hierarchy, divested of the above implications, is retained as a technical term. [169, 181]

Holism

A term coined by Jan Smuts* in his *Holism and Evolution* (1926). Smuts was concerned to argue that evolution is purposive, that nature has an inherent drive to create ever more complex integrated wholes. He tried to create a complex whole himself, of Darwinian evolution theory and Einsteinian physics. Neither his book nor its basic concept had any profound influence at the time, but from today's perspective they seem remarkably prescient. In theoretical physics, in the philosophy of GENERAL SYSTEMS THEORY and its diverse applications, and in particular areas such as medicine and ECOLOGY[7], holism and holistic approaches are being widely canvassed today.

Simply defined, holism is the theory that wholes are more than the sum of their parts. REDUCTIONISM takes the contrary view. Holistic approaches, in science, medicine, etc., may employ analytic methods, but synthesis, and consideration of the part in the context of the whole, constitute their governing principle.

See also HOLON, SYNERGY. [305]

Holon

A term coined by Arthur Koestler* in the context of GENERAL SYSTEMS THEORY to designate an entity which functions at once as a whole and as a part, and which manifests properties of independence in the one function and dependence in the other. In normal usage, the terms 'part' and 'whole' imply something incomplete or complete, fragmented or finished and contained, but in reality we do not find parts or wholes in this absolute sense. We find rather that there are ascending orders or levels of complexity, each level or order being at once a thing in itself and a component of a larger or more comprehensive entity.

Biological systems afford the clearest illustration of this. Molecules, organelles, cells, tissues, organs, and organisms, are progressively complex entities, each with its distinct inherent structure and properties and each at the same time comprising a part of the next entity in the series, or alternatively each self-determining in respect of the establishment and maintenance of its own structure and function, and determined from above in respect of its structural integration with and functioning in the larger totality. Koestler designated this dual nature of holons the 'Janus principle', implying that holons, like the Janus of legend, have two faces, one turned downward and preoccupied with the self, and one turned upward and concerned with its relation to the next level in the HIERARCHY. In other words, holons have two distinct tendencies or potentials, self-assertive on the one hand and integrative on the other. They seek both to be a whole and to belong to a whole.

Thus expressed, the holon concept may seem rather mystical, and indeed it does convey both ethical and metaphysical implications. But at the same time it has a wide range of practical applications, and serves as a conceptual tool for describing the nature and dynamics of a variety of phenomena. We can think, for instance, of behaviour, of language, of cognition, of societies, as hierarchical or multi-levelled structures comprised of dynamically interacting holons, sub-systems or sub-routines. Processes of growth, of communication, or of organization, are more comprehensively and realistically represented by the holon/hierarchy model which emphasizes part-whole reciprocity than by the mechanistic model of discrete 'building blocks' which have no meaning, dynamic or coherence until they are aggregated into a whole. [169]

Humanism

A word widely and loosely used, with variously approving or pejorative implications. Historically, Renaissance humanism was a repudiation of repressive dogma and abstraction and an exaltation of man as endowed with free will, reason, judgement, superiority over nature, and a special relationship to God. This humanism looked back to the Greek and Roman cultures and found in them a noble and ideal image of man and concept of his individual and social potentials. Man was made in the image of God, and his world was perfectible.

Subsequently, humanism became more secular, emphasizing man's autonomy, the importance of his unaided quest for truth and right, and dispensing with any idea of divine guidance or sanctions. In the nineteenth century there arose scientific humanism, MARXIST humanism, POSITIVIST humanism (Auguste Comte* proposed the establishment of a nontheistic 'religion of humanity') and PRAGMATIC humanism. In the present century we have had EXISTENTIALIST humanism, and also a resurgence of Christian humanism, which emphasizes the humanity of Christ and looks to him as a model of human perfection.

When humanism is described, it is generally for its naïvety for believing in the perfectibility of man and society, and its ignoring the problem of inherent evil. It is sometimes derogatorily paired with liberalism, and critics impugn its optimism, lack of vision, unrealistic meliorism, and insupportable beneficent view of human nature. Seventy years ago the philosopher T. E. Hulme* derided humanism for these faults, and subsequent history has underlined the relevance of his argument, at least in so far as liberal humanism has been seen to be ineffective in opposition to social and political evil, and sometimes its dupe. But although humanism may be faulted from a theoretical viewpoint, people who have repudiated it in practice have certainly not been exemplars of any desirable alternative. [140]

Idealism

In the vernacular, the word denotes a naïve optimism or aspiration which is considered incompatible with actual conditions or possibilities, and is opposed by and irreconcilable to realism. In philosophy the term has quite a different meaning, deriving not from 'ideal' but from 'idea'. Philosophical idealism is any doctrine which holds that reality is not fundamentally material, but mental. In Platonic idealism, phenomena were considered not real in themselves but as shadow-projections of a world of ideas, or ideal forms. In the idealism of Berkeley*, material things were held to have no existence independent of the mind; *esse est percipi*, to be is to be perceived, and perception is mental; things exist independent of the perception of finite minds, in the infinite mind of God. In Kant's* brand of idealism, the human mind is held capable of perception or knowledge only of appearances ('phenomena'), which derive from an independently existent transcendent reality. In Hegelian* idealism, a spiritual Absolute is held to be the ultimate reality, and finite minds and material things to be dependent fragments of it or illusory appearances generated by it. Generally, any philosophy which maintains a distinction between reality and appearances, that infers from the contradictoriness or illusoriness of appearances the existence of a reality lying behind them, is idealistic.

Ideology

A set of beliefs, ideas, values, and objectives subscribed to by a group of people, generally for motives of which they are not fully aware or will not admit. Ideologies may be regarded as secular religions, as worldviews determined and delimited by sectional bias, as value- and belief-systems designed to mobilize people for political action, or as social formulas designed to make intelligible a status quo or to justify a project of revolutionary change. Ideologies engage feelings and prejudices in their devotees which abrogate rational and ethical considerations, and thus furnish an incentive and a specious rationale for conflict with other ideologies.

Inner game

The concept of the 'inner game' is an importation of ZEN³ principles into sports psychology. It was first expounded by Timothy Gallwey*.

As anyone who has engaged in a competitive sport knows, there are times when one is on form, when there is ease and assurance in one's performance. Relaxation, not straining after an effect, being unanxious about performance and results, are characteristics of such times. The body is in tune, not only in itself but also with the total situation that is the game. In tennis, for instance, racket and ball are not like tools or instruments, they are extensions of the player's psyche. The inner game is the game that the body knows, instinctively, how to play. If a player has been coached, in an actual game he has to forget all principle and theory, and just let his body perform as it knows best. If the mind is involved, either criticizing the performance or urging greater effort or competence, it inhibits the body's performance. Athletics, golf and skiing are other sports to which the inner game principles have been specifically applied. [104]

Inner space

In the 1970s, the term 'inner space' started to be used to designate an area of exploration deemed as important as or even more than the exploration of outer space by the cosmonauts of the late 1960s. One of the cosmonauts, Edgar Mitchell, became an enthusiastic promoter of inner space research, through his 'Institute of Noetic Sciences'. Research into ALTERED STATES OF CONSCIOUSNESS⁴, studies of the psychic concomitants of drug ingestion and of sustained sensory deprivation conditions, and PSI⁵ research, all constituted 'inner space' exploration. The most dedicated and intrepid explorer was probably John Lilly*, who underwent bizarre risks and privations in his explorations, and reported his experiences in a number of books. The analogy to outer space exploration was further amplified when a reviewer dubbed Dr Lilly a 'psychenaut'. [190, 191]

Intentionality
See PHENOMENOLOGY.

Lateral thinking
A term coined by Edward de Bono* to describe an approach to problem-solving that transcends seemingly logical obstacles by reformulating the problem in a novel way. In the creation of novelty, in the realm of scientific thinking as well as of the arts, logic and reason play little part, and indeed may be positively inhibiting, for they are pattern-making and pattern-using mental functions that deal exclusively with the known and therefore cannot apprehend the unknown. For the unknown, the new, to become manifest, familiar patterns have to be disrupted, habitual modes of perception disoriented, novel insights and approaches provoked. Scientists have often attested that conceptual breakthroughs intractable to their reasoning powers have come to them adventitiously and illogically, as when the chemist Kekulé* saw the structure of the benzine ring in a dream in the form of a snake with its tail in its mouth. The techniques of lateral thinking seek to provoke and stimulate such insights and to give rise to novelty by introducing randomly selected words and concepts as stimuli into the mental processes of problem-solving. [36]

Linear thinking
Thinking in the linear as distinct from the LATERAL mode, is logical, sequential, step-by-step, and although appropriate to and necessary for many practical purposes it has inherent limitations, and if predominant positively inhibits creative, imaginative and innovative thinking.

Linguistic philosophy
Linguistic philosophy was developed by Ludwig Wittgenstein*, and the exemplary work in the *genre* is his *Philosophical Investigations*. Wittgenstein's method was to demonstrate the imprecision, ambiguities and contradictions in our use of language, which are symptomatic of inherent fallibilities of the human mind. He conceived his method as a 'therapy', a way of alleviating philosophical puzzlement, not by solving philosophical problems but by dissolving them. Linguistic philosophy was heir to LOGICAL POSITIVISM, but did not share its POSITIVIST bias or its deference to the laws of formal logic. It was more broadly and traditionally philosophical, in that it maintained that by holding up the mirror to language it was holding up the mirror to man, enabling man to live more authentically by dispelling the illusions, the ostensible but insubstantial meanings, implicit in his use of language. [361]

Logical positivism

A philosophical school which originated in the 'Vienna Circle' of the 1920s, and subsequently profoundly influenced academic philosophy throughout Europe and the US. Its main doctrine was the principle of verification, which held that a proposition must be verifiable either by reference to sense-experience or by philosophical analysis based on the laws of logic. It repudiated as meaningless both the questions and the propositions of METAPHYSICS, and statements of putative religious or ethical import. This reduced philosophy to a rather specialized academic discipline which was hard put to find questions meaningful enough to merit discussion. Ludwig Wittgenstein*, an original member of the Vienna Circle, led some logical positivists out of this impasse into LINGUISTIC PHILOSOPHY. [9]

Marxism

A complex of historical, economic, social and political theory developed by Karl Marx*. In its historical analysis, Marxism combined a philosophical DETERMINISM with a theory of EVOLUTION which extended the principles of DARWINISM[2] to processes of social change. Marx maintained that it is not the consciousness of men that determines their existence, but on the contrary, it is their social existence which determines their consciousness. The primary determinant of social existence was 'the mode of production in material life'. The capitalist mode of production had historically produced a class structure in which ownership of the means of production was concentrated in a minority class, the bourgeoisie, so that the majority class, the proletariat, was of necessity induced to secure its material needs by selling its labour. This structure gave rise to class antagonism and struggle, and herein lay the dynamic of evolutionary change. The proletariat, Marx maintained, would not indefinitely suffer the condition of 'alienation', i.e. forfeit of control over the processes of their work and the products of their labour. They would seek through revolution to redress the exploitation that capitalism subjected them to, and thus would come about inevitable changes in the structures of social existence, which in turn would bring about changes in human consciousness. Specifically, the means of production of the material needs of society would become common property and their distribution would be equitably determined. The blight of alienation and exploitation would be removed, and after a transitional period of 'the dictatorship of the proletariat' a classless, state-less, communist society would be naturally established.

Marxism derived much of its authority and influence from its claim to be scientific and its co-opting evolution theory to support a doctrine of historical inevitability. Its doctrines were persuasive in the nineteenth century not only because prevailing social conditions and unrest in Western industrialized countries made their relevance manifest, but also because they were consonant with

the prevailing POSITIVIST, DE-
TERMINIST, MECHANIST and
MATERIALIST modes of thought
in science and philosophy. But if
the test of a scientific theory is its
predictive power, doctrinaire Marxism (as distinct from Marx's own
prescient analyses of capitalist
social and economic dynamics)
must be considered disproved by
history. Not only has the industrial
working class not fulfilled its revolutionary role in western countries,
but rather has been assimilated
into a modified and less egregiously
exploitative capitalist social structure; but also where communist
revolutions with professed Marxist
principles have occurred, the resultant social orders have been far
from the UTOPIAN[7] ideal envisaged by Marx, and have tended
to take the doctrine of proletarian
dictatorship as a licence for a repressive authoritarianism and
covert elitism which implicitly repudiates rather than transitionally
defers millennial communism.

Although its predictive failure
may have eroded Marxism's claims
to scientific authority, specific
Marxist political, economic and
social analyses and concepts (e.g.
the theory of 'alienation'), have
proved more right and relevant
than the intellectual superstructure
in which they were embedded, in
such areas as aesthetics and literary
theory as well as in sociology, politics and economics. Modern
Marxian studies, furthermore,
have discovered under the
materialistic and deterministic
superstructure an 'ecological Marx'
expressing ORGANICIST views of
human and natural life. [124]

Materialism

In the vernacular, a primary concern for the acquisition of material
goods and the enjoyment of physical satisfactions, and a consequent
rejection of or indifference to the
spiritual, aesthetic, or ethical. In
philosophy, the belief that only
things that have the material properties of specific location and extension in space and time, and that
are accessible to human sensory
perception, really exist. Although
the two senses of the term are
clearly related, the discrediting of
philosophical materialism by
modern physical science has not
had a perceptible widespread effect
upon the popularity and social ac-
ceptability of materialism in the
vernacular sense of the term.

Mechanism

A body of philosophical and scientific theory which construes the
functioning of everything in the
material universe in terms analogous to the functioning of a
machine, and by implication discounts the reality of anything that
cannot be so construed. It presupposes that every phenomenon is
reducible to component parts, and
that the purpose of science is to
specify those parts and to determine the universal laws that
govern their functioning. It further
presupposes that every effect has
an antecedent cause which can be
precisely specified in terms of those
universal laws. The mechanistic
worldview was first expounded
in the seventeenth century by
Descartes*, and subsequently
Newton* created a synthesis of scientific knowledge and principle

which established the mechanistic model as the very foundation of science. It is indisputable that most of the great achievements of modern science and technology were accomplished through research and hypothesis determined by the mechanistic model, and indeed in many areas the model continues to serve as a powerful tool and to yield important discoveries (e.g. DNA[2]). But modern QUANTUM[2] physics has demonstrated that the mechanistic 'laws of nature' are not universal laws, and in particular that they do not apply to very small (subatomic) or very large (astrophysical) phenomena. This demonstration in a rather arcane department of physical science has had far-reaching effects, which collectively indicate that the philosophical assumptions of mechanism have long been felt to be inadequate and in many respects inimical. The realization that those assumptions underlie the dubiously beneficial practices of modern medicine and medical technology, both FREUDIAN[4] and BEHAVIOURIST[4] psychology, all influential schools of modern economic thinking, and that they are responsible for the severe ecological crises that the world is now experiencing, is becoming increasingly widespread. At the same time philosophical principles fundamentally opposed to mechanism, in particular HOLISM and ORGANICISM, are becoming increasingly influential. [45, 214, 273]

Metaphysics

The branch of philosophy which investigates questions that are not susceptible to empirical investigation, that may arise from the study of the physical world but are not answerable in terms of it or of the sciences that concern themselves exclusively with it. Metaphysical propositions, being unverifiable by reference to the empirical world, are held by some philosophers, notably the LOGICAL POSITIVISTS, to be therefore meaningless or nonsensical. By seeking to disembarrass philosophy of its metaphysical dimension, logical positivism diminished philosophy to an academic discipline addressing questions of rather arcane, if specific, relevance. Metaphysics addresses questions of general relevance, about nature, the universe, mind, knowledge, reality and appearance, purpose, meaning. Metaphysical questions may be meaningless for some philosophers, but for most people they constitute the fundamental concerns of philosophy. What really exists? Is the universe fundamentally one thing or unrelated congeries of things? Is the universe mechanistic? Do all effects have determinate causes? Is change only an appearance or is it fundamental? Are there such things as random or chance events, in nature and in human life? Do people possess free will? Has life a purpose? Is there a God? Do ethical values have any basis in the nature of things, or are they merely arbitrary human postulates? These are some of the basic metaphysical questions. Ironically, at the time when philosophers, seeking to be more scientific, were repudiating them, scientists such as Einstein*,

Bohr*, Heisenberg* and Pauli* were finding that their investigations led them beyond physics into metaphysics, and were unashamedly making metaphysical statements and speculations. It could be said that with the development of QUANTUM THEORY[2] physics became more metaphysical than philosophy.

Mind-body problem

The question of how mind and body relate to each other, and which is primary, has preoccupied philosophers of all ages and cultures. Within the two schools of thought, the MONIST and the DUALIST, there are fundamental differences between philosophers of materialistic and of spiritualistic or IDEALIST bias. In modern scientific culture the materialistic-monist view that only the material and the physical exist, in the sense that all phenomena, including those of mind, are governed by the laws of physics and biology, has tended to prevail. This view is seen at its most extreme in the psychology of BEHAVIOURISM[4], which totally repudiates the existence of mind. It also prevails in orthodox neurophysiology, where most research is premised on what is known as the hypothesis of neurophysiological determination, which proposes that mind and brain are the same thing and that there is a distinct brain-state corresponding to every mental state or event. Where the dualist view has been influential, for instance upon orthodox medicine, it has generally been the CARTESIAN view that mind and body are totally different

entities, and that the latter, as part of the material world, is entirely governed by mechanical principles and forces.

With the development of modern electrical instruments for monitoring brain functions, the question that is fundamental to the mind-body problem, i.e. whether mind and brain are the same thing, has become experimentally testable. The new experimental techniques have been employed both in orthodox neurophysiology and in PSI[5] research. Although research in the former area has tended to confirm the identity theory of mind and brain, it has still not been able to prove a causative link between mind events and brain events, but only correlations between them. This leaves open the possibility that brain and mind may be independent although correlated and interacting systems. This view has two distinguished advocates in the neuroscientist John Eccles* and the philosopher Karl Popper*, who in a co-authored book, significantly titled *The Self and its Brain*, argue the case for what they call 'dualistic interactionism'. Eccles has formulated the concept of a 'self-conscious mind' as a distinct entity that interacts with the 'liaison brain', and he elaborates a complex theory of how the mind continually scans the brain to select from the diverse patterns of cortical activity the components that it integrates into conscious experience in accordance with its present interests and purposes.

The evidence produced by modern PSI research, which has often used neurophysiological experimental techniques, has tended to support the dualist position. The results of many experiments in TELEPATHY[5] research, in which subtle physiological responses to remotely generated mental stimuli have been recorded, are not consistent with orthodox views of the powers of brains. Nor is the evidence for CLAIRVOYANCE[5] and PRECOGNITION[5], for according to orthodox views there is no way that brains, which are physical systems, could transcend the perceptual limitations of space and time that such systems are bound by. Equally difficult to explain in terms of brain functions is the evidence that mentally held intentions and wishes can be actualized without the mediation of the physical motor mechanisms, yet all the evidence for PSYCHOKINESIS[5] indicates that this occurs. Although such evidence is not accepted as proven by most scientists, the evidence for PSYCHOSOMATIC[6] interaction (see also BIOFEEDBACK[6]) cannot easily be repudiated, and points also to the conclusion that the effects of mind cannot always be explained in terms of physical brain activity.

Although it would be rash to say that the mind-body problem has been solved, it is certainly true today that both experimental and theoretical science have thrown light upon it, and that a solution in terms of interactionism or of the existence of a physical-mental continuum seems probable. [30, 43]

Monism

The theory that there exists only one substance or kind of thing in the universe. Any philosophy which maintains that all phenomena are fundamentally material, or spiritual, or mental, is monist. DUALISM, which holds that there are two distinct and irreducible kinds of thing – generally mind and matter – and pluralism, which holds that there are a multiplicity, are philosophical doctrines opposed to monism. Religious philosophies that maintain that all phenomena issue from or are imbued with a divine principle, or are significantly interrelated, tend to be monist, but religious thought has also espoused the dualist view, maintaining an opposition and irreconcilability between spirit and matter (see GNOSTICISM[3]), good and evil, God and Devil. The argument between monists and dualists has generally been conducted on an abstract level, but in the context of the MIND-BODY PROBLEM some empirical evidence has been adduced which is difficult to reconcile with a thoroughgoing monism.

New age

A term widely current in the 1970s and allied with an optimism that the astrological shift from the Piscean to the Aquarian age augured radical and evolutionary changes in human consciousness and society. As the changes then manifest have not on the whole sustained the momentum they initially developed, and indeed an age incompatible with and inhospitable to that optimism and idealism seems to have supervened, the implicit MILLENNIALISM[3] of the New Age concept tends today more to embarrass than to enthuse all but the intransigently cultic of its original proponents, the majority having accommodated their optimism to more gradualist beliefs and endeavours.

Noetics

The scientific study of mind and CONSCIOUSNESS[4] extended to embrace putative ways of knowing that orthodox science does not generally ackowledge as germane to its project or amenable to its methodology and tends therefore to repudiate as unreliable. Studies in the fields of psychic research and parapsychology, religious and mystical experience, non-ordinary states of consciousness, creativity, and modes of non-rational cognition, are all pertinent to the project of noetics, which is to study mind and its operations PHENOMENO-LOGICALLY and without the constraints of dogma, preconceptions or expectations as to its nature and limitations.

Occam's razor

In philosophy, the principle of parsimony in the creation of hypothesis. Propounded by William of Occam*, the principle enjoins the selection of the simplest hypothesis that fits the facts and the excision of any entity arbitrarily postulated and which the empirical situation does not necessitate.

Ontology

The department of METAPHYSICS that is concerned with establishing what exists. Ontology is the theory of being, or of existence. Some ontologies deny the existence of things that others assert. Questions of the existence of other minds, material objects, universals, objective ethical absolutes, for instance, are philosophically contentious. The fundamental problem is whether existence itself is a property, and whether it can be predicated of things in the same sense irrespective of the category of thing postulated as an existent. [125]

Open system

A system that interacts with its environment, as distinct from a 'closed system', which doesn't.

See DISSIPATIVE STRUC-TURE[2].

Organicism

The philosophical view that physical reality, at whatever level of complexity, manifests organic as distinct from mechanical properties. In other words, both micro- and macro-physical phenomena are not to be construed as aggregates of parts, but as complex wholes endowed with properties that are particular to the whole and neither exhibited by any of the parts in isolation nor predictable by physical or mechanical law from their aggregation. The philosopher A. N. Whitehead* first expounded a comprehensive philosophy of organicism in 1928-9. His statement that 'Biology is the study of the larger organisms, whereas physics is the study of the smaller organisms', was novel and unorthodox at the time, for physicists and biologists then considered their disciplines and research quite separate and unconnected. Since then the organicist conceptual approach has combined with research findings compatible with it to effect the convergence of the two areas. Whitehead proceeded to develop the organicist concept into a scheme of speculative or metaphysical philosophy. Its more specific applications were developed by others in the context of GENERAL SYSTEMS THEORY.

See also HOLISM, HOLON, GAIA HYPOTHESIS[7]. [350, 351]

Paradigm

A pattern or model. The term has acquired a particular contemporary relevance since it was employed by Thomas Kuhn* in 1962 to refer to a set of assumptions, derived from a particular achievement or discovery, about how scientific work should proceed, what kind of discoveries it might expect to make and what areas of investigation are relevant. Paradigms are necessary to facilitate scientific work of any kind, but no paradigm can ever 'explain all the facts with which it is confronted'. So paradigm-based science, according to Kuhn, becomes 'a strenuous and devoted attempt to force nature into the conceptual boxes supplied by a professional education', and it 'suppresses fundamental novelties because they are necessarily subversive of its basic commitments'.

Though paradigms exert a tenacious hold upon the scientific mind, they do eventually collapse under the weight of accumulated anomaly, to be replaced by a more inclusive formulation, which in turn becomes the prevailing paradigm. Thus do scientific revolutions occur, according to Kuhn's analysis. On the ground that revolutions in other areas of thought and life are analogous, the term 'paradigm' is now widely used to designate any consistent theory or body of knowledge and its underlying assumptions. [178]

Phenomenology

A method of philosophical investigation developed by Edmund Husserl*. The term means literally the study or description of appearances. The aim of phenomenology is to comprehend the totality or essence of a perceived object. This project presupposes that things have an essence or a meaning in and for themselves, which is a philosophically contentious proposition. Assuming that things have this essence or meaning, the phenomenologist proposes and pursues a method of revealing it. This method involves directing a particular type of attention towards the object, an attention which is aware of and sets aside ('brackets') all preconceptions about it. Such preconceptions may have been formed by personal experience, cultural influences, conceptual bias determined by historical, social, scientific, etc. modes of interpretation. Divesting perception or understanding of all these distorting factors, and thus enabling the inherent essence or meaning of a thing to reveal itself, is philosophical work as demanding as and analogous to the meditative disciplines of the mystic or the creative labours of the artist. As the phenomenologist Maurice Merleau-Ponty wrote: 'It is as painstaking as the works of Proust, Valéry, Balzac or Cézanne – by reason of the same kind of attentiveness and wonder, the same demand for awareness, the same will to seize the meaning of the world or of history as that meaning comes into being.'

Phenomenology seeks to set before our eyes the world as it is, to 'disclose' it, not by the traditional methods of proceeding from analysis to synthesis, or deriving truths through processes of deduction or induction, but by the engagement of 'attentiveness and wonder' in a perceptual or descriptive act which enables a total reality to show itself. Our preconceptions are a part of this totality. The phenomenologist does not reject them utterly, he consciously sets them aside, thus defamiliarizing the world by loosening the ties of intentionality that normally bind us to it and to a limited and conditioned perception of it. Thus arises 'wonder' in the face of the world, and only thus can we perceive it in all its strangeness and novelty.

'Intentionality' is a central concept in phenomenology. That our processes of perceiving and thinking about the world normally involve our intentions towards it, that we project such intentions upon the world, is a well-attested psychological fact. Phenomenology recognizes the intentionality of perception, and demands of its practitioners a complete awareness of the operations of intentionality in our perceptions and thought, but it does not denounce intentionality as a falsifier of reality; rather, it recognizes it as a component, a part of a total reality which would be falsified if it were left out just as it would be falsified if it were taken for the reality itself. While on the one hand unconscious intentionality may obscure reality from us, on the other conscious intentionality is inseparable from the philosophical project of disclosure of the world. And although some forms of intentional projection upon the world may distort it, Husserlian phenomenology proposes that in philosophically disciplined perception there is a correspondence between the intended perceptual act and the actual reality, a reciprocity between what other philosophies have considered irreconcilable subjective and objective worlds.

This correspondence holds good in respect of meaning and the perception of meaning. Meaning is neither entirely subjective, something added to phenomena by the human mind, nor entirely objective, something possibly inherent in phenomena but which the human mind cannot apprehend with certainty. Human consciousness is itself a project of the world, it is perpetually directed towards the world, it is intimately bound up in the complex network of facts and relationships that constitute the world, and by virtue of this directedness and involvement it is capable of apprehending meaning. In phenomenological observation, wrote Merleau-Ponty, 'perspectives blend, perceptions confirm each other, a meaning emerges'. This emergent meaning neither requires nor is capable of confirmation or verification by reference to any principle or doctrine, it exists in and can only be apprehended in a totality of facts and blending relationships of facts. When consciousness encompasses that totality, meaning discloses itself.

As Thomas Kuhn* has demonstrated, science is always constrained by its prevailing PARADIGMS and principles of verification to reject novelty and anomaly, but progress in science often depends upon attending to the anomalous and novel. Some theoretical and research scientists today, particularly in such 'borderline sciences' as parapsychology and sociology, have based their work upon the principles and methods of phenomenology. Because it does not prejudge what can happen or what is significant, because it not only is hospitable to novelty but positively expects it to arise from observation of phenomena, because it acknowledges – as QUANTUM² physics does – consciousness as a component of reality, and because it prescribes a mode of attention to the world that is at the same time detached and involved in the disclosure of its meaning, phenomenology arguably affords a better basis for scientific work and thought than such paradigmatic approaches as MECHANISM and POSITIVISM, in which intentionality is manifest but unacknowledged. [141, 215, 362]

Positivism

A philosophical doctrine developed by Auguste Comte* which holds that all true knowledge is scientific and seeks to extend the SCIENTIFIC METHOD² to the study and description of all phenomena, including those of human psychology and society. Comte argued by analogy to evolution theory that human thought had progressed from a theological stage through a metaphysical stage to a scientific stage, and that the latter rendered the two previous stages obsolete. Science was conceived as concerned exclusively with the observable and the quantifiable, and positivism held that any proposition that was not empirically or mathematically demonstrable was nonsensical. It was thus a form of REDUCTIONISM.

The positivist attitude is congenial to the type of mind that seeks certainty of knowledge and is confident of its possibility, and that is intolerant of anomaly and mystery. Such a mental attitude was arguably more supportable in the nineteenth century than it is today, when not only has science itself departed far from EMPIRICISM and become increasingly 'mystical', but the confidence in science to explain and manage everything has been largely eroded. However, the attenuated influence of positivism remains, particularly in academic philosophy, where LOGICAL POSITIVISM has been widely influential. [9]

Pragmatism

A body of theories about meaning and truth developed by the American philosophers Charles Peirce*, William James* and John Dewey*. Peirce made a distinction between concepts relating to the senses and emotions and those relating to the intellect, and held that the meaning of the latter was identified with the sum of their effects upon our actions and experiences. William James went further, arguing that concepts directly affect our senses, emotions and experiences, and that their truth lies in the satisfactoriness or effectiveness of the effects they have. Dewey, likewise, argued that knowledge should not be a matter for contemplation merely, but an instrument for action. A good example of applied pragmatism was William James's decision, after an inconclusive intellectual struggle with the problem of free will, to resolve the issue by stating: 'my first act of free will shall be to believe in free will'. Pragmatic truth is whatever agrees with our reality or experience, or whatever works for us. [10, 150]

Reductionism

Science and philosophy always seek to specify fundamental principles to explain phenomena, to proceed by analysis to reduce complexity to simplicity. The relevance and value of such a procedure cannot be denied, but a distinction has to be made between reduction as a method and reductionism as a form of doctrinaire exclusivism. Reductionism in this sense asserts that phenomena are *nothing but* what analysis has reduced them to. As the reductive method has proved a powerful tool of scientific thought, and the practical triumphs of science in the modern world are conspicuous and incontestable, doctrinaire reductionism has tended to become established orthodoxy,

particularly in areas of quasi-scientific thought. Thus we have the BEHAVIOURIST's[4] contention that human behaviour is nothing but a complex pattern of conditional responses; the neo-DARWINIST's[2] assertion that EVOLUTION is nothing but a process of natural selection operating upon chance mutations; the materialistic-MONIST view that all mind-events are nothing but electrochemical brain-events; the LOGICAL POSITIVIST view that philosophy is nothing but analysis and therefore unanalysable metaphysical propositions are nonsensical. Intellectual reductionists tend to be combative, zealous in the defence and promotion of their specific nothing-but-ism, and scornful of opposition that seeks to subvert their view with data or arguments that they consider soft or unscientific. The anti-reductionist's problem is to specify a *something more* with properties as assured and demonstrable as the reductionist's *nothing but*, in circumstances where the reductionist's belief system includes criteria of verification that automatically disqualify anomalies.

The opposite of reductionism is any view which regards phenomena as more than the sum of their parts, or explicable not in terms of single causes but in terms of a complex interaction of a plurality of causes. Such is the view of HOLISM, and a clear trend of modern thought in many areas is towards holistic as opposed to reductionist approaches. [170]

Scientism

The belief that the SCIENTIFIC

METHOD[2] alone can establish valid truth and knowledge, and in its dogmatic form the rejection as non-sensical any statements about man, nature or society that do not meet the EMPIRICAL criteria of verification of the scientific method.

Self-organization

In GENERAL SYSTEMS THEORY, systems which constitute ordered wholes manifest a capacity for self-organization. The more complex the system, the less rigidly determined and the more autonomous this capacity is. All systems have a determinate goal-orientation, a tendency to attain and stabilize themselves in a steady state. But the more complex a system or organism is, the more open it is to input of material or information from its environment, the more flexible, adaptable and, paradoxically, unstable it has to be in order to organize itself and maintain its structural coherence and integrity. Self-organization in the higher or more complex systems, therefore, is a process which always contains the possibility of self-transcendence, i.e. of self-*re*organization in a yet higher order of complexity. See DISSIPATIVE STRUCTURE[2]. [152, 181]

Serendipity

Luck, or seeming luck. The apocryphal tales of Archimedes in his bath and Newton being struck by a falling apple illustrate it. Propitious hazard seems to play a prominent part in many creative achievements, in scientific discovery as well as in the arts. When it does, the suspicion that 'something is going on', that there is a kind of occult complicity between the mind and external events, is often irresistible. The opposite side of the coin is accident proneness, equally uncanny seeming ill-luck, the clustering of unpropitious hazards. Mind-set, expectation and awareness no doubt play a part in it, but an exclusively psychological explanation seems inadequate.

See also COINCIDENCE. [168]

Symbiosis

A relationship between two different kinds of organism which works to their mutual advantage. For instance, when micro-organisms in an animal's digestive system assist the digestive process by breaking down food, a symbiotic relationship exists between the micro-organisms and the host. There are many such relationships between plants and insects, which facilitate breeding or feeding. To understand the patterns of symbiosis in nature is essential to ECOLOGY[7], for many ecological disasters have occurred through ignorance of such patterns, by the destruction, generally unwitting, of one of the symbionts. If man has learnt, in recent times, to comprehend and preserve symbiotic relationships in nature, he may also have drawn the inference that competition and aggression are not the only 'laws of nature' that his own conduct might be modelled upon. [127]

Synchronicity

Carl Jung*, who coined the term, defined it as 'an acausal connecting principle'. Many personal experiences had led him to the conclusion that there is a class of events, by no means uncommon, which are meaningfully but not causally connected. Such events we normally call coincidences and attribute to chance, but, Jung insisted, there is an important distinction to be made between 'meaningful coincidences' and 'meaningless chance groupings'. Esoteric and Eastern philosophies recognize this distinction, but in classical Western physics CAUSALITY is the only acknowledged mode of connection between events. Jung's own thinking had been greatly stimulated by the classic of ancient Chinese philosophy and divination, the I CHING[3], which he regarded as the supreme endorsement and illustration of the validity of the principle of synchronicity. A person who consults the *I Ching* is guided to the relevant text in it by performing the apparently arbitrary act of tossing three coins six times and noting the patterns of 'heads' and 'tails' in which they fall. This method, Jung wrote, 'like all divinatory or intuitive techniques, is based on an acausal or synchronistic connecting principle'.

The UNCONSCIOUS[4], Jung proposed, has three distinct levels, the personal unconscious, the collective unconscious and the 'psychoid' level, and it is the latter two levels that are involved in synchronistic events. At these levels the psyche is unbounded, transpersonal; it is a microcosm that interacts with and reflects the macrocosm. From Leibniz's* philosophy Jung adopted the model of the universe as a 'pre-established harmony', composed of a multiplicity of interrelated monads each of which contains an image of the whole. 'Every body', wrote Leibniz, 'responds to all that happens in the universe, so that he who saw all could read in each one what is happening everywhere, and even what has happened and what will happen.' This corresponds remarkably with the philosophy underlying the *I Ching*, and Jung based his conception of the psyche and its relations with the external world on the Leibnizian model of interrelated wholeness, maintaining that at the collective unconscious and psychoid levels the psyche is thrown open to influences from all points on the continuum which is the universe at any given moment. The human being at a conscious level is enmeshed in a complex of social, economic and personal relations which he partially manipulates and is partially manipulated by; and at the deep unconscious level he is enmeshed in another complex of relations, transcending space, time and causality, which continually form meaningful patterns, or synchronicities, across the continuum of the universe.

Towards the end of his life, Jung put a great deal of time and effort into canvassing his idea of synchronicity among physicists, and gained at least one distinguished supporter in Wolfgang Pauli*. Pauli was the creator of a key concept of QUANTUM THEORY[2], the 'Exclusion Principle'. The philosopher of science Henry Margenau has described Pauli's principle as 'a mathematical symmetry imposed upon the basic equations of nature producing what appears like a dynamic effect'. In the light of this, it is easy to see what drew Jung and Pauli to each other. They had in common the idea that symmetry can produce an apparently dynamic effect, and they brought evidence for it from areas of investigation that according to traditional scientific thinking are widely divergent. One of Jung's profoundest convictions was that the physical and the psychological sciences had been arbitrarily differentiated and must eventually converge. Recent developments in physics (see NONLOCAL CONNECTIONS[2], IMPLICATE ORDER[2]) have not only constituted such a convergence, but also have made the concept of synchronicity less outlandish than it appeared when Jung first proposed it. [161]

Synergy

Basically, the principle that a whole is something greater or other than the sum of its parts, or that when sub-systems coalesce to form a larger system the totality may accrue a bonus benefit resultant from the coalescence. Although originally a term specific to biological science, it has developed wider connotations, for instance in business management, where the bonus benefit may be construed as resulting from corporate mergers. Strictly speaking, however, synergies are not always or necessarily beneficial, for in some cases a coalescence can give rise to problems that disadvantage the totality and diminish its efficiency.

Transcendental ego

Edmund Husserl* took over from Kant* the term 'transcendental ego' to designate the pure consciousness that engages in PHENO-MENOLOGICAL observation. Divested of INTENTIONALITY, of bias, of personality, decontaminated from all influence upon its modes of perception and understanding, the transcendental ego is capable of direct intuitive knowledge of the world; reality 'discloses' itself to it. The concept is a radical departure from the scientific-rational approach to knowledge, although it involves a rigorous intellectual discipline. It has an affinity to mystical concepts, and relevance in the context of the philosophy of CONSCIOUS-NESS[4]. [141]

Vitalism

The belief that there exists in animate organisms a principle or process that distinguishes them from inanimate matter and that is not explicable in terms of mechanistic or physico-chemical processes. The idea goes back to Aristotle, who called this principle ENTE-LECHY[2]. Kepler's *facultas formatrix*, Galvani's 'life force', Goethe's *Gestaltung*, and Bergson's *élan vital*, are other names for it. In the nineteenth and early twentieth centuries vitalist ideas were popular, because they seemed the only alternative to MECHANISM, but as vitalists could not support their ideas with demonstrable proofs, and as physical and biological science made great advances by acting on the assumption that all vital activities could be explained in terms of physico-chemical processes, vitalism tended to fall into disrepute as an unnecessary and rather metaphysical concept. It has not been entirely discredited, however, and indeed it is arguable that there has emerged in modern science a kind of neo-vitalism, and that for instance Schrödinger's* concept of NEGENTROPY[2], Szent-György's* 'SYNTROPY'[2], and Sheldrake's* MORPHIC RESONANCE[2], are fundamentally vitalist concepts, as are some of the basic propositions of GENERAL SYSTEMS THEORY. The fact that the higher and more complex an organism becomes, the more properties it manifests that are not explicable in terms of its component parts or their known modes of interaction, such as self-regulation and purposive drive, supports the vitalist hypothesis. So does the fact that modern physical science acknowledges that causality is not necessarily energetic, for in this case it is possible that a non-physical force or principle could influence physical events without its influence being physically detectable. The fact that microphysical events are now known to be probabilistic and not deterministic also makes plausible the proposition that the proba-

bility of their occurrence could be governed by a non-physical 'field of influence'. [71]

Zeitgeist

The 'spirit of the age', exhibited in convergent tendencies in the arts, science, religion and sometimes more diffuse cultural phenomena such as fashion and modes of speech and interpersonal conduct. That a historical period may be invested with a spirit that is not a product of an interplay of the ideas and developments that spontaneously arise in it, but rather a dynamic substratum from which those ideas and developments take their complexion, is not a concept that generally endears itself to historians, who tend to regard it as itself a product of the German Romantic *Zeitgeist* of the last century, which tended to imbue everything, from nature to the nation-state, with a crypto-spiritual essence. Divested of such implications, however, the term is often descriptively useful when cultural manifestations can be seen to cluster or converge around a related congeries of ideas, beliefs and aspirations, as happened for instance in the 1960s.

See COUNTERCULTURE[7].

2
SCIENCE

Antimatter

RELATIVITY THEORY established the equivalence of matter and energy, and led to the experimental creation of material particles from energy. In 1930 the mathematical physicist Paul Dirac* predicted that for every particle that comes into being there must be a corresponding antiparticle, of equal mass but opposite electrical charge. Two years later the positron, or antiparticle of the electron, was discovered. Theoretically, material objects composed entirely of antimatter could exist, and may exist elsewhere in the universe, but as mutual annihilation results from the collision of particle and antiparticle, the only antimatter that exists in our world – and that only transiently – is in the physics laboratory.

Atom

Originally believed to be the smallest unit of matter and the basic building block of the physical world, the atom has been shown by modern physics to be constituted of a number of subatomic PARTICLES which are themselves quanta of energy. But although atoms are no longer conceivable as solid objects, they are entities in the sense that they are distinguishable from each other according to their weights and structures. Just over a hundred types are known, the majority of which correspond with the natural occurring elements. [328]

Bell's theorem

A mathematical demonstration of the principle of NONLOCAL CON-NECTIONS, worked out by John Bell* in the 1960s, and suggested by the Einstein–Rosen–Podolski thought experiment (see ERP EXPERIMENT) of three decades before. Similarly based upon the behaviour of paired particles that are spatially separated, Bell's theorem conclusively demonstrates that correlations between them not only occur but also that they cannot be attributed to the effect of local 'hidden variables', as physicists concerned to maintain the classical and Einsteinian view of causality had proposed. The predictions advanced by Bell's theorem have subsequently been experimentally tested and proved to be correct. Clauser and Freedman in the US and Alain Aspect in France have independently demonstrated that split correlated pairs of particles behave as if each one of a pair instantaneously 'knows' what happens to the other one, rather like closely connected human beings are sometimes said to know, telepathically, when something drastic happens to one or the other. The implications of Bell's theorem may, in fact, be relevant to understanding TELEPATHY[5]. It is sometimes said that the 'irrationality' of quantum events is confined to the subatomic realm, but, as physicist Henry Stapp* has written: 'The important thing about Bell's theorem is that it puts the dilemma posed by quantum phenomena clearly into the realm of macroscopic phenomena ... [it] shows that our ordinary ideas about the world are somehow profoundly deficient even on the macroscopic level.' [45, 308]

Big bang

The idea that the universe originated in an immense explosion of a dense aggregate of matter is known as the 'big bang hypothesis', and it is held by the majority of present-day cosmologists. According to the theory, the universe came into existence *ex nihilo* between 10,000 and 20,000 million years ago in a cosmic flash which generated all the energy and matter that constitute the universe today. The explosion first generated radiation, and the discovery, in 1965, of cosmic background radiation, a kind of residual glow from the primeval heat, is strong supportive evidence for the big bang hypothesis.

The expansion of the universe initiated by the big bang has been ongoing ever since, and calculations of the rate of expansion have shown that it is precisely the rate that would prevent the cosmos collapsing – if it were fractionally slower – or rapidly dispersing all the cosmic material – if it were fractionally faster. Furthermore, the expansion is uniform, in the sense that it is the same in every direction, which means that the big bang must have been an extraordinarily coherent event, an explosion of exactly the same magnitude at every point. How such coherence, and such fine tuning of the vigour of the explosion, could have occurred by chance, is one of the awesome mysteries of cosmology. [64, 346]

Black hole

A hypothetical astrophysical phenomenon the existence of which is implied by RELATIVITY THEORY. In time every large star must burn away its mass and reach a critical size at which it begins to collapse in upon itself under its own gravitation. Its component matter becomes steadily denser, its surface gravitation stronger, and the space-time around it more curved. Not even light can escape from its ambience, so it becomes unobservable, except through the effects of its gravitational influence on neighbouring bodies. The probable existence of specific black holes has been inferred from observed astronomical perturbations not otherwise explicable. [321]

Bootstrap theory

The story of the boy who fell into a bog and pulled himself out by his own bootstraps is familiar to most modern physicists. Whereas the classical physicist believed in and sought fundamental laws governing physical reality, and sometimes believed these laws God-ordained, the modern physicist has to face the fact that there are no such laws, there is no looking beyond physical reality for the principles that govern it. The analogy points to the fact that for the physicist there is no escape from the conceptual bog unless he relinquishes the expectation of ultimate authoritative answers, and that having relinquished it he might find answers after all, just by accepting and contemplating the very bogginess of the bog.

What is known as bootstrap theory was developed by physicist Geoffrey Chew* in the 1960s, and

Classical physics

has been evolved by him and others since, specifically in an area of particle physics known as S-matrix theory which is concerned with the description of strong particle interactions, but with radical theoretical implications for the whole of physics. Fritjof Capra* has expounded these implications. He writes: 'The bootstrap philosophy not only abandons the idea of fundamental building blocks of matter, but accepts no fundamental entities whatsoever – no fundamental constants, laws, or equations. The universe is seen as a dynamic web of interrelated events. None of the properties of any part of this web is fundamental; they all follow from the properties of the other parts, and the overall consistency of their interrelations determines the structure of the entire web.'

Physical theories are approximations; they apply and work in respect of a limited area of observation, but no one theory yields a coherent overview. A 'bootstrapper' acknowledges this fact, is not dismayed by it, does not conclude from it that nature is basically incoherent and ambiguous. Rather, he recognizes the relevance of a plurality of theories, all of which are the human mind's conceptual approximations, or models, and looks for patterns of mutual consistency between them. If in nature everything is involved with everything else in a dynamic process, if interactions and patterns are more basic phenomena than entities and forces, no single fixed theory or supposedly fundamental law can possibly represent this reality. Boot-strap theory begins by relinquishing the need and quest for such laws, and goes on to seek to comprehend physical reality as it discloses itself in its multiplicity, as a self-consistent and self-governing system of dynamic interactions, which may be locally indeterminate but is coherent overall. [45, 52]

Classical physics

Physics is the science that concerns itself with describing the nature of the physical universe, from the microcosm to the macrocosm, and ascertaining the laws that govern phenomena occurring within it. The descriptions and the body of knowledge of physical laws that were developed in science between the sixteenth and the present century are known as classical physics. In the present century the accuracy of these descriptions and the absoluteness of these laws have been undermined by RELATIVITY and QUANTUM THEORY. Although most of the great discoveries of the modern scientific era, and the great developments in technology, are attributable to the practice of the SCIENTIFIC METHOD and the application of the laws of classical physics, in recent decades a new physics has arisen which has shown the descriptions and the laws of classical physics to be either wrong, approximate, or relevant only in limited spheres.

Fundamental to classical physics was the atomistic concept of matter. It was believed that all material substance was composed of basic 'building blocks', and therefore that anything could be broken down into its component parts to determine its fundamental nature. Nature and the universe were conceived as constituted of things and forces. Physical laws were laws of force and motion, which described how the parts of physical systems worked together. The assumptions that wholes were nothing but aggregates of parts, and that absolute laws governing activity within and between physical systems could be ascertained, led to the adoption of a MECHANISTIC[1] model of physical reality. Absolute concepts of DETERMINISM[1] and CAUSALITY[1] were implicit in this model. The correctness of the model and its underlying assumptions appeared to be confirmed by the great synthesis of scientific knowledge and elucidation of mechanical laws accomplished in the seventeenth century by Isaac Newton*. For two centuries thereafter, classical Newtonian physics and mechanics reigned supreme in science. In whatever field they were applied, the laws held good, and they enabled phenomenal progress in science and technology to be made.

There were problem areas, however. Observations in the fields of electromagnetism and thermal physics were not always easily reconcilable to the Newtonian laws and the mechanistic model, but researchers in these fields were generally able to extend the laws and modify the model to accommodate their observations. The laws of nineteenth-century THERMODYNAMICS are an example of such an accommodation. Although the mechanistic bias of their formulation led to a conclusion irreconcilable with EVOLUTION[1] theory – i.e. that in all physical systems ENTROPY inexorably increases – the general practical applicability and experimental verifiability of the laws caused such theoretical problems to be set aside as anomalous and irrelevant. Greater difficulties, however, were inherent in the classical atomistic model of matter, and in the idea of space and time as absolutes. RELATIVITY THEORY demolished the idea of absolute space and time, and the new experimental techniques for investigating subatomic phenomena demolished the idea of the existence of any fundamental material 'building blocks'. QUANTUM THEORY further undermined the edifice of classical physics by demonstrating that the supposed absolute laws of its mechanics did not hold good for subatomic phenomena, and even that its foundation stone of causality and determinism was shaky. It also demonstrated that the very project of classical physics – the project of objective observation and description of nature and the universe – was impossible.

It cannot be said that a science that led to the development of the internal combustion engine and the understanding of the structure of DNA – to name but two of its thousands of triumphs – was wrong. What was wrong with classical physics was its claims to infallibility and absoluteness, and its fundamental mechanistic bias. The new physics of today makes no such claims and is cautiously aware of the pitfalls of paradigmatic bias. [105]

Clock paradox
See RELATIVITY THEORY.

Coherent light
Light radiation in which all the excited atoms vibrate together, producing waves of the same phase. The generation of coherent light, and its amplification by means of mirrors, is the basis of laser technology. Coherent light produces a beam of energy whose intensity and focus can be finely controlled. On the one hand it can be used as a destructive military weapon, and on the other for the purposes of microsurgery.

Complementarity
A term introduced into the vocabulary of QUANTUM THEORY by the Danish physicist Niels Bohr* to explain the phenomenon of WAVE-PARTICLE DUALITY. The fact that in different experimental situations light can manifest either wave-like or particle-like characteristics suggested to Bohr the idea that these apparently mutually exclusive characteristics should be conceived not in terms of an irreconcilable dualism but rather as complementary properties of a fundamental reality. It was not a question of either-or, but of both-and; light was both wave-like and particle-like, and both descriptions were essential to a complete understanding of the phenomenon. Bohr saw a parallel between his concept of complementarity and the ancient Chinese idea of the dynamic interaction of the polar opposite principles of YIN AND YANG[3], and he believed that the principle had relevance not only in physics but also to life and philosophy. In science generally, the principle of complementarity draws attention to the fact that an experimenter or observer cannot but be involved in determining the results of his experiment or observation. Different experimental strategies will yield different and maybe paradoxical conclusions, but knowledge is not advanced by championing a particular conclusion but rather by embracing all conclusions under the umbrella of complementarity, even if this leaves a paradox unresolved. [35]

Critical mass
For a nuclear chain reaction to occur a specific minimum quantity of radioactive material must be available. This quantity is known as the critical mass. The term is sometimes used metaphorically, in contexts where a cumulative build-up, for instance of dissonant elements within a population or within a body of information, reaches a point where an explosive reaction or revolutionary change suddenly occurs.

Curved space
See RELATIVITY THEORY.

Darwinism
The theory of EVOLUTION[1] expounded by the English naturalist Charles Darwin*. The cornerstone of the Darwinian theory, explaining both the diversity of species

and the process of their evolution, is the principle of natural selection. This principle regards the characteristics of living beings as determined by passive adaptation to environmental conditions. Alternative theories take the view that living organisms are active in their environment and develop through their initiative in adapting to or exploiting it (see LAMARCKISM).

Darwinian theory holds that the hereditary process throws up occasional variations, and that those variations that are beneficial to an organism in its environment will be 'selected' for survival, i.e. the variations best 'fitted' to the environment will prevail while others die out. Existence or survival are conceived in terms of a struggle or battle; the Tennysonian concept of 'nature red in tooth and claw' is quintessentially Darwinian, as are 'laissez faire' and 'monetarist' economics. According to Darwinism, variations occur entirely by chance. Evolution is in no way purposive. Moreover, it is a closed system in the sense that nothing outside the process governs it or can intervene in it. Man therefore has no unique status in the order of nature except as the dominant – because best adapted – form of animal life. It was because such implications contradicted religious ideas of the omnipotence and omnipresence of God (Samuel Butler* said that Darwin had 'banished God from the universe'), and of the unique spiritual nature of human beings, that Darwinism sparked off vehement controversy when it was first propounded.

It is clear today that Darwinism owed its success in part to its compatibility with POSITIVISM[1], MATERIALISM[1] and MECHANISM[1], philosophies that reigned in the nineteenth century. Early critics drew attention to the circularity of the argument of the survival of the fittest (the fittest being by definition those who survive). Darwin himself acknowledged that his theory could not answer certain fundamental problems, such as the emergence of new characteristics in the evolution of species. Contemporary biological theory assumed that offspring inherited about equal proportions of characteristics from each parent, and if this were true it was impossible to explain how beneficial variations could ever become established, since they would be rapidly diluted from generation to generation. It was not until the work of Gregor Mendel* on the laws of inheritance was rediscovered at the turn of the century that the answer was found. The science of GENETICS that developed from it helped to establish Darwinism as a scientific theory, and the reformulation of the theory in terms of Mendelian genetics became known as neo-Darwinism.

In neo-Darwinist evolution theory, the appearance of chance variations in the hereditary process is attributed to genetic mutation, which occurs through miscopying of the genetic structure of DNA in the process of reproduction. However, it is known that the copying process is remarkably accurate, and that when miscopyings (or 'point mutations') occur they are usually deleterious or neutral, so the idea of random mutation throwing up beneficial variations sufficiently robust or profuse for natural selection to bring about the appearance of new species is open to question. Furthermore, an evolutionary improvement in an organism requires several coherent, co-ordinated and simultaneous mutations. As the very principles of coherence and co-ordination are incompatible with randomness, the neo-Darwinian hypothesis seems to be at a logical impasse. Moreover, the principle of random mutation seems irreconcilable with certain observed facts, such as that the placental and marsupial mammals, although they evolved independently of each other for several hundred million years (after Australia became an island), diversified along parallel lines. 'Missing links' in the fossil record – the fact that evidence for major evolutionary transitions, such as from reptiles to mammals or birds, have not been found – also call into question the Darwinian notion of evolution as a gradual progression from the most rudimentary life forms to the most complex. [61, 62, 65, 136, 198, 266]

Dimensions
See HYPERSPACE.

Dissipative structure
A term coined by the Nobel laureate Belgian chemist Ilya Prigogine* to describe the characteristics of physical systems in far-from-equilibrium states. According to the laws of THERMODYNAMICS, in physical systems ENTROPY steadily increases until the whole system runs down into a state of equilibrium.

While the MECHANISTIC[1] paradigm was paramount in science, the idea prevailed that everything eventually 'ran down' – biological systems through senescence, the universe through HEAT-DEATH, civilizations through a process of degradation into disorder – even though the (also mechanistic) theory of EVOLUTION[1] was not easily reconcilable to it. To accommodate evolution, a distinction had to be made between non-living and living physical systems, in terms of the former being 'closed' systems which would degrade to a state of equilibrium, and the latter being 'open' systems (i.e. open to interaction with their environment and consequently capable of growth, reproduction, etc.). 'Open' systems maintain themselves in far-from-equilibrium states and manifest dynamic characteristics; they change and evolve.

Prigogine's research has been of physical systems in far-from-equilibrium states. In the light of it, a distinction between living and non-living systems in terms of conventional thermodynamic or entropy theory has proved untenable. Certain chemical systems have been observed to manifest properties of change, self-organization and stability in far-from-equilibrium states that make them look structurally and dynamically like living systems. It was to describe such systems that Prigogine coined the term 'dissipative structure'. What is dissipated in such structures is entropy. They manifest an internal dynamic which combats the build-up of entropy and prevents the onset of equilibrium.

The internal dynamic of a dissipative structure governs not only a self-organizing and self-maintaining process, but also a self-changing one. A highly volatile condition of perturbation and fluctuation in the system is essential to this process. Paradoxically, the more volatile a system is, the greater the perturbations within it, the more stable it is. An illustrative analogy is a vortex in a flowing river: it requires a fast rate of flow of water into it and through it to maintain its stability. This analogy does not, however, illustrate the most significant characteristic of dissipative structures, which is that when a critical point of fluctuation in a system is reached, when it is apparently most volatile and perturbed, it can suddenly 'jump' into a new stable order that had not been manifest in it before, but had existed, as in the systems of QUANTUM mechanics, only as one of its many potentialities.

This dynamic process has suggestive correspondences with physicist David Bohm's* concept of the 'unfolding' of the IMPLICATE ORDER into the explicate. It has implications, too, for evolution theory (see PUNCTUATED EQUILIBRIUM). In fact, so suggestive is the dissipative structure theory that it appears rapidly to be acquiring the status of a new PARADIGM[1]. Order, and the creation or emergence of new forms of order, are primary concerns of human beings, both as individuals and as societies, and the demonstration that new and higher forms of order may manifest spontaneously in highly perturbed systems carries obvious implications for psychology, for sociology and for history. Such extensions of the theory carry it into the realm of metaphor, which in itself is not reprehensible and certainly does not discredit the scientific value of the theory, although, as with the HOLOGRAPHIC PARADIGM and the many speculations upon the implications of quantum theory, the distinction between scientific fact and scientific metaphor needs to be clearly understood. [255]

DNA

The DNA (deoxyribonucleic acid) molecule is the component of the genes that carries hereditary instructions. Its function was first discovered in the 1940s by scientists at the Rockefeller Institute for Medical Research in New York led by immunologist Oswald Avery. This led to a scientific race to determine its precise structure, a race which was won in 1953 by Maurice Wilkins*, James Watson* and Francis Crick*, who shared a 1962 Nobel Prize for their discovery. What they discovered was that DNA is structured in the form of a double helix, i.e. two nucleotide chains twisted around each other. To look at, what is known as the Watson-Crick model of DNA is a jumble of tight-packed different coloured balls (representing the different nucleotides) comprising two strings twisted together. Precisely how this chain constitutes the 'genetic code' of information and controls the functioning of cells was elucidated by subsequent research.

A code is a system of correspondences between two different sequences of events. Say, for instance, I had four picture cards, of an apple, an orange, a pear and a lemon. I could decide that a combination of any three in a particular order would stand for a letter, and could work out an alphabet on this basis. In the DNA code the letters are the four base nucleotides – A, T, G and C. Each sequence of three of them on the chain spells out a 'word', or a specification for a particular amino acid. As a DNA molecule can contain up to 10 million nucleotides in its two chains, a lot of 'words' can be spelled out. The amino acid chains – or 'sentences' – that are formed of these 'three-letter words' specify particular proteins. The 'sentences' are the genes. Each gene instructs the making of a specific enzyme, a special protein which in turn controls a particular chemical reaction within the cell. In order to produce a specific result – for instance, the manufacture of a hair-colour pigment – the interaction of several genes and their associated enzymes may be required. And as different cells perform different functions, usually only a small section of the DNA chain will be used. Whether the rest remains dormant or whether it serves some other function (Fritjof Capra* has suggested that it 'may well be used for integrative activities which biologists are likely to remain ignorant of as long as they adhere to reductionist models') is not at present known. [45, 340]

Electromagnetic spectrum
The fact that electricity and mag-

netism are not two distinct forces but manifestations of the same force was demonstrated in the mid-nineteenth century, experimentally by Michael Faraday* and theoretically by James Clerk Maxwell*. The postulate of the existence of force fields (see FIELD THEORY) led to that of electromagnetic waves, of different lengths or periodic undulations, which travel through the fields. Maxwell worked out equations for the speed of wave propagation, and mathematically predicted the existence of radio waves before they were experimentally produced in the laboratory by Heinrich Hertz*. Subsequent research established the existence of a range of electromagnetic waves, differing in the frequency of their oscillations, from cosmic rays to gamma rays, X-rays, light rays (including the invisible ultra-violet and infra-red), radar and radio waves, and these constitute what is known as the electromagnetic spectrum.

Entelechy
An Aristotelian term adopted by the German embryologist Hans Driesch* to denote a vital principle in organic systems which governs their attainment of their goal or end. Driesch observed that when a part of an embryo is removed the remaining part is able to generate a more or less normal adult organism. He argued from this observation that living systems are not MECHANISTIC[1], because no machine can remain a whole after parts of it are removed, and therefore that their ultimate form must

be determined by an inherent formative principle which is itself non-physical and non-energetic.

See MORPHOGENESIS and VITALISM[1]. [71]

Entropy

Coined by Rudolf Clausius* in 1865 in the context of the second law of THERMODYNAMICS, the word 'entropy' is a quantifiable term which refers to the degree of thermal dissipation in an isolated physical system. It is a measure of the degree of order in a system – low entropy equating with a high degree and high entropy with the reverse. Closed systems are subject to an irreversible process of entropy increase, leading ultimately to a state of equilibrium where all activity has ceased (see HEAT-DEATH). However, in living systems, a reverse process, of the generation of higher degrees of order out of lower, takes place, and the terms NEGENTROPY and SYNTROPY have been coined to describe this.

See DISSIPATIVE STRUCTURE. [265]

ERP experiment

The ERP experiment or ERP paradox is a thought experiment proposed in 1935 by Einstein* and two colleagues, Nathan Rosen and Boris Podolski. It was designed to demonstrate a supposed fundamental flaw in QUANTUM THEORY, but ironically it has been employed most effectively to illustrate precisely the interpretation of quantum mechanics that Einstein found antipathetic to his fundamentally MECHANISTIC[1] and DE-TERMINISTIC[1] concept of the physical universe.

The original ERP experiment proposed that an atom comprising two electrons be split and the electrons made to fly off in opposite directions at high speed. Quantum theory maintains that the momentum and position of the two separate particles will remain correlated: a proposition which is not inconsistent with the laws of classical physics. But according to the Heisenberg* UNCERTAINTY PRINCIPLE, if the position of one of the particles were to be measured, its momentum would become indeterminable. How, Einstein and his colleagues asked, would this affect the second particle? Paradoxically, according to quantum theory, the measurement of the position of particle A would enable both the momentum and position of particle B to be ascertained, which would violate the uncertainty principle.

Physicist David Bohm* later refined the ERP experiment by proposing that the 'spin' of one of the particles be measured. According to quantum mechanics, in a two-particle system the spin of the two components will always be equal and opposite, so that if the spin of particle A is *up*, that of particle B will be *down*, or if A has a spin *right*, B will have a spin *left*. Further, the axis of rotation of a spinning electron is indeterminable, that is to say it exists only as a probability until an observation or measurement is made. And the act of measurement itself perturbs the electron spin. This implies not only that a measurement of particle A will give information about particle B, but also that a physical effect upon particle A will simultaneously affect particle B. It is in fact possible to orient the spin of a particle with a magnetic field, so even if particle B is tens of thousands of miles apart from particle A, its spin can still be changed if that of particle A is experimentally perturbed.

This violated the classical, and Einsteinian, concept of cause and effect. It was manifestly impossible, Einstein said, that what we do to particle A should simultaneously affect the independent and spatially separated particle B, for there could be no causal link between the two events. Even if some kind of information transfer were supposed to take place between the two particles, this could not occur instantaneously, for information cannot travel faster than the speed of light, and theoretically the particles could be separated by an immense distance.

What was manifestly impossible to Einstein and his colleagues has, however, been accepted by later physicists as fundamental to quantum reality. In that reality any physical system is an 'undivided wholeness' (Bohm's term), and effects occurring in any part of it will simultaneously affect both other parts and the whole without the operation of any physically determinate mode of interaction.

See also NONLOCAL CONNECTIONS, BELL'S THEOREM, SYNCHRONICITY[1]. [34]

Ethology

The scientific observation of animal behaviour. Ethology has developed in the present century as a science distinct from zoology through its emphasis upon studying behaviour under natural conditions, without experimental interference. Ethologists observe and describe the structures of animal behaviours, develop hypotheses about the ways these behaviours relate and the purposes they serve, and make further observations to test their hypotheses. Behaviours such as courtship habits, play, aggressiveness, maternal caring, and territorialism are typically studied.

Ethology undoubtedly throws light on human behaviour, and some contributions to the literature (e.g. Lorenz's* *On Aggression*, Morris's* *The Naked Ape*, and Tiger* and Fox's* *The Imperial Animal*) have significantly influenced popular attitudes to and understanding of human behaviour. Such works have, however, been criticized for interpreting animal behaviour in human terms, and then drawing conclusions which, applied back to human behaviours, reinforce them as 'only natural'. Patriarchal dominance and territorialism may be cited as examples of such dubiously sanctioned behaviours. [194, 225, 323]

Exobiology

Exobiology is said by its proponents to be 'the science of extraterrestrial life', although purists would object that there cannot be a science of something the very existence of which is conjectural. However, the hypothesis that life exists elsewhere in the universe can be scientifically investigated, even if it does not meet the requirement of FALSIFIABILITY that is demanded of a truly scientific hypothesis. Exobiology is perhaps a misnomer since the sciences involved in the investigative procedures are not exclusively the biological sciences. All that the latter can do is specify the physical conditions necessary for the occurrence and sustenance of biological life at varying levels of complexity, and study extraterrestrial material, for instance meteorites, for evidence of its existence. Such studies have, in fact, been positive, and lend the theory of PANSPERMIA some credibility. The question whether intelligent, as distinct from rudimentary biological, life exists extraterrestrially is a matter of multidisciplinary conjecture, and astronomers, communications technologists, anthropologists and historians, and students of anomalous phenomena such as UFOs, have all made contributions to the investigation without any clear conclusion having yet been reached. [280]

Experimenter effect

The fact that in a scientific observation or experiment the observer or experimenter himself has an effect which must be taken into account is a fundamental principle of QUANTUM THEORY.

In classical, Newtonian mechanics, a system or object was taken to be in a single, constant state, and to be observable at any time in that state. When physicists got down to the observation of the subatomic world, this single-state principle was found to be quite inadequate. Subatomic systems are in a state of continual fluctuation, and as these fluctuations are not determined by laws of motion or of force-fields it is not possible to predict what state the system will be in at any particular time; it is only possible to describe the system in terms of calculable probabilities. So between observations a system is in a combination of mutually exclusive states. This combination is known as the 'state vector', and a complete description of the system is the description of its state vector.

When an observation of a system is made, the state vector is said to 'collapse'; i.e. to become fixed in one of its probabilities or component states. This fixing is the experimenter effect. The observation or measurement thus accomplished is not of the system in its totality, but only in one of its probabilities, and therefore must be construed as only approximate, and certainly no universal relevance can be claimed for it.

The above describes how the idea of the experimenter effect arose in the context of the quantum theory of measurement. This has led in other contexts to an understanding of the relativity and approximateness of scientific experiments and their results. An experiment is a device for posing a question, and experimental results, or answers, are conditioned by the method of questioning, i.e. by the experimenter's consciousness and its limitations. This does not only mean that science can only get the right answers if it asks the right

Field theory

questions, but also that in the actual conduct of an experiment the consciousness of the experimenter may play a part in determining the results. In PSI[5] research, for instance, it is now generally recognized that some experimenters appear to have a psi-conducive and others a psi-inhibiting effect on the experiment, and also that the 'set and setting' of the experimental design may similarly have a positive or an inhibiting influence. [135]

Falsifiability

A principle proposed by the philosopher Karl Popper* to define scientific theory. The efforts of science, Popper proposed, should be directed not towards proving theories, but towards disproving them. A theory arrived at by the inductive method of making observations or doing experiments designed to prove it is not a scientific truth, according to Popper, because a single negative observation or result can demolish it, and there can never be total certainty that such an observation or result will not occur. A sound scientific theory is one that leads to the formulation of predictions that can be tested experimentally and thus shown to be false. By this criterion, most theories proposed in the areas of psychology, sociology, and parapsychology, for instance, would not qualify. [254]

Field theory

Experimental and theoretical physics in the nineteenth and early twentieth centuries led to the abandonment of the classical concept of physical reality as constituted of particles in favour of the concept of fields. In classical physical theory material objects and the space around them were distinct things; matter existed in space, but that space was itself void. Gravitation was a force emanating from material bodies which propagated across this empty space. Investigation of the phenomena of electricity and magnetism in the mid nineteenth century by Faraday* and Maxwell* led to the introduction of the concept of fields, as complex patterns of energy emanating from electrically charged bodies which could affect other similarly charged bodies within their ambience. The assumptions of classical physics were not fundamentally perturbed by the field concept, however, until Einstein* developed his theory of General RELATIVITY. Einstein's theory not only unified the gravitational and electromagnetic fields, but also established the primacy of the field. It was not a case of material bodies emanating from a field, but rather of them manifesting within fields as intense condensations of the forces there deployed. The concept of matter as a transient phenomenon manifesting within a field was further developed in QUANTUM THEORY, which demonstrated that at the subatomic level the very concept of a material particle was insupportable, for ostensible particles could manifest as waves under different experimental conditions. Moreover, in quantum field theory the concept of force has been radically revised. When subatomic particles interact, they do so not by exerting force upon each other but by exchanging sub-particles, or 'virtual' particles, which only exist for the duration of the interaction. No laws determine these interactions. Order and lawfulness exist only as properties of the field. The metaphor of a web or network is often used to represent the field and the interactions that occur within it, for it conveys the fact that there is no separateness, that everything is interconnected and involved in a dynamic of interaction.

Field theory has suggested to some philosophically minded physicists and science writers a new model of reality and of the universe, for when the concept of order developed in relativity and quantum field theory is extended to the macroscopic world it implies a fundamental unity, wholeness and interconnectedness which not only make observed phenomena coherent but also turn out to be consistent with principles of religious and esoteric philosophy. [44, 105, 135]

Fission

A nuclear reaction in which the atomic nucleus is split, by being bombarded with neutrons, resulting in the release of energy and radioactivity. Nuclear power stations and the atomic bomb work on the principle of deriving energy from fission.

Formative causation

The proposition that there exists in nature a formative or causative principle which produces effects upon living organisms and their behaviours but is itself immaterial and non-energetic was put forward by Rupert Sheldrake* in 1981.

In the life sciences as at present understood a mechanistic view of causation prevails. This applies equally to neo-Darwinian EVOLUTION[1] theory, which explains evolution in terms of random mutation and the process of natural selection, and to orthodox embryology, which explains the growth and regeneration of biological structures in terms of genetic programmes carried by DNA molecules. But these mechanistic interpretations run up against problems: in evolution, the problems of explaining evolutionary 'jumps', the emergence of new forms, and the fact that like characteristics develop independently in different species; and in biology, the problem of how cells constituted of the same DNA become specified for different functions. An even greater problem is posed by behaviour, both instinctual behaviour such as spiders' ability to spin webs, and learned behaviour, such as the maze-running and other abilities developed in laboratory rats. Mechanistic principles of causation cannot convincingly overcome these problems, and Sheldrake's argument is that his hypothesis of formative causation not only overcomes them but also offers more plausible explanations than MECHANISM[1] does of the processes of evolution, biogenesis, healing, learning and memory, and furthermore affords a possible approach to the comprehension of a whole range of phenomena that present science ignores and categorizes as paranormal or supernatural.

Sheldrake's hypothesis brings FIELD THEORY into biology. While field theory has long been respectable in physics, because electromagnetic field-effects are demonstrable and measurable, it has not been accepted in orthodox biology because of the dominant bias towards explaining things in terms of chemical processes. Sheldrake's proposition is that the patterning for the genesis of biological structures is not chemically coded in DNA but is laid down in a 'morphogenetic field', i.e. a field which determines shape and form. Such fields are not empirically detectable because they do not have an energy component; but they work in synchrony with energetic causation to create form and spatial order in developing or regenerating biological systems. Sheldrake calls this non-energetic influence 'morphic resonance', and he further hypothesizes that this resonance builds up cumulatively so that the past forms of a structure or system determine the form adopted when new forms are generated. With regard to behaviour, the hypothesis holds that learned behaviours are reinforced in species by morphic resonance. Furthermore, because field-effects, being non-energetic, are not attenuated by travelling through space, it is possible that increased facility in learning and in the exercise of newly learned skills should manifest in different groups of a species in widely separated locations without any mode of physical communication or influence exist-

ing between these groups – which is a phenomenon that has in fact been observed. Sheldrake cites the results of experiments conducted with rats in the 1920s and 1930s, independently in Edinburgh, Harvard and Melbourne, which were designed to test the Lamarckian proposition that learned characteristics and behaviours can be inherited. In all three of these experimental situations the rates of learning of the rats markedly improved from generation to generation, but the improvement was not consistent with Lamarckian theory, for it was quite uncorrelated with the animals' breeding or training. Sheldrake argues that not only are the results compatible with his theory of formative causation, but would even have been predicted by it.

See also MORPHOGENESIS. [294]

Fourth dimension
See RELATIVITY THEORY.

Fusion
A nuclear reaction in which an atomic nucleus is produced from the union of two lighter nuclei. Greater amounts of energy can be thus produced than by FISSION, but because fusion requires far higher operating temperatures the process is not used for nuclear power generation. The hydrogen bomb, however, derives its power from fusion.

Genetics
The science of heredity. Its founder was Gregor Mendel*. Experimenting with the common pea, Mendel developed and cross-bred strains

with specific characteristics and observed what happened to those characteristics as they passed through several generations. He found that they were inherited according to very specific laws, and he proposed that there must exist in the reproductive cell distinct 'units of heredity' that carry particular characteristics. He published his findings in 1865, but it was not until the early 1900s that scientists began to realize that the laws of heredity that Mendel had formulated for plants applied to all living things, including human beings. Then William Bateson* coined the term 'gene' for Mendel's 'unit of heredity', and 'genetics' for the new science.

Genetics furnished the answer to the fundamental problem of Darwinian EVOLUTION[1] theory: how beneficial variations within species became hereditarily established. It explained the mechanism of evolution. Throughout the present century it has been the central area of research in biology. With the discovery by the biologist Thomas Hunt Morgan* that genes are grouped together to form chromosomes a further breakthrough was made in the science of heredity. But precisely what genes were, how they worked and how heredity information was coded into them remained a mystery until in the 1940s a number of scientists began to investigate the function and structure of the DNA molecule – research which led in 1953 to the so-called breaking of the genetic code by Maurice Wilkins*, Francis Crick* and James Watson*. This work elucidated the biochemical processes involved in the transmission of hereditary information, but it did not elucidate precisely what kinds of information can be so transmitted. There developed from it a school of biological determinism that proposed that all aspects of human character and behaviour, individual and social, are genetically encoded and transmitted: a view which carries sinister implications.

See SOCIOBIOLOGY. [17, 273, 340]

Geometrodynamics

A term coined by physicist John A. Wheeler* for a theory developed by himself and others from Einstein's General Theory of RELATIVITY. It is concerned with the dynamics of curved space, and proposes that the Einsteinian concept of four-dimensional space-time is of limited validity. What Wheeler calls 'superspace' is multi-dimensional. The access points to other dimensions are what he calls 'worm-holes' in the curved surface of space-time, and the dynamics of these worm-holes are similar to the dynamics of cosmological BLACK HOLES. The theory proposes that superspace could serve as a short cut between locations distantly separated in four-dimensional space-time, and that the multiplicity of the worm-holes in its surface could imply that space-time is 'multiply connected'. A consequence of the theory is that 'one has to forgo that view of nature in which every event, past, present or future, occupies its preordained position in a grand catalog called "space-time". There is no space-time, there is no time, there is no before, there is no after'. Wheeler's theories have been regarded as a breakthrough in orthodox science wich may make explicable many things that have long been rejected as incomprehensible and probably delusory PARANORMAL PHENOMENA[5]. [325, 349]

Gödel's theorem

A modern mathematical restatement of the logical dilemma presented by the ancient Cretan philosopher Epeminides when he stated: 'All Cretans are liars.' The dilemma arises from the fact that the statement is self-referring and although apparently coherent has an inherent irreducible contradiction which renders logic powerless to assert its truth or falsehood. In 1931 Kurt Gödel* demonstrated that every formal language, including mathematics, contains meaningful formulations that are nonsensical because neither they nor their negations can be deduced from their fundamental axioms. The implications for theoretical science were profoundly disturbing, for fundamental to the scientific endeavour as it was then conceived was the principle of deductive derivation of scientific truth from established axioms and its formulation in the precise language of mathematics.

Gödel's theorem proved that there could be no such thing as expressible scientific truth, that any descriptive statement must be regarded as approximate and suspect, and that no scientific system could ever be complete (it was formally known as the 'Incompleteness Theorem'). At about the same time as Gödel published his theorem, QUANTUM physics was producing observations and theories that likewise required the abandonment of the totalizing scientific endeavour, and the BOOTSTRAP THEORY that later developed in physics was an approach designed to accommodate scientific observation and description to the implications of Gödel's theorem.

Those implications reach beyond science, into whatever area man has conceived the project of comprehending totality, ultimate truth or meaning. They are particularly unsettling for religious thought, and for the formulation and pursuit of projects generally associated with the religious life, such as knowing God or achieving enlightenment. Such concepts imply a progress towards a goal, but the theorem shows the goal to be illusory, so the idea of progress becomes meaningless. Certain esoteric and mystical religious traditions accommodate better to this situation than do orthodox attitudes, for instance ZEN[3] Buddhism, which mocks the totalizing and discursive projects of the human mind, and with its puzzles and KOANS[3] systematically confounds them in its devotees. [233]

Half-life

Individual PARTICLES decay randomly and unpredictably, but in a large population of identical particles it is possible to predict on a statistical basis how long it will take for that population to be depleted by 50 per cent. This duration is known as the half-life of the particular particle.

Heat-death

The application to cosmology of the second law of THERMO-DYNAMICS leads to the conclusion that gradually ENTROPY must increase in the universe, resulting in an ultimate run-down state of dissipated heat energy that cannot be converted into anything else. This hypothetical end-state is known as the heat-death of the universe.

Holographic paradigm

A theoretical model or metaphor for an emergent new worldview which conceives physical systems as indivisible wholes. Whereas formerly science tended to regard physical systems as aggregates of independent parts, in the holographic PARADIGM[1] parts are interdependent; and as well as the whole being conceived as containing parts, the parts are conceived as reciprocally containing the whole. The paradigm is derived from the process of three-dimensional photography by laser known as holography. A characteristic of a holographic plate is that if it is cut up into small pieces an image of the original whole structure can be retrieved from every single fragment. This characteristic has suggested to scientists in various fields new theoretical and experimental strategies. In physics, the holographic paradigm is more consonant with developments in QUANTUM THEORY than was the MECH-ANISTIC[1] paradigm, and theoretical physicist David Bohm* has developed a theoretical model of the universe as holographic. In neuroscience, Karl Pribram* has applied the holographic paradigm to his study of the brain, and has found it more consistent with experimental findings, for instance that specific memories are not stored in specific sites in the brain but appear to be distributed throughout, than was the model of the brain as a telephone exchange or a computer.

The holographic paradigm, it must be emphasized, is a suggestive working model for theoretical and experimental science, though one with limitations. For instance, it is intrinsically static and cannot represent dynamic processes. It is an approximation, a new and provocative paradigm certainly, but not a comprehensive one. [354]

Holomovement

A term coined by the theoretical physicist David Bohm* in the context of his theory of the IMPLIC-ATE ORDER. In a sense analogous to the way that a radio wave 'carries' an ordered structure that can be aurally or visually decoded, so the holomovement 'carries' an implicate order. Aspects of the implicate order may in certain circumstances become explicate or be 'unfolded' through the holomovement. Laws governing these processes of unfolding may be ascertained, for instance the laws pertaining to electromagnetic or sound waves, but the relevance of these laws is limited to specific circumstances and they should not be taken as universal. In the holomovement, phenomena become explicate and perceived as lawful, but the holomovement itself cannot be so perceived. Physics

cannot undertake the project of ascertaining the law of the whole.
Newtonian mechanics was long
thought to have accomplished this,
but RELATIVITY and QUANTUM
THEORY showed that the Newtonian laws had only limited relevance. It could be said that the
world of relativity and quantum
physics was an implicate order underlying the order of CLASSICAL
PHYSICS, and that in the present
century this formerly unperceived
implicate order has become explicate. But underlying it are other
implicate orders, the totality of
which constitutes the holomovement, which itself is 'undefinable
and immeasurable'. [34]

Hyperspace
RELATIVITY   THEORY   established that the classical manner of
conceiving physical reality in terms
of a three-dimensional space and
an entirely independent dimension
of time was untenable. Micro- and
macro-physical phenomena could
only be described in terms of
a four-dimensional continuum,
'space-time'. The space-time concept explained the 'force' of gravitation in terms of geometry. But it
did not enable all known physical
forces and effects to be so explained; in particular it did not
explain electromagnetism. To accommodate electromagnetism, suggested the Polish physicist Theodor
Kaluza in 1921, another space
dimension had to be postulated,
making physical reality five-dimen-
sional. Although the mathematical
demonstration of the existence of
the fifth dimension was elegant,
physical evidence for it was non-

existent and it was virtually impossible to visualize. The fact that
inhabitants of a two-dimensional
'Flatland' would not be able to
visualize our ostensibly three-
dimensional universe argued for
the possibility of the existence of
the postulated extra dimension,
but where was it? A Swedish physicist, Oscar Klein, suggested in
1926 that it might be 'rolled up' so
infinitesimally small that it eluded
observation. The Kaluza–Klein
theory was designed to accommodate electromagnetism into a unified
FIELD THEORY. Since it was formulated two other fundamental
forces of nature have been discovered, the strong and the weak
nuclear forces, and to accommodate these mathematical physics has
had to postulate an eleven-dimen-
sional universe. The extra dimensions are often referred to as
'hyperspace' or 'superspace', and
these concepts have sometimes
been invoked to explain PARA-
NORMAL PHENOMENA[5] occurring within perceived space-time
as involving intrusion or transition
interactions with these dimensions.
   See also GEOMETRODYNAM-
ICS. [64, 349]

Implicate order
That the universe is in some
manner ordered is an assumption
fundamental to all science. MECH-
ANISTIC[1] science assumes that the
order is machine-like in the sense
of being an assemblage of parts
into wholes, with action and interaction governed by the laws pertaining to energy. This model is
not consistent with QUANTUM
physics. The theoretical physicist

David Bohm* has developed a new concept of order which is so consistent. He has proposed that we think in terms of an order of 'undivided wholeness' in which phenomena have two potential states, the 'enfolded' or 'implicate' state and the 'unfolded' or 'explicate' state.

To illustrate how in the implicate order everything is enfolded in everything else, and how the implicate order may become explicate through a process of unfolding, Bohm cites a simple laboratory experiment. If an insoluble droplet of ink is put into glycerine, in a container equipped with a device that will stir the glycerine slowly, the droplet will become attenuated to a thread and will eventually disappear as the fluid is stirred. But if the direction of the stirring is reversed, the droplet will appear again, reconstituted. When it had apparently disappeared it was 'implicated' or 'enfolded' in the glycerine; and the manner of its reappearance illustrates the principle of 'unfolding'. When it was enfolded, the particles that comprised it were apparently randomly distributed in the glycerine, but the fact that they could be reconstituted into the droplet indicates that some sort of order pertained in their implicate state.

Another illustration of Bohm's is the hologram. If any part of a holographic plate is illuminated, the whole picture can be seen in it; i.e. the totality is implicit, or enfolded, in the part. Lens photography, on the other hand, emphasizes the point-to-point correspondence of object and image, and its employment in science to

isolate for inspection very minute or very distant objects tended to confirm the mechanistic view of life and the universe. The new scientific world view, Bohm suggests, should be based on the HOLOGRAPHIC PARADIGM, and on the idea that 'a total order is contained, in some implicit sense, in each region of space and time'.

Until very recently, physical science has concerned itself exclusively with the precise description of the explicate order, but now progress lies in the direction of giving primary relevance to the implicate order, to the undivided wholeness. When science attends to the explicate order in which elements manifest as independent of and outside each other, this apparent separateness not only determines the mode of scientific inquiry but is also taken as constituting a fundamental reality. It is assumed that there is nothing but the manifest explicate order. This assumption cannot be squared with QUANTUM THEORY.

Both the mathematical equations and the actual experiments of quantum physics, according to Bohm, point to the existence of a multi-dimensional reality. He proposes that 'there is a second implicate order which organises the primary order'. The ink-in-glycerine and hologram analogies illustrate the process of enfoldment and unfoldment in three dimensions, but QUANTUM THEORY suggests the existence of a 'super-implicate order', or 'quantum formative field' which relates fields in different parts of space and in fact encompasses the entire universe.

Bohm's theoretical formulations are an attempt to make coherent the apparently lawless world of quantum physics and to create a new PARADIGM[1] which may suggest directions for innovative research. But they also have wider implications. As the underlying assumptions of MECHANISM[1] extended beyond the science that gave rise to them, so the underlying assumptions of the 'undivided wholeness' order of reality might have an extended influence. If, instead of thinking in terms of separate entities and the forces that govern their interactions, we think in terms of a fundamental wholeness that embraces and interrelates all the elements that constitute it, this very mode of thought will determine new approaches, for instance to medicine, economics, and ecology.

Bohm's theory also has relevance to the philosophy and psychology of CONSCIOUSNESS[4]. What we consider normal consciousness attends to the explicate order. But there are modes of consciousness (and the work of the psychologist Jean Piaget* suggests that they are primary in the experience of young children) that focus awareness upon the implicate order. And there are also modes – those of MYSTICISM[3] – that consist in awareness of the higher dimensionalities of the implicate order and of their relation to the lower dimensionalities and also to the explicate order, and in which the world is seen and experienced as an undivided wholeness.

See Also HOLISM[1], HOLOMOVEMENT, STATE-SPECIFIC SCIENCE. [34]

Indeterminacy principle
See QUANTUM THEORY.

Lamarckism
The theory of EVOLUTION[1] proposed by the French zoologist Pierre Antoine de Monet, le Chevalier de Lamarck*. Lamarck proposed that in living organisms evolution results from the cumulative efforts of many generations to cope with the exigencies of the environment and to exploit its opportunities. In the classic example, the giraffe developed a long neck in order to browse on the higher foliage of trees; will and purpose determined its distinctive characteristic, which was passed on in the hereditary process. DARWINISM proposed an alternative theory of evolution, by natural selection working on random variations in species over generations, which became – and remains in modified form – the orthodox scientific viewpoint. However, Darwin himself was a less convinced Darwinist than many of his followers, and towards the end of his life wrote to his cousin Francis Galton that each year he felt himself more compelled to revert to the theory of acquired characteristics.

Lamarckism appeals to many because it suggests that human will and effort are significant in the evolutionary process, whereas Darwinism regards chance and accident as paramount. The fact that Lamarckism was enthusiastically embraced by Joseph Stalin, who made a form of it known as Lysenkoism official Communist doctrine, contributed to its disrepute in the twentieth century. Orthodox science, too, appeared to discredit the theory, for a central principle of molecular biology is that genetic information is transmitted only from chromosomal nucleic acid to protein and not in the reverse direction, and this principle renders impossible the transmission of acquired characteristics from generation to generation.

However, Lamarckism is not totally discredited. Darwinism prevailed in part because it was able to specify a mechanism for evolution which science could apparently verify, whereas Lamarckism could not. But the scientific evidence for the Darwinian hypothesis is by no means conclusive (see DARWINISM), and evidence that acquired characteristics can sometimes be inherited has been accumulating.

The difficulty of proving any evolutionary theory is that the rate of change is so slow that the process is not susceptible to experimental verification, at least in the larger mammalian species. But fast-reproducing species such as fruit-flies, flatworms, mice and rats can be used to test whether acquired characteristics can be passed on from one generation to the next. Experiments by James McConnell with flatworms at the University of Michigan, by William Byrne with rats at the University of Tennessee, and by George Ungar with mice at the University of Texas, have all indicated that learned behaviour might be passed on. Also, an experiment by Conrad Waddington* with fruit-flies at the University of Edinburgh produced some evidence that abnormal physi-

cal characteristics produced under conditions of environmental stress persist in offspring raised under normal, nonstressful conditions. Although these experiments have not reinstated Lamarckism, they have persuaded some scientists that the hypothesis may have some merit. The fact that many animal species have characteristics specific to their environment and needs, such as callosities on the knees of camels and on the bellies of ostriches, and that these characteristics cannot easily be explained as a result of random mutation and natural selection, also suggest that Lamarckism may explain one of the causative factors in the process of evolutionary change. [136, 169, 167]

Life, nature of

The problem of specifying the nature of life and of defining a precise borderline between animate and inanimate matter, is one fraught with ambiguity. Complexity of organization, the ability to reproduce, and the capacity to grow by taking material from the environment and re-organizing it or shaping it to a predetermined pattern, are acknowledged properties of living systems. However, a single protein molecule manifests organized complexity, crystals shape materials from their environment, and viruses reproduce themselves, but whether a macromolecule, a crystal or a virus should be said to be alive is a moot question.

The borderline definition problem aside, modern biochemistry has made great progress towards understanding the nature of life. When Erwin Schrödinger*, in 1944, suggested that genes might carry information coded into their physical structure, molecular biologists began to concentrate their efforts upon 'cracking the genetic code'. In the early 1960s James Watson* and Francis Crick* were successful in specifying the precise structure of the DNA molecule, a macromolecule which carries coded information and is capable of self-replication and protein synthesis. A rather similar macromolecule, RNA, was also found to carry coded information, and to serve as a 'messenger' for such information in the process of protein synthesis. It is generally believed that RNA evolved first in the most rudimentary living systems, and DNA at a later stage. Some known viruses have only RNA.

Self-reproduction in rudimentary living systems takes place by cell-division, and in more complex systems by genetic exchange. Cell-division, however, does not produce diversity, and after several hundred reproductions in this manner the process tends to slow down and eventually to cease. When reproduction takes place by genetic exchange, both the random pairing-off of the chromosomes and the occasional 'copying errors' or mutations in their genetic DNA ensure diversity, and it is this potential for diversity that characterizes the nature of life in its more evolved manifestations.

The chemical complexity of life is staggering. Protein molecules have different properties, and are of different kinds, depending on the way in which their constituent amino acids are located in relation to each other. In the insulin molecule, for instance, there are two chains of amino acids, with respectively 280 million million and 510 million million million possible locational permutations. The simplest indisputably living organism, the bacterial cell, consists of some 5,000 different kinds of proteins. Whether the complex combinational processes fundamental to life came about by chance is the basic question posed by the discoveries of modern molecular biologists, although it is a question few of them address. It may indeed be beyond the competence of science, although if the question is posed differently, if we ask what force or principle determines the inherent organization of a living system, it should not be so considered. The difficulty is that the problem will probably not yield a solution in terms of biochemical processes, and the indisputable triumphs of molecular biology have biased most scientists towards research based on the assumption that life is not only fundamentally but also exclusively a biochemical phenomenon. The biochemical model of the nature of life is a sophisticated version of MECHANISM[1], and in this may lie its basic limitation. Francis Crick* has written that: 'Now that the programme of genetic and molecular biological research has been completed, we have come full circle – back to the problems ... left behind unsolved.'

For some indications as to possible alternative or more

comprehensive answers to the question of the nature of life, see the entries on GENERAL SYSTEMS THEORY[1], VITALISM[1], LIFE-FIELDS, MORPHOGENESIS, and FORMATIVE CAUSATION. [59, 272, 285]

Life, origin of

Theories of the origin of life fall into three categories: those that attribute it to a supernatural event, those that see it in terms of a spontaneous and chance event, and those that propose an extraterrestrial origin.

The philosophers of the ancient world taught that life is generated spontaneously out of inanimate matter. The ancient Mesopotamian, Egyptian and Hebrew religions had in common the belief that man was made of clay and had the breath of life breathed into him by a god. But the ancients did not have the benefit of the microscope, and until this instrument was invented nobody suspected the existence of the swarming world of micro-organisms. This invention, and in particular Leeuwenhoek's* observations of the wonders of the world of microbiology, contributed to the popularity, in the eighteenth and nineteenth centuries, of the belief that the lower forms of life were 'bred from corruption', i.e. were somehow spontaneously generated. Leeuwenhoek himself maintained that the seeds of life came out of the air, and Pasteur* later proved him right. But proof that the spontaneous generation of life does not occur does not necessarily imply that it did not occur at some time in the primordial past.

In the 1920s J. B. S. Haldane* in England and A. I. Oparin* in Russia independently proposed a theory that life originated in a primordial 'hot, dilute soup' of chemicals, sloshing about on the earth's surface and going through a series of chemical reactions. Under normal circumstances such a mixture would eventually settle into equilibrium and a state of low energy, but, the theory held, circumstances in the environment of the primitive earth were not as we know them today. Instead of oxygen, the earth's atmosphere contained primarily carbon dioxide, according to Haldane, or perhaps methane, according to Oparin. Due to the low concentration of oxygen, there would have been no ozone layer to filter ultra-violet radiation. The primordial soup would have been kept in a state of imbalance by a combination of volcanic action, ocean currents, rivers pouring fresh minerals into the mix, and deluges of carbon and nitrogen compounds from the atmosphere. Eventually, through the action of ultra-violet radiation upon the chemical soup, the first organic molecules would have been formed.

The Haldane-Oparin theory of the spontaneous genesis of life is still widely accepted today. But it has been undermined by subsequent revelations of the staggering complexity of the protein macromolecules and their constituent amino acids (see LIFE, NATURE OF). The theory held that life originated in an event which was statistically highly improbable but nevertheless virtually bound to occur given enough time. Recent discoveries have so increased the factor of statistical improbability that some scientists, for instance Fred Hoyle* and Francis Crick*, have been led to doubt whether life in fact originated on earth at all, and to propose variations on the old idea of PANSPERMIA, or extraterrestrial origin. [22, 59, 136, 239]

Life-fields

Electrodynamic fields associated with living organisms. Their existence was postulated by Professor Harold Saxton Burr* of Yale University in 1972. Burr's evidence, based on 30 years of research, constitutes indisputable proof that wherever there is life there are electrical properties. Several of his discoveries were of practical value. He found that it was possible to pinpoint the monthly occurrence of ovulation in females by monitoring their L-fields and looking for a sharp rise in voltage; also that L-field measurements could help locate malignancies in the body and measure the rate of healing of internal wounds after operations. And when measurements were taken of seeds, it was possible to predict how strong and healthy the plants would grow.

Burr developed theoretical proposals from his observations which ran counter to scientific orthodoxy. He proposed that modern biology's bias towards a chemical interpretation of life processes had prevented it from recognizing the primacy of the electrical field. The L-field, he proposed, was the organizing principle in living systems. As iron filings scattered on a card over a magnet will invariably arrange themselves in the patterns of the lines of force of the magnet's field, so in living organisms the constantly renewed molecules and cells 'are rebuilt as before and arrange themselves in the same pattern as the old'. This hypothesis plausibly accounts for the self-maintenance of living systems, but whether it accounts for MORPHOGENESIS, as Burr maintained, is arguable, for this would imply that the organizing field has an existence independent of and prior to the physical substance that it organizes. The claim made by a follower of Burr's, Edward W. Russell*, that 'science has revealed the Soul', is an extravagant extrapolation from Burr's own observations and reflections upon them, although perhaps Burr did invite such conjectures by titling one of his books *Blueprint for Immortality*. About the same time as Burr published his book the phenomenon known as KIRLIAN PHOTOGRAPHY[5], which appeared to reveal life-fields, was widely publicized, and Burr's discoveries and theoretical proposals probably suffered from the doubts subsequently cast upon the ostensible evidence of Kirlian photography.

Burr's experimental findings and their practical potentials remain valuable and indisputable. Arguably his most important discovery was that through changes in their L-fields living organisms respond to many environmental influences, some emanating even from extraterrestrial sources. He recorded L-field measurements of a large maple tree in his garden over a period of years, and found voltage changes corresponding with lunar cycles and sun-spot variations. Human beings, he suggested, must also be subject to such influences, and he proposed that L-fields are not only the organizing principle in living systems but also our 'antennae to the universe'. He did not make any claims for the validity of ASTROLOGY[3], but one can see that more orthodox colleagues might have feared that he was tending that way. [42, 278]

Maxwell's demon

A theoretical paradox conceived by James Clerk Maxwell* to thwart the second law of THERMO-DYNAMICS. The chambers, each containing a gas at a constant temperature and pressure, are separated by a shutter that is presided over by a demon, who operates the shutter to let fast molecules of the gas through in one direction and slow ones through in the other. This traffic would eventually result in the system being out of equilibrium, with a temperature difference between the two chambers. The heat in one of the chambers could then be converted into energy, and when it was dissipated and a state of high ENTROPY again prevailed, the process could be repeated again, and then yet again and so on.

The possibility of confounding the entropic process, and of achieving perpetual motion in an isolated system, was intriguing not only to engineers but also to theologians, who saw in the demon's activity an analogy to God's intervention to rescue his creation from the fate of HEAT-DEATH. Unfortunately, however, flaws show up in the argument when RELATIVITY and QUANTUM THEORY are applied to it, and the second law of thermodynamics remains undefeated by it. [265]

Morphic resonance
See FORMATIVE CAUSATION.

Morphogenesis
The process of the creation or change of forms in living systems. The question how the forms of things are determined is a contentious one, both in philosophy and in science. Plato taught that the forms of things in the material world are reflections of transcendent ideal forms, and as this conception was compatible with that of a divine Creator it prevailed until the modern scientific era. However, it could not satisfactorily account for the fact that in the phenomenal world forms changed and evolved. This fact was better explained on the Aristotelian principle that forms are immanent rather than transcendent, that they are accountable to some active principle inherent in organic systems. But the problem of identifying this active principle has proved difficult. MECHANISM[1] proposes that in biological morphogenesis form is 'programmed' in the DNA molecule, but it cannot explain the processes involved in the original specification of the forms thus programmed (and of course the very metaphor implies the existence of a 'programmer' or creator), nor can it explain how cells imprinted with

identical genetic information become specified for different biological functions, or how regeneration takes place in damaged organic structures. The ascription of morphogenesis to chemical and physical causation is thus unproved and raises formidable difficulties for the mechanistic hypothesis. An alternative hypothesis is that of VITALISM[1], which proposes that there exists a non-physical vital factor which acts upon a physical system but is not itself a part of it. This factor, which specifies the goal of a developmental process and allows for that goal to be reached by a variety of alternative pathways, has been called ENTELECHY, and modern QUANTUM THEORY, with its emphasis on indeterminism and the possibility of prediction only in terms of probabilities, lends some support to it. However, vitalism is dualistic, and it runs up against the problem of how a non-physical factor could act upon a physical system. This problem is overcome in ORGANICIST[1] views of morphogenesis by proposing the existence of formative fields, analogous to electromagnetic fields. This proposition, though plausible, remains descriptive rather than explanatory so long as it fails to specify the provenance and nature of these fields in terms of processes that are scientifically testable. A promising recent breakthrough to a coherent theory of morphogenesis is Rupert Sheldrake's* hypothesis of FORMATIVE CAUSATION. [294]

Natural selection
See DARWINISM.

Negentropy
A term coined by physicist Erwin Schrödinger* to designate the innate property of living organisms to build themselves up into more complex and functionally coordinated structures, in defiance of the physical law of ENTROPY, which Schrödinger pointed out applies only to closed physical and mechanical systems. [285]

Non-Euclidean geometry
Geometry, the study of spatial structures and relationships, was believed by the Greeks to be the first of the sciences, to furnish the foundations of philosophy, logic and art, and to manifest the mind of God, the creator of universal order. Euclid's *Elements of Geometry*, which dates from about 300 BC, set down the geometrical laws of three-dimensional spaces, and constituted a model of deductive reasoning from fundamental axioms that was central to CLASSICAL PHYSICS. That Euclidean geometry was the only geometry, and that its laws were not constructs of the human intellect but inherent properties of the physical world, were propositions that remained unquestioned until the early nineteenth century. Then the Euclidean postulates, and particularly the fifth postulate, which states that parallel lines will never meet, were shown by a number of mathematicians, notably Georg Riemann*, to be false in respect of curved spaces. The development of non-Euclidean geometries remained a branch of esoteric mathematics until RELATIVITY THEORY demonstrated that space

is in fact curved, and that the universe as a whole can only be comprehended in non-Euclidean terms. The proven fact that the postulates of Euclidean geometry are not absolute truths, but merely intellectual constructs that hold good only relatively and in specific limited conditions, required a fundamental reappraisal of the basic principles and methods of physical science as a truth-seeking endeavour. [130]

Nonlocal connections
According to the laws of CLASSI-CAL PHYSICS, connections between events must be local, i.e. there must be some causal link between them. It is impossible for nonlocalized events to occur. Yet the fact that such events do occur is demonstrated by QUANTUM THEORY (see particularly ERP EXPERIMENT and BELL'S THEOREM). In quantum reality two entities, such as electrons, can manifest corresponding behaviours even though there is no causal connection between them or, more precisely, no connection determinable in terms of energy transfer.

Two alternative, though closely related, possible explanations of this situation have been proposed. One is that information transfer may occur superluminally (i.e. beyond the speed of light), in which case the information 'carrier' cannot be a known thing such as an electromagnetic wave, for it is generally accepted that electromagnetic propagation must be subluminal. The second explanation conceives physical systems, from the atom to the universe,

as wholes indivisible into discrete or independent parts and in which events occurring anywhere will have effects everywhere, or alternatively where events are correlated in a manner that makes the very idea of causation misleading.

See also SYNCHRONICITY[1]. [34, 44]

Nuclear physics
Up to the 1930s, experimental and theoretical physics had been primarily concerned with determining the structure of the ATOM, and the laws governing the behaviour of its component electrons. QUANTUM THEORY had made great progress towards comprehending that structure and those laws, but whether its discoveries would apply equally to the interior world of the atomic nucleus remained to be seen. About 100,000 times smaller than the atom itself but comprising most of its mass, the nucleus was difficult to explore not only because of its size and density, but also because of the strength of the internal nuclear force that held its components together. Only with the development of accelerators capable of bombarding the nucleus with penetrating particles at velocities close to the speed of light, did it become possible to investigate its structure.

If at first some physicists thought that the atomic nucleus would prove to be the ultimate 'building block' of matter, they were soon proved wrong. It, too, turned out to be a composite and dynamic entity, with a multitude of smaller PARTICLES whizzing about inside it at near the speed of light. RELATIVITY THEORY had to be combined with quantum theory to comprehend subnuclear events and forces, as what became alternatively known as high energy physics demonstrated the actual creation of matter from energy that Einstein's theory had predicted. The discovery, in 1932, of the positron by Carl Anderson*, and of the neutron by J. Chadwick*, heralded an era of some four decades over which about 200 different particles were identified. Physicists spoke of 'the particle zoo', and were often bewildered by the diversity and complexity of the subnuclear world, but gradually relativistic quantum theory and mathematical analysis discovered symmetries within it and laws governing its activity, and today some physicists are foreseeing that, with the solution of a few problems that are currently being worked upon, all will be explained and fundamental physics will have accomplished its project and will come to an end.

Nuclear physics has given us nuclear power and the nuclear bomb. Extrapolated cosmologically, it has also given us a new understanding of the universe and its origins in the so-called BIG BANG. These have been indisputably great achievements, even if their benefit to mankind is dubious. It now aspires to wrap up everything in a Grand Unified Theory of the four fundamental forces of nature. Only gravity remains recalcitrant, or so we are told. But it may not be irrelevant to recall that just about a century ago, with Maxwell's*

grand unification of the forces of electricity and magnetism, physicists were also saying that all there remained to do was the dotting of the 'i's and the crossing of the 't's. [105, 135]

Panspermia

Among theories of the origin of life on earth, variations on the theory of panspermia have been held by a number of nineteenth- and twentieth-century scientists. In the nineteenth century Hermann von Helmholtz* and Lord Kelvin* independently proposed that the seeds of life were carried to earth from elsewhere in the cosmos as 'passengers' on comets or meteorites. In 1908 the Swedish chemist Svente Arrhenius* expounded the theory and coined the term 'panspermia', which implied that organic materials were abundant in the universe. The Haldane-Oparin 'chemical soup' theory (see LIFE, ORIGIN OF) of the spontaneous generation of life on earth made the panspermic hypothesis unpopular for a time, particularly as it seemed extravagant and speculative and open to the objection that organic material could not survive the radiation and heat it would be subjected to in space and on entering the earth's atmosphere. However, with the expanding knowledge of the complexity of the chemistry of life and the statistical improbability of its occurrence, the spontaneous generation theory has been called in question, and some scientists, notably Fred Hoyle* and Francis Crick*, have proposed a theory of 'directed panspermia', which holds that the seeds of life were sent to our planet by an intelligent civilization elsewhere in the universe. [5, 59, 137]

Particles

A term used by physicists to designate the fundamental components of ATOMS. Hundreds of distinct types of particle have been identified, distinguished by their mass, electric charge, duration and spin. Most of these are unstable, i.e. the duration of their existence is short, while others, notably electrons, protons, photons and neutrinos, are relatively stable. Particles are divisible into two categories, the 'leptons', which respond only to the weak nuclear force, and the 'hadrons', which respond to both the weak and the strong forces and to gravity. Electrons and neutrinos belong to the former category, protons and neutrons and most of the unstable particles to the latter. The multiplicity and variety of the hadron group was bewildering until in the 1960s the 'quark' theory was developed by Murray Gell-Mann* and George Zweig*. The theory proposed that hadrons are made up of yet smaller particles, which were called 'quarks'. Initially, three distinct types, or 'flavours', of quark were proposed, and different combinations of them were shown to make up the different hadrons. With the discovery of more hadrons, other quark 'flavours' had to be postulated, but the theory has held good, and evidence for the existence of quarks has come with the increasing sophistication and power of experimental high-energy particle accelerators. [328]

Primordial soup

The conjectural prebiotic state of the earth.

See LIFE, ORIGIN OF.

Probability

The mathematics of events and processes that are inherently indeterminate as singularities but manifest pattern and lawfulness in aggregates. Professional gaming and actuarial practice have long applied probability calculations in fairly crude practical ways, but in the present century probability theory has become a sophisticated branch of pure mathematics, largely on account of its relevance to QUANTUM THEORY subsequent to Heisenberg's* propounding his 'Indeterminacy Principle', and also because of the increasingly widespread applications of statistical studies and forecasting techniques.

Punctuated equilibrium

A theory of EVOLUTION[1] proposed independently by Harvard palaeontologist Stephen Jay Gould* and by Niles Eldredge of the American Museum of Natural History, in 1977–8. The theory proposes that evolution was not a gradual process, as DARWINISM maintains, but occurred in periodic 'jumps'. The absence from the fossil record of transitional life forms, for instance between reptiles and mammals, is a major problem for Darwinian theory, as is evidence for the coexistence of species that according to Darwinian theory should have appeared in a progressive sequence. These two facts are consistent with punctuated equilibrium. If evolutionary jumps occur, there will be no transitional forms, and if, as the theory holds, these jumps are made initially by small groups within larger populations, the coexistence of individuals at different evolutionary levels can be expected. The theory proposes that these evolutionary jumps occur when isolated small groups within a larger population are abnormally stressed. Stress would 'punctuate' the equilibrium of a society, setting up internal perturbations which could only be resolved through a jump that established a new equilibrium at a higher level. This view is consistent with GENERAL SYSTEMS THEORY[1] and DISSIPATIVE STRUCTURES theory. [111]

Quantum theory

Two distinct bodies of theory are central to the twentieth-century revolution in physical science. RELATIVITY THEORY, the work of one man, has to do with the universe at large, while quantum theory, the cumulative work of many minds, has to do with events in the realm of the very small, the subatomic world. The theories have overlapped and cross-fertilized each other over the decades, throwing off in the process a multitude of discoveries and technologies, from nuclear power to TV, that have revolutionized the world, and at the same time revolutionized concepts of the nature and origin of the universe.

Quantum theory began unspectacularly in 1900 when Max Planck* was constrained by his investigations into the phenomenon known as black body radiation to propose that the energy of light is delivered in packets, or 'quanta'. Planck was able to establish a rule to enable the quantum of energy for any particular frequency in the ELECTROMAGNETIC SPECTRUM to be calculated, and 'Planck's constant' was to become one of the cornerstones of the new physics. However, the theory did not enjoy instant acclaim for it seemed radically incompatible with the prevailing idea that light travelled not in discrete packets but in waves: an idea triumphantly established by James Clerk Maxwell* only three decades previously and since proved by experiment and the discovery of radio waves. The quantum theory of light seemed to revive the Newtonian 'corpuscular' theory that Maxwell and others had supposedly laid to rest. It did not seem in 1900 that progress lay in the direction pointed by Planck.

But there were anomalies in the wave theory, and one of these, known as the photoelectric effect, received the attention of Einstein*, who in 1905, some months before he published his 'Special Theory of Relativity', produced a paper on the photoelectric effect which demonstrated that light must indeed consist of packets of energy, which he called 'photons'. Yet the experimental evidence for the wave theory – in particular the study of 'interference patterns' produced on a screen when light projected through two pinholes in another screen falls upon it – stood its ground and was incontrovertible. To explain the interference patterns in terms of the particle theory required the seemingly preposterous proposition that the same particle passed simultaneously through both pinholes. There seemed to be a stalemate situation, with the wave theory explaining some observed phenomena and the particle theory others, and the two being radically irreconcilable.

But what is a particle? The term suggests that it is an entity endowed with the quantifiable properties of material things: mass, location, momentum. As such, some kind of mechanical laws must be formulable to describe its behaviour. What became known as quantum mechanics was the attempt to establish such laws, which were found not to be the same as the laws of Newtonian mechanics, formerly thought to be universal but then found to break down in respect of subatomic events. While the wave-particle dilemma remained unresolved, some progress was made towards comprehending the mechanics of the subatomic world, although it was progress in the manner of two steps forward and one back, as theory after theory rose and fell, yielding in their demise theoretical, mathematical or experimental contributions to the new physics. Investigative technique developments such as the invention in 1911 of the cloud chamber, which enables particle paths to be observed, also facilitated research progress.

In the 1890s J. J. Thomson* had discovered the electron, and in the following decade Ernest Rutherford*, having harnessed the power of radioactivity to bombard the atom and knock electrons out of it, produced a model of atomic structure, comprising a positively charged nucleus with a number of negatively charged electrons whirling around it with relatively vast distances separating them, the whole system being analogous to a planetary system and likewise consisting mainly of empty space. It was the formulation of this model that led to the realization that quantum mechanics must develop its own laws because the observed behaviour of electrons was not compatible with those of Newtonian mechanics. Working with the model, the Danish physicist Niels Bohr* established mathematical laws to explain and predict the orbital behaviour of electrons, which had to incorporate a curious observed phenomenon: the ability of electrons to jump from one orbit to another, an event which involved a loss or a gain of energy. Bohr drew upon the work of Planck, and his work initiated the quantum theory of the atom and instigated numerous valuable experiments, but neither his theory nor Rutherford's model that it was based on was to survive intact for long.

In Rutherford's and Bohr's work there was an implicit bias towards the particle theory, but the old dilemma remained unresolved and the wave theory would not just go away. It was Prince Louis de Broglie* who led the way out of the dilemma: surely the most original exercise ever of the principle of *noblesse oblige*. Invoking relativity theory's principle of the equivalence of mass and energy, de Broglie proposed that particles pulsate with energy and emanate waves. The existence of 'matter waves' had never been experimentally observed, but de Broglie pursued his intuition, mathematically working out the wavelengths of the then known particles, photons and electrons, and proposing an equation capable of predicting the wavelength of any particle. His equations and predictions were upheld by subsequent experiment and observation. The principle of wave-particle duality became fundamental in the evolution of quantum theory.

To propose that particles have wave functions and that waves can manifest particle properties may seem like a satisfactory reconciliation, but when the wave characteristics of particles and the particle characteristics of waves come under scrutiny some queer and disconcerting implications arise. Take the interference-pattern experiment above-mentioned. It makes sense, on the principle that particles can behave like waves, that when a beam of electrons is fired at the screen with the two pinholes, a wavelike pattern should appear on the detector screen. But what if the electrons are shot off one at a time? In theory there should be no interference pattern, but just two bright patches on the screen, but in fact the interference pattern does gradually build up, which implies either that the individual electrons are endowed with some sort of memory or symmetry-seeking property or again that each electron passed through both holes. A preposterous

alternative, but if it is put to the test by incorporating detectors at the holes, what happens? The electrons pass in sequence through one hole or the other, though now no interference pattern appears but just the two bright patches. It seems that the experimental set-up has determined the behaviour of the electron, that when it is observed it behaves like a particle and when not observed like a wave.

The fact that the act of observation or measurement affects the phenomenon being observed or measured brought into quantum theory an element of indeterminacy that Einstein, for one, found profoundly unsettling. Out had to go the idea of the scientist as the detached objective observer. 'What we observe', wrote Werner Heisenberg*, 'is not nature in itself but nature exposed to our method of questioning.' Heisenberg formulated his 'indeterminacy principle', which demonstrated that it is impossible to ascertain both the momentum and the position of a particle. Chance appeared to reign supreme in the quantum world, and events could not be predicted with certainty but only on a basis of statistical probability. That an electron observed at point A would be at point B when next observed, could be predicted in terms of high probability, but there was always the outside chance that it would pop up at point X, and indeed sometimes it would.

But to speak in such terms still implies that an electron is some kind of entity. To conceive it as such is permissible in quantum theory, but only with the understanding that language is a conceptual tool and its referents do not necessarily exist in the modes it implies. And if we want to go on conceptualizing atomic processes in terms of mechanics we can do so, only we had better mitigate the crudity of the approach and speak rather of 'wave mechanics'. On the other hand, this does not mean that material reality is dematerialized into a phantom world of mere mathematical probabilities. There is always an 'on the other hand' in quantum physics. Indeterminacy rules, but on the other hand statistical probability makes prediction virtually certain for large aggregates of events. Matter may appear to be spirited away into energy quanta and a mathematical 'tendency' to manifest material properties, but on the other hand energy is convertible into matter with substantial and quantifiable properties. There are always two aspects to quantum phenomena, but these must not be conceived in terms of a radical dualism but rather, in Bohr's term, as COMPLEMENTARITY.

Strangely, Heisenberg's indeterminacy principle did not undermine further research work in quantum physics, but rather afforded it a new and more assured foundation. With the development of new techniques for accelerating particles, experimental probes not only of the atom but also of its nucleus became possible, and a new dimension of mystery and discovery was opened up (see NUCLEAR PHYSICS).

A brief article on quantum theory cannot aspire to be comprehensive or to review all the relevant experimental and theoretical contributions to the subject. And as for the metaphysical implications, they are legion and endlessly beguiling. So any conclusion cannot be in the nature of a summing-up, but only – and aptly in the context – a pointer to certain possibilities. One of the more esoteric concepts in quantum theory is that of 'exchange'. In his early but eloquent and still relevant book, *The Strange Story of the Quantum*, Banesh Hoffmann* ruminates on it thus: 'It is still a strange and awe-inspiring thought that you and I are thus rhythmically exchanging particles with one another, and with the earth and the beasts of the earth, and the sun and the moon and the stars, to the utmost galaxy.' If quantum theory, in one of its aspects, seems reductively to steal the world away from us, in another aspect it gives us it back most bountifully, implying a wholeness, coherence and interactivity that formerly only mystics and poets had spoken of. Quantum theory may be a tangled web of ideas in which the lay mind can become perilously enmeshed, but – again 'on the other hand' – it implies that the universe itself is a tangled web of interconnections, and affords a basis for belief that the human aspiration to apprehend meaning, purpose and wholeness, and to participate in whatever the universe is about, may not after all be a vain dream.

See also BOOTSTRAP THEORY, ERP EXPERIMENT, EXPERIMENTER EFFECT, IMPLICATE ORDER. [44, 105, 126, 135]

Quarks
See PARTICLES.

Quasars
Quasi-stellar objects, believed to be located in the furthest reaches of the universe, and which emit intense radiation of uncertain provenance, conjectured by some astronomers to result from collisions between galaxies composed of matter and ANTIMATTER.

Relativity theory
Both the major theoretical and many of the technological developments of modern science, including the fission bomb and the nuclear reactor, originate in three academic papers published by Albert Einstein* in 1905. One of these, originally titled *On the Electrodynamics of Moving Bodies*, became more widely known as the 'Special Theory of Relativity', and it revolutionized scientific, and in due course philosophical and popular thought, about the nature and properties of time, space, matter and motion.

With relativity theory there began the process of the confounding of common-sense conceptualizing based upon our direct experience of the physical world that was later to develop bizarre proportions in QUANTUM THEORY. In respect of motion, for a start, common sense would say that, by analogy for instance to one moving train passing another, different velocities would be measured by an observer depending on whether the passing train was going in the same or the opposite direction. But this is not the case with light. Light

has motion, in a vacuum it has a precisely measurable velocity of 300,000 kilometres a second, but – and this is where common sense is confounded – when this velocity is measured it never varies in relation to the motion of the observer, no matter from which direction the beam of light comes. This paradox had been demonstrated in 1888 in the Michelson-Morley experiment (named after its American co-formulators), and had since been a disquieting puzzle for scientists because it was irreconcilable with the basic principles of Newtonian mechanics. Einstein's starting point was the construction of a mathematical framework that could coherently accommodate the observed phenomenon of the constancy of the speed of light. The cornerstone of this framework was the principle that different reference frames travelling at a constant speed in a straight line will always, relative to each other, be coherent and symmetrical, the laws of physics will obtain in them, and they will appear, from the point of view of those who inhabit them, to be at rest.

It is from the proviso, 'relative to each other', that the revolutionary implications of Einstein's theory arise. The cost of establishing coherence within and between specific frames of reference requires the abandonment of the idea of the possibility of any absolute or ultimate coherence or of the primacy of any particular frame of reference. At a stroke one of the pillars of CLASSICAL PHYSICS has been demolished leaving the whole edifice tottering.

When asymmetrical frames of reference are contemplated the paradoxes engendered put common sense and credulity under greater stress. Our notions of time, in particular, are out of joint. From different frames of reference, i.e. in respect of observers moving differently in relation to each other, clocks and other temporal processes move relatively slower or quicker. The speed of light has to be approached for any gross variation to manifest, but the principle has been demonstrated by experiments in which small time differentials have been registered between clocks flown around the world and others in a laboratory. This 'time dilation effect' is often illustrated in the 'twin paradox', which has us suppose that an astronaut twin returns to earth after a high-speed space journey to find his twin brother many years older than himself. This fanciful idea illustrates another fundamental principle of relativity theory: that space and time are not separate things but are inextricably bound together and constitute a 'space-time continuum'. In our common-sense and consensual modes of perception we perceive three dimensions of space around us, and time as a one-dimensional line or arrow proceeding inexorably from past to future. But in fact we exist in a four-dimensional space-time, and all our common-sense assumptions about time, which inform our thinking and our attitudes to life and living in profound and generally unexamined ways, · are merely provisional constructs, true and relevant only relatively.

Whether we infer positive or negative, meaning-enhancing or meaning-annulling, conclusions from the liberation from time that relativity theory confers upon us, depends upon the philosophical accom- modations we choose to make, but the fact that we live in a world where the space and time of our common-sense perceptions and experiences are provisional and illusory is incontrovertible.

If the space-time continuum of relativity theory had disturbing philosophical implications, the mass-energy equivalence deductions from it had even more disturbing practical ones, in particular the development of the nuclear bomb. The celebrated equation $E = mc^2$ states that matter is a form of locked-up energy, and enables a prediction to be made of the amount of energy that will be released when a given mass is annihilated, as it is when it is accelerated to near the speed of light (which is represented by the symbol 'c'). The technology to achieve such accelerations has been incorporated for practical purposes in nuclear reactors, and for research and experimental purposes in particle accelerators, both of which have yielded abundant evidence of the correctness of Einstein's theoretical deductions.

All the above follows from the 1905 Special Relativity Theory. Ten years later Einstein published his General Theory, in which the earlier work was extended to include gravity and which introduced concepts about the geometry of space-time and the universe that were as revolutionary

Scientific method

for cosmology as the earlier work had been for physics, and likewise were subsequently proved to be correct by experiment and observation. The primary postulate of the General Theory is that the space-time continuum is not, as in the 'special' conditions of the earlier theory, geometrically flat, but curved. This curvature is the effect of gravity, the force that massive material bodies exert upon one another. Just as Newtonian mechanics holds good only relatively, under special conditions that do not universally obtain, so likewise does Euclidean geometry, which pertains to flat surfaces but not to curved ones. And as space is 'warped' by gravity, so too must time be, manifesting different characteristics and rates of flow in different parts of the universe.

Science fiction writers have made much play with the Einsteinian concepts of 'space warps' and 'time warps', and thus made people aware, if rather vaguely and approximately, of some of the implications of general relativity. But those implications go much further, and were not completely foreseen even by Einstein himself. He conceived, as did all his contemporaries, a STEADY-STATE universe, a closed and overall stable, although in particular locations gravitationally perturbed, spherical entity. Some of his equations implied that this was not the case, that in fact the universe must be either expanding or contracting, and in order to adjust them to the steady-state view he had to introduce into the equations an extra term, which he called the 'cosmical

constant'. He later referred to this accommodation as the greatest blunder of his life, in the light of the discovery, in the 1920s, that the universe was expanding. But the discovery only went to prove the tremendous predictive power of relativity theory, which extended even beyond the capacity of the phenomenal faculties of its creator fully to comprehend. [77, 105, 135]

Scientific method

The procedures by means of which scientific laws are established and verified constitute what is known as the scientific method. These procedures were established in the seventeenth century, by Galileo*, Bacon* and Descartes*. Galileo laid the foundations of modern science by basing it upon experiment and the mathematical formulation of the laws of nature thus established. Bacon, too, stressed the importance of the empirical or experimental approach, and formulated the inductive procedure, which consists in deriving general principles from experiments and then devising further experiments to test these principles. Descartes' contribution was to base the quest for scientific truth on an intellectual procedure of radical doubt which would ultimately uncover self-evident and incontrovertible first principles. Like Galileo, Descartes believed that mathematics was the appropriate language for exact science, and that everything in nature was quantifiable. Underlying his scientific method was the assumption that the universe and all phenomena within it are analysable, and that when analysis has succeeded in breaking down a phenomenon into its component parts reason and logic can then ascertain how the parts relate to each other or work together. This assumption was shared by Newton*, who accomplished a grand synthesis of scientific knowledge and formulation of scientific law in terms of mechanics which was the great triumph of the classical scientific method and remained unchallenged until the present century.

In the present century, however, with the development of RELATIVITY and QUANTUM THEORY, flaws have been revealed in the assumptions and procedures of the classical scientific method. In particular, its assumptions that absolute truths can be ascertained, that nature can be looked upon objectively and read like a book by someone familiar with the language, that mathematics itself is by definition logical, that wholes can be comprehended in terms of their parts and their interrelations or interactions, have been called in question. Notwithstanding its achievements, the scientific method of Galileo, Bacon, Descartes and Newton has been shown actually to inhibit the progress of scientific understanding in the twentieth century. It has been realized that scientists can only get answers to the questions they put to nature, and that the answers they get are in part dependent on the method of questioning. As Thomas Kuhn* has shown, all science is PARADIGM[1]-based, and

normal science is a puzzle-solving activity which does not 'aim to produce major novelties, conceptual or phenomenal'. Yet science only progresses through the production of 'major novelties', and inflexible principles of method are not conducive to such production. It is widely conceded that a paradigm shift has been taking place in science in recent decades, and with this shift there has occurred a rethinking of the basic principles of scientific method. Karl Popper* modified the classical concept of method by proposing that the job of theoretical science was to make predictions which could be tested experimentally, but entered the caveat that no theory or experimental 'proof' could ever be considered final and absolute. He also helped to distinguish science from metaphysics and mysticism by proposing the principle of FALSIFIABILITY. Other theorists have been more radical, for instance Charles Tart* with his proposals for STATE-SPECIFIC SCIENCES, and have proposed revisions of the principles of scientific method to admit to investigation phenomena generally considered PARANORMAL[5]. [44, 254]

Sociobiology

When E. O. Wilson* published *Sociobiology: The New Synthesis* in 1975 he proposed his subject as a new science devoted to 'the systematic study of the biological basis of all social behavior'. Sociobiology was quickly accepted by academic communities as the new science that it purported to be, and a good

State-specific science

deal of literature, both academic and popular, has been generated by it. However, the fundamental argument of sociobiology, that all human social behaviour is coded in the genes, is highly dubious and certainly not proven. As a theory of human nature and human society, sociobiology is radically DETERMINIST[1] and REDUCT-IONIST[1]. It tends to the conclusion that as all human behaviour is genetically determined, and has been formed by the process of natural selection, it is folly to expect or work for any improvement in the status quo. It may well be that its appeal as a new science lies in its tendency to legitimize human behaviour and social organization, with all their imperfections, as somehow natural and inevitable. The bias of sociobiological theory is well expressed in the title of one of its best-known texts, Richard Dawkins's* *The Selfish Gene.*

Although Dawkins and other sociobiologists would deny that their purpose is to exculpate selfishness, greed, territoriality and exploitation in human behaviour, such exculpation is implicit in their arguments. [65, 273, 360]

Space-time
In addition to the three dimensions of space that we normally experience, RELATIVITY THEORY proposes the existence of a fourth dimension which is a continuum in which space and time are integrated.

State-specific science
A term coined by the parapsy-chologist Charles T. Tart. Arguing that orthodox science is a science of one state of consciousness, Tart has proposed the development of 'state-of-consciousness-specific sciences'. Opposing the BE-HAVIOURIST[4] contention that mental states are irrelevant to the scientific study of man, Tart argues that subjective experiences, particularly in ALTERED STATES OF CONSCIOUSNESS[4], are real and meaningful, and that to dismiss them as mere imagination or hallucination is to impose arbitrary and unnecessary limitations upon knowledge. 'Observations of internal processes', he writes, 'are probably much more difficult to make than those of external physical processes, because of their inherently greater complexity. The essence of science, however, is that we observe what there is to be observed whether it is difficult or not.' Mental states, he suggests, can be studied and compared and common features can be charted using experimenters trained in the PHENOMENOLOGICAL[1] method. If such experimenters can experience an ASC and report on the specific states they go through, and such reports are subsequently analysed and compared, a number of maps of specific states of consciousness will be obtained, which because of the elements of consensus and repetition will stand as objective and scientifically acceptable descriptions of realities.

To assist the experimenter-subject to make specific state-of-consciousness reports, Tart has prepared scales of levels of consciousness and in the experimental situation has required subjects to name at intervals the level they have reached. He has discovered by this method a pattern of correspondences between levels of consciousness and the occurrence of particular phenomena and experiences. Tart's work has attracted the attention of other parapsychologists, and it looks likely that the 'state-specific' approach will become increasingly common in PSI^5 research in the future, replacing the statistical method and the use of ordinary subjects in normal states of consciousness, and enabling researchers to plot with accuracy the experimental, cognitive, conative and physiological correlates of a range and variety of states of consciousness. [317]

Steady-state theory

The cosmological steady-state theory was put forward by Fred Hoyle* and colleagues in 1948. It proposed the continuous creation of matter in the universe, and attributed its observed expansion to this process. According to the theory, the average density of the universe would have remained constant throughout time, with the newly created matter aggregating into new galaxies which would push apart existing ones. Today the steady-state theory has few supporters, although Hoyle himself has endeavoured to modify it to bring it into line with new findings. But astronomical observation has disproved its hypothesis of a constant average density, and the discovery, in 1965, of cosmic background microwave radiation constituted persuasive evidence to support the rival BIG BANG theory. [136]

Stochastic

Adjective applied to processes that are constituted of random or indeterminate events, such as the flow of traffic, the spread of an epidemic, or the behaviour of an electorate or an economy. PROBABILITY theory seeks to comprehend such processes by developing mathematical models of them.

Superconductivity

An electrical property of metals when cooled to near-zero temperatures: the capacity to conduct an electrical current without resistance, so that it persists for a very long time and does not require an electromotive force from a battery or generator to sustain its flow. Whereas in an ordinary circuit the electrical flow is constituted of separate charged electrons through the metal's atomic structure, in a superconducting circuit the electrons are no longer separate but combine their momentum to constitute a collective fluid-like electrical force which becomes coordinated with the metal's atomic structure and meets no resistance from it. Superconductivity is a good example of $SYNERGY^1$ – a bonus that accrues from the interaction of two distinct entities or systems. Practically, the principle has been applied in computers and to generate magnetic fields to power vehicles elevated above superconducting tracks. Current research is concentrating on inducing superconductivity at higher temperatures, and other practical applications are anticipated.

Syntropy
A term proposed by biochemist Albert Szent-Gyorgi* as the opposite of ENTROPY. While entropy is a process of the progressive collapse into disorder of a mechanical system, syntropy, which operates in living systems, is an inherent drive towards greater order and the progressive incorporation of greater complexity. There is, wrote Szent-Gyorgi, an analogous psychological drive 'towards synthesis, towards growth, towards wholeness and self-perfection'. [314]

Thermodynamics, laws of
Thermodynamics, the 'science of heat', or 'science of complexity', evolved from the early nineteenth century as a distinct branch of physics, allied to the development of engines and mechanical systems that used heat conversion as a source of energy. Three fundamental laws were established:

1 The law of conservation of energy states that although the energy involved in a process may change its form, its total remains constant and none of it is lost.

2 The second law states that although no energy is ever lost, the amount of useful energy in a system or process steadily diminishes, dissipating into forms from which it cannot be recovered, for instance when hot water mingles with cold it cannot be retrieved from the resultant tepid mix. The implication of this is that in any physical system there is an irreversible process of energy dissipation which eventually runs the system down into a state of low-energy equilibrium. The term ENTROPY was coined as a quantifiable measure of this dis-ordering process. So long as systems and processes were conceived in mechanical terms they had to be presumed subject to the second law, to increasing entropy (but see DISSIPATIVE STRUCTURE).

3 The third law is the logical consequence of the first two, and states that a system cannot cool down to an absolute zero temperature. [255]

Uncertainty principle
Another name for Heisenberg's 'Indeterminacy Principle'.
  See QUANTUM THEORY.

Wave-particle duality
See QUANTUM THEORY.

3
SPIRITUALITY AND ESOTERIC THOUGHT

Agni yoga

Literally, 'union by fire'. A YOGA technique developed in recent times from ancient Indian and Chinese sources by Russell Paul Schofield*. Dissatisfied with techniques of psychological transformation that relied merely on the conscious recognition of disruptive or restricting psychic material, Schofield developed in Agni yoga techniques for 'burning out' unwanted and inhibiting psychic residues. Based on the principle that 'energy is concentrated where thought is focused', Agni yoga employs VISUALIZATION⁶ together with postural and physical techniques to facilitate the controlled flow of energy, or the 'inner fire', which is essential to the work of psychic clearance, integration and transformation. [217]

Akashic record

In ESOTERICISM, a cosmic reservoir of information and memories to which the gifted psychic can gain access. The phenomena of 'mental mediumship' have always intrigued and awed witnesses, particularly when the 'channel's' utterances manifest knowledge, wisdom or prescience beyond his or her imaginable human capability, and explanations have generally been proposed attributing the content of the communications to gods, spirits, reclusive 'masters of wisdom' with telepathic powers, or extraterrestrials. The Akashic record idea is an alternative explanation, but one no less *ad hoc*, and with the disadvantage that it postulates an impalpable entity to explain a palpable mystery. [311]

Alchemy

Alchemy, the 'royal art' of the HERMETIC philosophers, was ostensibly a pseudoscientific quest for a means of transmuting base metal into gold, but this quest was in fact an analogue of the GNOSTIC striving to liberate the divine element imprisoned in matter, to transmute the alchemist's own spiritual substance by ridding it of contaminating impurities and thus enabling the pure soul or spirit to become manifest and free. No doubt some of the medieval and Renaissance alchemists were misguided dabblers in chemistry or avaricious charlatans, but the alchemical tradition itself was intellectually subtle and practically demanding. Modern chemical science had its origins in the work of the alchemists, but the work itself was informed by a purpose and a philosophy that most modern scientists would find alien and all of them would find inapposite to the scientific project.

Carl Jung* discovered the alchemical literature late in life, but not too late to devote two of his major works, *Psychology and Alchemy* and *Mysterium Coniunctionis*, to it. Jung's basic insight was that the stages of the alchemical process correlate with stages of the INDIVIDUATION⁴ process, by which a person becomes psychically whole, and that alchemical symbolism referred not only to occult metallurgic experimentation but also to episodes of psychic experience and growth. For instance, alchemists wrote of three processes which the volatile spirit mercury must be subjected to: the *nigredo* (blackening), *albedo* (whitening), and *rubedo* (reddening). In descriptions of the *nigredo* process, metaphors of torturing, breaking down, grinding, immersing, separating, killing, represented the agonizing death experience (the descent into Hell, the 'dark night of the soul') that must initiate spiritual change. The *albedo* stage was described in imagery of dawn, light, emergence, washing, cleansing: it was the stage of spiritual rebirth. The *rubedo* was represented by imagery of the sun, royalty, power, dominion, signifying an achieved totality of fulfilment and awareness. Some alchemists, it is said, literally died in the practice of their art, and not through scientific ignorance or ineptitude, but through intolerable psychic trauma, failure to accomplish the transition from the *nigredo* to the *albedo* stage of the work. Fatal or irreversible psychoses are certainly not uncommon in modern man's experience, and one reason why alchemy is not just an interesting anachronism is that it contextualizes psychotic episodes, demonstrates that, although they may come unbidden, they are states of soul that harbour potentials as well as hazards.

Alchemy, ASTROLOGY, KABBALISM and the other 'occult sciences' furnish maps of the subconscious and strategies of spiritual development that many people today find as relevant and useful as did their devotees in so-called pre-scientific times and cultures. [158, 253, 296]

Anthroposophy

A spiritual philosophy developed by the Austrian scientist/mystic Rudolf Steiner*. A scholarly polymath, Steiner was an early follower of Helena Blavatsky* and THEOSOPHY, and the Anthroposophical Society that he founded in 1909 owed much to their influence. It also owed a great deal to German Romanticism and Idealistic philosophy, and in particular to the works and life of Goethe*. Steiner sought the expression of the spiritual in and through art, not only painting and sculpture but also poetry and drama, and he himself created works in these several media as well as influencing others to do so. He also designed and had built two extraordinary buildings, which he called 'Goetheanums', to serve as headquarters of the Anthroposophical Society and as arts centres. The first was burnt down (Nazi sabotage was suspected), but at the second, near Basle in Switzerland, Steiner's mystery plays are still performed.

In connection with the drama, Steiner developed 'eurythmy', which is used by anthroposophists both as a performance art and as a therapy. Eurythmy, or eurythmics, is sound made manifest through gesture. Steiner taught that the sounds that constitute language have associated body postures and movements, and that medical cures can be effected by an expert therapist prescribing appropriate sounds and movements. Eurythmy is one aspect of anthroposophical medicine, which is today practised by physicians throughout the world. Another area where Steiner's ideas have had a lasting influence is that of organic farming.

But undoubtedly the primary area is that of education. There are over 100 Rudolf Steiner schools worldwide, and the principles and methods of his educational system have been adopted piecemeal in many others. [310, 311]

Astral body

In occult anatomy, the astral body is a counterpart of the physical body, said to be composed of 'finer matter' or a 'semifluid substance' which is not perceptible to the normal senses but sometimes is to the paranormal or psychic senses in the form of an AURA[5]. Alternatively called the 'etheric' or 'spiritual' body, this replica is said to be capable of separation from the physical body and of existing independently of it, both in life and in death. In some individuals it is 'looser' than in others, and such people are capable of ASTRAL TRAVEL[5] or projection. KIRLIAN PHOTOGRAPHY[5] has been claimed as evidential of the existence of the astral body, and the BIOPLASMA[5] theory developed by colleagues of Kirlian* seeks to explain the phenomenon in physical terms. One of the most curious effects claimed as evidential of the reality of the astral body and its close relation to the physical is the performance of medical operations upon it – what to observers would look like mime operations – which have alleviated chronic physical conditions. Death-bed observations of the separation of an ethereal entity from the physical body – reports of which are transcultural but consonant in detail – have also been cited as evidence,

as too have 'phantasms of the living' – apparitions of close relatives or friends seen by people in moments of crisis – many cases of which have been recorded by psychical researchers. [223, 295]

Astrology

'Astrology' literally means 'science of the stars', and it is arguably man's oldest science, developed worldwide as a system of DIVINATION and of character interpretation over a period of some four thousand years. Views of and attitudes to it are invariably biased. Modern scientific orthodoxy is biased towards its total rejection as a pseudo-science. Alternative views regard the development of astrology as the gradual discovery, by means of observation and inductive reasoning, of the laws of life and the universe, or as the elaboration of an interpretative system so flexible and ambiguous that it allows the fullest scope for the exercise of human cognitive faculties, including perhaps paranormal ones such as CLAIRVOYANCE[5].

Newspaper and magazine horoscopes cause many people to dismiss astrology as an idle concern of frivolous minds, but a number of modern objective studies, often conducted by people expecting to disprove its claims, indicate that there is more to it than that. The French researcher Michel Gauquelin* has conducted extensive studies of correlations between birth times, temperaments, and professions, and has come up with findings that would appear to be inexplicable on any hypothesis save that of planetary influence at the moment of birth. When Gauquelin studied astrologically the birth times of 576 members of the French Academy of Medicine, he found a very pronounced bias towards the planets Mars and Saturn having just risen or culminated in the sky. A control study of the same number of randomly selected ordinary people did not show the same bias, but in a second sample of 508 physicians it was distinctly reproduced. This strange finding prompted Gauquelin to research the horoscopes of thousands of people who had distinguished themselves in some way, and as the data accumulated quite clear correlations were observed to occur with a frequency far beyond chance expectancy. Jupiter was dominant for a sample of 1,409 famous actors with odds of 1,000 to one, for a sample of 1,003 politicians with odds of 100 to one, and again for a sample of journalists with odds also of 100 to one. The moon was in culmination in the birth horoscopes of 352 writers with odds of 100,000 to one; and Mars again was dominant for a sample of 202 large industrial managers with odds of over 200 to one. These planetary effects, however, did not show with subjects who were undistinguished in these professions, and moreover, Gauquelin wrote, 'the greater the heights reached by an individual in his chosen profession, the more likely he is to have been born in "planetary conformity" with his peers'.

Gauquelin found no statistical evidence that the sign of the zodiac that a person was born under, the 'aspects' of the planets or the 'houses' they were in at the moment of his birth, have any influence on character or destiny. But other researchers of equal scientific probity have turned up data that would appear to validate these components of traditional astrology.

Hans Eysenck* is among the most distinguished of contemporary psychologists, and he is certainly not known to have any leanings towards the occult. But he has published a paper reporting a study project in which he collaborated with an astrologer, Jeff Mayo, which was designed to test a sample of 2,323 people to see if there were any correspondences between their birth signs and the personality characteristics said to be associated with these signs. Rather to Eysenck's surprise, when the results of the objective personality evaluation test were computed and correlated with the individuals' birth signs, there were clear correspondences which were totally consistent with astrological principles. For instance, people with odd-numbered birth signs showed a distinct tendency towards extroversion, while those with even-numbered signs tended towards introversion, and people born under the 'water signs', Cancer, Scorpio and Pisces, showed an inclination to be emotional and neurotic. Cautiously, Eysenck concluded that the result of the study was that 'the astrological hypotheses tested have not been disconfirmed'.

Another way of testing the claims of astrology is to test the efficiency of astrologers, and a number of people have set up experiments designed to do this. The German psychologist Hans Bender* tested more than 100 astrologers, requiring them either to do a 'blind diagnosis' of an anonymous horoscope so that he could compare the readings with known facts about the person concerned, or to unscramble a mixed batch of horoscopes and detailed notes about certain people and see if they could match the horoscopes with the appropriate personal descriptions. Bender found a number of astrologers who were consistently successful in these types of test. A US psychologist, Vernon Clarke*, has conducted a series of experiments similar to Bender's, and his astrologers were so successful that he concluded: 'Never again will it be possible to dismiss the astrological technique as a vague, spooky, and mystical business – or as the plaything of undisciplined psychics – or as merely the profitable device of unscrupulous cranks.'

There is clearly much more to astrology than we can rationally comprehend, and it does seem to constitute significant evidence for an interactionist view of life and the universe. However, it is far from being a reliable predictive or interpretative tool. Perhaps it should be regarded, as Gauquelin has proposed, as a key to self-knowlege, a means of knowing individual temperamental biases and characterological 'unfavorable aspects'. It should certainly be borne in mind that astrological principles are considered indicative only of probabilities, and that it is a tra-vesty of astrology to conceive of individual fates 'written in the stars'. [106, 107, 166, 253]

Atman

In Hindu religion, the manifestation in the human soul of the ultimate and all-encompassing spiritual reality, which is called *Brahman*. The distinction between the inner reality of Atman and the outer reality of Brahman is held to be merely a convenient linguistic one, but in reality and essence they are the same. '*Tat tvam asi*' – 'That art thou' – is the Upanishadic succinct expression of this identity.

Avatar

In Hindu religion, an incarnation of divinity.

Bardo

The *Tibetan Book of the Dead*, the *Bardo Thodol*, teaches that human beings have a non-physical 'Bardo body' which separates from the physical body after death. The separation is said to take three days to complete, during which time the second body wanders around a 'Bardo region' where it encounters forms both radiantly beautiful and hideous and has to make choices between paths which determine the quality of its future existence. The *Bardo Thodol* is a manual of instruction and guidance to enable the Bardo body to make the right choices. [83]

Bodhisattva

In Buddhism, one who has achieved ENLIGHTENMENT but has chosen to stop short of the ultimate step of passage to NIRVANA in order to remain and work in the world to help others to achieve it; thus the embodiment of the Buddha-nature of perfect love, selflessness, compassion and wisdom.

Chakras

According to Indian occult anatomy, the 'subtle' human body has seven *chakras*, or energy-centres, each of which correlates with both psycho-physical and emotional-spiritual aspects of behaviour and personality. In ascending order, they are:

1 The root chakra, located at the base of the spine, which relates to primitive energy and the fulfilment of basic survival needs.
2 The sacral chakra, located in the sexual-genital region, which relates to sexuality and primary interpersonal relationships.
3 The navel chakra, or solar plexus, which relates to emotional responses, assertiveness, and social identity and expression.
4 The heart chakra, which relates to self-expression and feelings of affection and love.
5 The throat chakra, which relates to cultural and social creativity, self-expression and communication.
6 The frontal chakra, located between the eyebrows, which relates to heightened mental activity and self-awareness.
7 The crown chakra, located at the top of the head, which relates to the highest spiritual experience, self-realization and ENLIGHTENMENT.

Like the ACUPUNCTURE[6] points of Chinese medicine, the existence and location of the chakras has not been verified by Western science, and there is a tendency therefore to regard them as sym-bolic foci that serve the purposes of meditation. However, psychics often maintain that they can see them and can ascertain people's physical and psychological states from their relative brightness, and studies of practitioners of KUN-DALINI YOGA have shown that there are distinct physiological correlates to the experience of activating or 'opening' the chakras. [73, 185]

Ch'i

In Chinese philosophy, the vital breath of the cosmos, or the energy that animates all things. In man, the meridians that are the foci of ACUPUNCTURE[6] therapy are known as 'pathways of *ch'i*'. [102]

Cosmic consciousness

The Canadian psychologist Richard M. Bucke* coined the term to designate a transpersonal experience and resultant awareness. The experience, generally coming unsought and without warning, is emotionally one of joy and assurance, of belonging to and participating in an abundant living reality of cosmic dimensions. Intellectually, it is an experience of illumination or revelation, a visionary insight into 'the meaning and drift of the universe', an understanding 'that the life which is in man is eternal, as all life is eternal; that the soul of man is as immortal as God is; that the universe is so built and ordered that without any peradventure all things work together for the good of each and all; that the foundation principle of the world is what we call love; and that the happiness of every individual is in the long run absolutely certain'. The attainment of or entry into cosmic consciousness, according to Bucke, is the experience that has initiated the work of all the great spiritual teachers and informed the writings of some of the greatest poets, such as Dante, Wordsworth and Whitman. [41, 149]

Divination

The obtaining of information about the unknown or about the future, generally by employing some mechanical aid (a crystal ball, a pack of cards, tossed coins) or esoteric 'reading' procedure (palmistry, I CHING, ASTROLOGY, dream interpretation). It is distinguished from PRECOGNITION[5] by its employment of such means, and by being a deliberate rather than an involuntary eliciting of information. Although diviners' procedures often smack of charlatanism, the information they vouchsafe is often uncannily correct. This fact may signify the existence of a paranormal, psychic faculty in human beings, an inadequacy in 'common-sense' views of time, or the operation of 'an acausal connecting principle' in the universe (see SYNCHRONICITY[1]). However, no one of these three 'explanations' of divination adequately explains all its forms, and as they are not mutually con- tradictory it seems probable that all three would have to be taken into account in any comprehensive view of the phenomenon. [333]

Enlightenment

In the Hindu and Buddhist religions, the ego-transcendent state of consciousness that is the ultimate objective of the religious life and disciplines. ZEN Buddhism, and the various schools of YOGA, afford different methods of attainment of enlightenment, which enables individuals of different temperament to find the method most suitable for them. Experientially, enlightenment is the attainment of union with the divine, which is generally conceived as having both objective and subjective reality. Its necessary precursor is the experience of liberation, of freedom from the conceptual and physical ties to the material world that confine consciousness to the ego-dimension. The stages in the progression towards enlightenment are basically the same as the progressive stages of Western MYSTICISM, and the experience of enlightenment itself may be compared with COSMIC CONSCIOUSNESS. The fundamental difference between Eastern and Western religions lies in the centrality of the experience in the former, and the development in them of a variety of ways of attainment that make the experience potentially accessible to all rather than the exclusive property of the exceptionally gifted or of a putatively 'chosen' priesthood. [81]

Esotericism

Most religions have distinct exoteric and esoteric aspects. Its institutional structure, established dogma and ritual, and canonical scriptures constitute a religion's exoteric aspect. They prescribe and circumscribe the modes of religious observance and belief for the many. The esoteric is the concern of the few who are more intensely engaged in the spiritual life, and who seek teachings, rituals and disciplines that minister to a need for inner experience and transformation. Often its relations with the exoteric and its custodians are fraught, for mystical and heretical ideas may spring from it that threaten to subvert orthodoxy. Examples of esoteric movements are: in Christianity, GNOSTICISM, in Islam, SUFISM, and in Hinduism, TANTRISM.

In modern times, the term has been closely associated with the movement and teachings of THEOSOPHY, which affirms the existence of an 'esoteric hierarchy', the fount of a corpus of knowlege known as 'the ageless wisdom' or 'the secret doctrine', portions of which have from time to time been 'revealed', or communicated to mankind through various mediumistic channels, the most recent of whom have been Helena Blavatsky* and Alice Bailey*.

Feng-shui

(Pronounced 'foong-shway'.) The ancient Chinese art of geomancy, which was concerned with the propitious siting and orienting of towns, houses, palaces, tombs, etc., having regard to the influence of subtle earth forces and attunement to the elements (*feng-shui* means 'wind and water'). The basic principle of the philosophy of TAO, that success and happiness come from understanding the natural order and living in harmony with it, is central also in *feng-shui*, which seeks to relate man harmoniously to his environment. It regards the earth as a living entity, through which the life force, or CH'I energy, flows like an underground stream, just as the same energy flows through the acupuncture meridians of the human body. These earth-currents are known as 'dragon paths', and have been compared with LEY LINES. The *feng-shui* expert was known as a 'dragon man', and his skill lay in identifying the *ch'i* currents and manipulating the land surface so as to trap and pool their energy, thus enhancing the fertility of the land and the health, prosperity and contentment of its inhabitants. [218, 303]

Gnosticism

The religion of gnosticism rivalled Christianity during the first three centuries of the Christian era. Its chief tenet was that man is saved not by virtue of his faith or conduct but by knowledge (*gnosis*). Deriving mainly from Eastern sources, gnosticism opposed the state Christianity of Rome with a visionary, individualistic and implicitly elitist prescription for salvation, a cosmology that made God unapproachably transcendent and detached from the affairs of the world and stationed a hierarchy of tyrannical and inimical demons between him and man, a philosophy of dualism that regarded eternal strife as the law of life and nature, and an image of man that combined grandeur and despair, for it sharply dichotomized his spiritual and physical existence and made him a 'stranger' on the earth.

The universe, in the gnostic

view, is a prison, and the earth is its deepest dungeon, and just as man is imprisoned in this dungeon so there is imprisoned in the depths of man's being a portion of the divine substance, the spirit or 'spark' (*pneuma*), which longs to be reunited with the transcendent Godhead, but is prevented by the archons, or demons, who are at once in the universe and in man's soul, in the form of his appetites, passions, and attachments to worldly things. The spirit, the divine portion, sleeps in matter, unconscious of itself, and the only worthwhile purpose of life is to awaken and liberate it through knowledge. But the knowledge that awakens and liberates is not rational knowledge attained through processes of argument and cerebration, but the knowledge vouchsafed by secret lore or obtained through mystical illumination. It is knowledge both of the Being of God and of the Way the spirit must travel to escape from the prison of the world, and this practical knowledge of the Way involves immensely detailed knowledge of magical and ceremonial preparations for each stage of the long journey and for combating the powers of the demons.

This religion of *gnosis* was ruthlessly suppressed by state Christianity. The burning of the great library at Alexandria was an attempt to destroy all evidence of the existence of such rivals to the official religion that was becoming the orthodoxy of the Western world. The recent discovery of libraries of sacred texts at Nag Hamadi in Egypt and near the Dead Sea in Israel has given an indication of how widespread gnostic and other similar sects were in the early Christian centuries. As the secular empire of Rome crumbled, religions that offered the hope of self-realization and personal salvation prospered. Consciousness turned inward and sought strategies to liberate the spirit from the dross of the world. Gnosticism had its day, but ultimately the ecclesiastical empire of Rome triumphed where the secular empire had failed, the hegemony of Europe under the rule of the Church was established, and the gnostic religion went underground. It was never completely suppressed, though. Its message and myth were too close to perennial aspects of human experience and aspiration. It survived particularly in KABBALISM, and the *Zohar*, a kabbalist text written in Spain in the thirteenth century, contains many gnostic elements. It surfaced again in the fifteenth century, when the ancient HERMETIC writings were rediscovered and translated. The Hermetic tradition, which supplied the philosophical foundation for ALCHEMY, combined classical Greek and gnostic influences. The 'royal art' of the alchemists, the transmutation of base metal to gold, was an analogue of the gnostic striving to liberate the divine element imprisoned in matter, a task that could only be accomplished by an initiate possessed of arcane knowledge. When orthodox science combined with orthodox religion to suppress alchemy, the gnostic tradition again went underground and survived in secret societies, such as the Rosicrucians and the Freemasons.

It survived, too, as a cultural influence. EXISTENTIALISM[1], from Nietzsche* and Kierkegaard* to Sartre* and Heidegger*, often expressed aspects of the gnostic myth and message. The alien God, the loneliness, homesickness, forlornness of the man in whom the spirit is quickened, the sense of being a stranger in the world, the agonizing over attaining freedom and authentic existence, the contempt for the physical and the sense of nausea that man experiences confronted with the mindlessness and proliferation of nature: these are *motifs* common to both philosophies. Though what is missing in existentialism is the doctrine of *gnosis*, of salvation through knowledge. For the existentialist there is no salvation; existentialism is gnosticism divested of its mysticism and hope. [155, 211]

God

The deity. Whether He, She or It exists, and if so in what manner and endowed with what attributes, are questions that have exercised the human mind since time immemorial. They have also most remarkably engaged man's passions, inciting to murder and martyrdom on a scale difficult to reconcile on the one hand with the abstractness of the questions, and on the other with the generally alleged benevolence of the Divinity towards his creation and creatures. Whether man is created in God's image or vice versa has also been a vexed question, upon which perhaps the

most pertinent observation was made by the Greek philosopher Euhemeros, who said that if a horse could conceive of God he would be in the form of a horse.

Common sense may scoff at the idea of a partisan or an anthropomorphic God, and suspect that the Heavenly Father figure – 'old Nobodaddy aloft', as the great religious poet William Blake irreverently called him – is but a comforting transcendental counterpart of an idealized psychic archetype, but the idea of God as the Creator is not so easily dismissed. Modern cosmological theory holds that the universe originated in a 'BIG BANG[2]', and that this primordial event appears to have been planned and controlled, its power and uniformity being so precisely calculated that a fractional variation would have resulted in the annihilation rather than the creation of matter. 'God', said the physicist Sir James Jeans* some fifty years ago, 'is a mathematician', and the more we learn about the cosmos the more convincing the statement becomes. But not entirely convincing, because if science can ascertain the laws that governed Creation, and can show that the universe could only have come into being and only continues to exist in conformity with those laws, then God must have been bound by those laws, and therefore could not have been omnipotent. The supernatural God standing outside his creation and fashioning it to his will is a grand concept, but the divine stature becomes greatly diminished if he was not free to do otherwise. And a God who just set the ball rolling (the 'Prime Mover' of the traditional 'cosmological proof') is not a particularly inspiring object of worship.

Eastern religions generally postulate a divinity immanent in the natural order, suffusing and sustaining it, and such a concept accords better with science than that of a transcendent deity. Nor need it be construed as a reductive accommodation of the divine to the natural, because the natural is certainly awesome and wonderful enough to inspire in human beings the attitudes and responses generally considered appropriate in a finite being privileged to participate in and at least partly comprehend the totality. [63, 153]

Hermetic

A term applied to an esoteric tradition and group of writings from ancient and early medieval times, the most famous of which, the Smaragdine Tablet, expresses, elliptically and aphoristically, a mystical and magical philosophy. Attributed to Hermes Trismegistus (Hermes the thrice greatest), the Greek name for the Egyptian god Thoth, who was believed to be the scribe of the gods and the inventor of writing and all the arts, the Hermetic writings are replete with occult symbolism and allusive meanings incomprehensible to the uninitiated, hence the term hermetic is often used as synonymous with arcane. Much of the symbolism refers to ALCHEMY, which was known as 'the Hermetic Art'. The principle 'As above, so below' was the cornerstone of the Hermetic philosophy. It expressed the belief that the universe was a *cosmos*, an ordered whole, and that all its parts were interdependent and interactive. The interrelationship of the parts was believed to be governed by laws of sympathy and antipathy which could be understood only by divine revelation. The Hermetic writings included an elaborate system of occult correspondences between apparently unconnected phenomena and parts of the universe, which formed the basis of the magical tradition. Science discredited this tradition, but some modern thinkers have found deeper meanings in it than mere superstition or charlatanry could have endowed it with. In particular, Carl Jung* found in the Hermetic writings a rich store of 'archetypal motifs that ... appear in the dreams of modern individuals', and in the idea of occult connections and interactions a correspondence with his own concept of SYNCHRONICITY[1]. [296]

Hexagram

See I CHING.

I Ching

(Pronounced *ee-jing*.) The ancient Chinese 'Book of Changes', a gnomic text used for DIVINATION, based on the principle that man and his cosmic and terrestrial environments constitute an interacting unity governed by the activity of the complementary forces of YIN AND YANG.

The *I Ching* contains 64 figurations, each of a different combination of six broken and unbroken lines known as a hexagram. The broken lines represent yin, the unbroken ones yang. Each hexagram has a symbolic name signifying a different condition of life, and is accompanied by a short explanatory text. There is also a commentary on the text, attributed to Confucius, as well as explanations of the symbolism of the hexagram and the meaning of the separate lines in it. To find out which hexagram is relevant, a questioner tosses three coins six times (the original method uses division of a bunch of fifty yarrow stalks). Each toss indicates a line of the hexagram working up from the bottom. For instance, if the first toss produces two tails and one head, the bottom line is an unbroken one. The hexagram formed in this way by the six tosses is the one to be consulted and interpreted.

The philosophy of the *I Ching* is not determinist. It does not regard the future as fixed or purport to tell those who consult it what will happen. It emphasizes man's responsibility for his own fate. Change is fundamental to life; it does not occur haphazardly, but is rather governed by universal principles and patterning processes which are heralded by signs and tokens, and the divinatory art consists in understanding the principles and interpreting the signs. The *I Ching* texts are gnomic and nonspecific, and yield their meaning only to a perceptive interpretation undertaken in a serious frame of mind.

Since the *I Ching* was first translated in 1882, it has gained many Western followers. Carl Jung* attested from personal experience its ability to give remarkably accurate information and guidance, and was led by contemplation of its implications to develop his own concept of SYNCHRONICITY[1]. [253, 355]

Immortality

'Life everlasting' is specifically promised in the Christian and other religions, and many people the world over fervently believe in it, with varying degrees of conceptual sophistication. Just what is immortal, in what manner it continues to exist, and where, are questions that have engendered a wealth of imaginative myth and doctrinal ingenuity, which resolves into consensus primarily with regard to the existence of a nonphysical component of the personality, the soul or spirit, and secondarily with regard to the existence of a transmundane location, a heaven or hell, that is its appropriate milieu and which it is destined to inhabit for eternity.

Religions generally agree that what will continue to exist in the afterlife will be a something divested of its physical attributes, appetites and passions – although some incorporate ideas of reward and punishment that attribute to a governing deity the will to pay infinite dividends or to exact infinite retribution for acts of finite goodness or turpitude, and imagine the soul enjoying or suffering for eternity boons or banes of a positively physical nature. The idea that mind and body are separate and separable things can be plausibly argued (see MIND-BODY PROBLEM[1]), and some kind of posthumous existence of a quintessence of individual personality may be conjectured based upon it. But the idea of immortality implies ongoing existence in time. And RELATIVITY THEORY[2] has destroyed the naïve idea of time as absolute and universal, and the cosmological scenario that developed from it demonstrates that the universe had a beginning and probably will have an end – as the planetary systems within it certainly will have. The idea of 'life everlasting' must therefore be regarded as a promise or hope – both time-dependent concepts – that has long been misconstrued and has to be relinquished.

Kabbalism

The mystical branch of Judaism, which in turn developed two branching traditions, the speculative-metaphysical and the practical-magical. The texts collectively known as the Kabbalah comprise two major works, the *Sepher Yetzirah*, or Book of Creation, written in about the third century AD, and the *Zohar*, or Book of Splendour, written in the thirteenth century, and a number of lesser works and commentaries. The tradition has close associations with GNOSTICISM, and some of its fundamental ideas originated in early Judaism.

Central to kabbalism in both its aspects is the diagram known as the Tree of Life, which consists of ten circles, known as the *Sefiroth*, which represent emanations of the Godhead, or Ground of Being, known as the *En-Sof*, each corresponding with an attribute of God, which is also potentially an attribute of man. The diagram can be variously regarded as a schema of Creation, or as a map for the guidance of the soul in its upward journey from its entrapment in matter to its liberation and fulfilment in spirit. The ten Sefiroth are joined by twenty-two paths, which represent alternative ways to work towards union with God. The spiritual journey is beset by hazards, and the kabbalists symbolized these hazards as demons or animals that might be encountered on the paths. The 'magical' aspect of kabbalism, with its incantations, amulets, spells and talismans, developed out of this tradition, for these were conceived as devices to protect the traveller or control the forces that sought to subvert his endeavour.

The kabbalists were much occupied with the mystical significance of numbers and letters. In the practice known as *Gematria* the letters of words are converted into numerical equivalents, and correspondences are established with other words of the same numerical value. Thus are evolved what are known as 'Names of Power', secret names used in magical conjuration, the most important of which is the Tetragrammaton (YHVH), the name of Jehovah.

Although kabbalism was sometimes degraded into the practice of 'magic' to secure mundane or material advantage for the practitioner, in its origin and essence it was and remains one of the most comprehensive, subtle, poetic and rewarding systems of mystical philosophy. [91, 209, 253]

Karma

A central concept in Hindu and Buddhist thought. Originally, and in a cosmic sense, karma was the elemental force of creation. Later, transposed to a psychological and religious context, it became the chain of cause and effect that binds the soul to this world. Associated with the idea of reincarnation, karma was conceived as the store of rewards and punishments that the soul carries through from one life to another, a property modified, for better or worse, by what a person does in and with his life. The goal of the religious life, ENLIGHTENMENT, was conceived as a severance from bondage to karma, the ultimate annihilation of desire and individuality. [148]

Koan

In ZEN Buddhism, a riddle or paradox designed to show the inadequacy of conceptual and logical approaches to knowledge and reality. The well-known examples are: 'What is the sound of one hand clapping?' and 'What was your face before you were born?' The Zen trainee is given koans not just as illustrations of the fact that linguistic formulations can be syntactically faultless but at the same time meaningless, but also as riddles demanding intense concentration and ultimate resolution. He has to experience perplexity as mental anguish, and dwell in it until enlightenment, the jump to another level of awareness, occurs. An interesting parallel, pointed out by Fritjof Capra*, is with the situation modern theoretical physicists have often found themselves in,

confronted by nature itself with paradoxes that required for their solution a radical shift in the scientific mode of thought. [222, 345]

Kundalini yoga

Closely associated with TANTRA, kundalini yoga is a psychophysical discipline which seeks the attainment of ENLIGHTENMENT through the successive awakening and integrating of the seven energy centres known in Indian occult anatomy as the CHAKRAS. Symbolically represented as a serpent which lies coiled in the 'root chakra' at the base of the spine, the kundalini energy is, by the practice of yogic disciplines, raised through the intervening chakras ultimately to energize the 'crown chakra' at the top of the head. According to the yogi Gopi Krishna*, once kundalini is awakened it can be a psychically and physically disruptive, even destructive, force, and to seek to awaken it without having full knowledge of and commitment to the yogic disciplines that enable it to be contained and directed can be highly dangerous. Probably because it was naïvely understood as a means of sublimating sexual energy to attain a spiritual state of consciousness, kundalini yoga had a cultic following in the West in the 1970s. However, largely through the work of Gopi Krishna and his 'Kundalini Research Institute', at the same time the biophysical, psychological and metaphysical aspects of kundalini and tantrism were brought to the attention of Western scientists and philosophers. [174]

Latihan
See SUBUD.

Ley lines
Hypothetical straight tracks across the countryside. They are sometimes considered to be parts of a prehistoric communications network, but are also sometimes imbued with a more mystical significance. Their existence was first proposed in 1924 by Alfred Watkins*, a retired businessman who had lived all his life and travelled widely in the Welsh border country. He later told how his discovery had come to him as a kind of visionary experience one day in June 1920, when from a hill overlooking a panoramic landscape he had clearly seen lines of connection between ancient monuments, standing stones, churches and paths which he believed was a revelation of how that particular countryside had looked in the distant past. Subsequent research with maps convinced him that what he called ley lines (from the Anglo-Saxon *ley* or *lea*, meaning grassland) were a genuine phenomenon, since both natural and manmade features were often aligned over both short and long distances in far greater number than they were on lines arbitrarily drawn on the map.

Watkins himself did not attribute any mystical significance to his discovery. But in the late 1940s a dowser named Guy Underwood announced that he had discovered an underground magnetic force which ran in straight tracks which corresponded with certain ley lines and was concentrated in sacred sites such as Stonehenge, and he suggested that there was a link between ley lines and the religion of ancient man. Recent revived interest in ley lines stems largely from Underwood's* *The Pattern of the Past*, and also from John Michell's* *A View over Atlantis*, which drew attention to the fact that the Chinese have a traditional science concerned with linear earth forces and their sacred implications.

See FENG SHUI. [218, 330, 339]

Maya
In Hindu religion and philosophy, the mistaking the appearances of things for their intrinsic reality. The term is widely misunderstood as implying that the phenomenal world itself is an illusion and insubstantial. What it in fact implies is that our sensory experience of the world and the conceptual formulations we base upon that experience can inhibit us from apprehending its fundamental and essential nature, its divine *Brahman* nature which underlies and unites all manifest phenomena.

Meditation
The practice of a mental discipline designed to alter one's state of consciousness, either for the purpose of promoting relaxation and reducing stress, or of inducing mystical or visionary experience.

Dissociated from its religious associations, meditation can be considered simply as a 'relaxation response'. Dr Herbert Benson* of the Harvard Medical School, a specialist in stress-related ailments, contrasts the relaxation response with the 'flight or fight' response. The latter is a co-ordinated response to a challenge or threat which involves increase of oxygen consumption and of blood pressure, heart and respiration rate and the amount of blood pumped into the muscles. In the relaxation response all these functions are decreased, and Benson found that regular elicitation of the relaxation response has such beneficial effects as a general lowering of blood pressure and reducing or eliminating dependence on drugs, alcohol or nicotine products. He observes that over 50 per cent of the US population die of stress-related ailments, because in the conditions of modern life and business the flight or fight response is continually being elicited although in very few circumstances are fighting or running away appropriate behaviours, and therefore tensions and chemical byproducts such as cortisone tend to accumulate in the body, and he recommends that to alleviate these conditions or restore balance in their physical systems people should regularly elicit the relaxation response.

To engage in meditation as a means of combating the stressful conditions of life is one thing. To seek through its visionary, illuminative, ecstatic or mystical experience is quite another. All religions advocate meditation or prayer as a means of achieving an experience of unity, either with the divine or with the totality of what is, and prescribe techniques for doing so. All techniques involve the training of attention. There are two basic ways of doing this, through concentration or through 'mindfulness'. Concentration techniques are, for instance, focusing attention on an object such as a candle, a pebble, a twig, or concentrating on a KOAN, or reciting a *mantra*, a repeated word or sound, or counting one's breaths, and trying to expunge every other thought from consciousness. 'Mindfulness' is the cultivation of awareness of what happens to us or in us from moment to moment, and may take the form of detached observation of one's body, one's feelings or one's mental states, simply noting what goes on in them from moment to moment.

In his instructional booklet, *How to Meditate*, Lawrence LeShan* distinguishes four basic paths: of the intellect, of the emotions, of the body, and of action. The person who follows the path of the intellect meditates long and deeply on such topics as the alternative ways of perceiving and relating to the world and on philosophical and intellectual questions that force him to probe more deeply into the ambiguities of reality. He who follows the path of the emotions is the devotional type of mystic, whose meditations focus on love, praise and worship. He who follows the way of the body may practise, for instance, Hatha YOGA, T'AI CHI[6], the formal martial arts of the East, or dancing in the manner of the dervishes; through any of these disciplines he can learn concentration and the art of doing just one thing at a time. The path of action is a similar discipline, and involves doing ordinary things, such as flower arrangement, rug weaving, archery, or even the humdrum tasks of everyday life, with total and undivided attention. [20, 110, 189]

Millennialism

The belief that a change for the better, both in personal and sociopolitical life, will occur at the end of a specific period of time (the 'millennium' of Christian doctrine), and the adoption and prescription of codes of conduct in the present supposed to constitute a preparation for the anticipated change. Although millennialist cults and movements are generally religious and salvationist and look to divine intervention as the instrument of change, the idea clearly has appeal in any society where life conditions are hard and seem immutable, and it sometimes acquires a political complexion, as in the MARXIST[1] doctrine of the ultimate 'withering away of the State'. [56]

Mysticism

'Mystic' and 'mysticism' are terms often used pejoratively, with the implication that to seek 'the spiritual apprehension of truths beyond the understanding' (*Oxford Dictionary*) and their expression in language is to pursue chimeras and to license incoherent utterances. Mysticism, in this view (which FREUDIAN PSYCHOLOGY[4] has fostered), sinisterly abrogates rationality, and constitutes a regression to infantile states of consciousness or states often manifested by psychotics. On the other hand, mysticism has been regarded as the core-experience of all religions and spiritual philosophies, and its expression, in scriptural and literary texts, as the acme of human creativity.

Evelyn Underhill*, in the classic study of the subject, defined mysticism as: 'the expression of the innate tendency of the human spirit towards complete harmony with the transcendent order; whatever the theological formula under which that order is understood'. This 'tendency of the human spirit' is often expressed in mystical literature in the metaphor of a journey or quest. Underhill specified five distinct stages of the mystical journey or experience:

1 'The Awakening of the Self'. This may be a sudden conversion experience, an awareness or intuition of a transcendent reality and of an aspect of the self that belongs to it or can participate in it.
2 'The Purification of the Self'. Asceticism, renunciation, dying to the world and being reborn, incarnating a new self that has discarded the habits and attachments of the old, characterize this second stage.
3 'The Illumination of the Self'. The third stage is 'the great swing back into sunshine which is the reward of that painful descent into "the cell of self-knowledge"'. It is characterized by expressions of joy, bliss, ecstasy, rapture, 'God-intoxification', soaring lyricism, rhapsodic celebration of the immanence of a divine reality in the physical world or of a transcendent Absolute.
4 'The Dark Night of the Soul'. Suddenly the ecstatic illuminative experiences cease and seem to be negated by a profound sense of alienation and depression, of forlornness, being abandoned by God, irretrievably cast out into a joyless, desolate wasteland. This,

however, is a second and necessary purgative stage on the 'Mystic Way', a final excoriation of ego-consciousness.

5 'The Unitive Life'. Tranquillity and peace, at-one-ment with God and the Absolute, total obliteration of the self and even the senses, a sense of existence as pure consciousness, the resolution of the fret of becoming into a sense of a state of pure being, are characteristics of the consummation of the mystic's journey. Now another journey may begin, back into the objective, social world, where the mystic may become the great teacher, saint, healer, poet.

Only a tendentious or ignorant parody of mysticism can portray it as infantile or regressive, whatever correspondences there may be between the schizophrenic's and the mystic's transports and depressions or between the bliss of the blastopheric embryo and of the mystic's 'unitive life'. And only an impoverished view of human nature, relationships and societies can fail to see that the experiences and insights that mysticism yields are relevant, not only religiously or aesthetically but also quite practically, particularly in a world where divisive modes of thought and action prevail. [149, 330]

Nirvana
In Buddhism, the ultimate blessed state, the goal of the religious life, deliverance from the wheel of life and death and rebirth, the final annihilation of desire, ego-consciousness and attachment to the physical world, the absorption of the soul into divine reality.

Noosphere
In the evolutionary philosophy of Pierre Teilhard de Chardin*, the layer of consciousness that encompasses the earth. The planet may be conceived as composed of a series of concentric layers: the metallic barysphere, the rocky lithosphere, the fluid hydrosphere and atmosphere, the living membrane of flora and fauna that comprises the biosphere, and finally the noosphere, which, according to Teilhard, is what the genesis of the other layers was for. Geogenesis led to biogenesis, which in turn led to 'noogenesis', which is ongoing, drawn to the goal of the OMEGA POINT. Consciousness emerged and developed in man, and in this process, wrote Teilhard, 'the earth "got a new skin"; better still, it found its soul'. [51]

Occultism
Commonly associated on the one hand with crass superstition, and on the other with disreputable trafficking with ideas and practices disruptive of psychic, social and theological order, occultism has generally had a bad press. The word occult means 'covered over' or 'hidden', which hasn't helped, because it can be taken as implying either that occultists engage in secret or nefarious practices, or that the consensus order of science and society is a 'cover-up' that occultists are engaged in subverting. It is arguable that all scientific progress is an uncovering of what was previously hidden, and that electromagnetism for instance was occult before Maxwell* elucidated it, and even that the universe and the forces that modern physical science studies have notable correspondences with some ancient oc-

Perennial philosophy

cultist concepts. It is also true that the 'occult sciences' have not been held in such ill-esteem by some of the founders of modern science, such as Roger Bacon* and Isaac Newton*, as they are by most of today's scientists. But although science may sometimes lend support to occultism, and occultism may sometimes suggest experimental strategies for science, there will always remain the fundamental difference that occultism is basically a congeries of metaphysical systems which branch into psycho-spiritual disciplines on the one hand and divinatory disciplines on the other, whereas science is and must remain strictly empirical. Some of the systems and practices that are generally considered occult are dealt with in the separate entries of ASTROLOGY, ALCHEMY, I CHING, KABBALISM and TAROT. [253, 357]

Oceanic feeling
An alternative term for COSMIC CONSCIOUSNESS.

Omega point
In the evolutionary philosophy of Pierre Teilhard de Chardin*, the 'Omega point' is both the goal of the evolutionary process and the dynamic principle which governs it. It is 'the Prime Mover ahead'. The evolution of consciousness or spirit in humanity is not simply a process of ongoing complexification, or of going ever onward and upward; it is rather a process of convergence towards an ultimate point or state. Omega is ultimate, but it is also actual, and it exerts a persistent attractive influence upon human consciousness. It is beyond space and time, but it radiates its influence back into the space-time dimension of the NOOSPHERE.

Teilhard was a palaeontologist and a philosopher, but at the same time a Jesuit priest, and his Omega point is clearly a theological concept. In fact he sometimes writes of 'God-Omega'. His main work, *The Phenomenon of Man*, is an attempt to reconcile and synthesize modern scientific knowledge, evolution theory, and Christian doctrine. [51]

Pantheism
The identification of the divine with nature and the worship of it therein. A religious orientation towards the physical world which dispenses with the idea of a transcendent deity, pantheism could be regarded as a sophisticated form of primitive animism, which worshipped the gods of specific mountains, rivers, etc. But if 'nature' is understood more broadly, as comprehending the laws that govern the physical world, it could be argued that while modern science and cosmology have rendered redundant the idea of a transcendent and supernatural GOD, they have furnished support for the proposition of the existence of an immanent and natural God.

Perennial philosophy
The term *philosophia perennis* was coined by Leibniz* and later adopted by Aldous Huxley* to describe the 'highest common factors' of religions and spiritual and esoteric philosophies. It is religion

divested of doctrine, the time-honoured and quintessential wisdom or knowledge vouchsafed by the religious experience. In Huxley's words, it is 'the metaphysic that recognizes a divine Reality substantial to the world of things and lives and minds; the psychology that finds in the soul something similar to, or even identical with, divine Reality; the ethic that places man's final end in the knowledge of the immanent and transcendent Ground of all being'.

The perennial philosophy originates in experience, and conceptual formulations of it cannot adequately convey what the experience is like or what it signifies. Verbal formulations of it tend to be paradoxical or gnomic, as for instance the Sanskrit formula *tat tvam asi* ('thou art that'), or Kabir's aphorism, 'Behold but One in all things; it is the second that leads you astray.' The experience is basically of oneness, of human consciousness being integral and co-extensive with a universal consciousness. It is what Bucke* called the experience of COSMIC CONSCIOUSNESS. In the light of this experience, ordinary experience and ordinary consciousness appear as a kind of sleep, and much that masquerades as knowledge or learning seems manifest illusion. Metaphors of sleep and awakening characterize statements of the perennial philosophy. Human potentials are limitless, but generally go unfulfilled, even unrecognized. But when they are recognized, when the unitary experience awakens the soul to growth, illusions and all divisive modes of thought and being are

shed, and the human being discovers 'the Kingdom of Heaven within', himself becomes godlike, understanding and participating in the universal evolutionary process.

The perennial philosophy has been re-stated in all ages and cultures, and has sometimes surfaced in strange contexts, for instance in ALCHEMY and the HERMETIC philosophy. In our time, it has influenced and been practically applied in TRANSPERSONAL PSYCHOLOGY[4], and has surfaced even in the work of theoretical physicists such as David Bohm* and Fritjof Capra*. It is not generally the philosophy of philosophers or philosophical schools, although, as Jacob Needleman* has argued, philosophers such as Descartes*, Kant* and, in our time, Wittgenstein*, have expressed aspects of it or urged and facilitated the 'awakening' that is the precondition of comprehending it and living in accord with it. [143, 235]

Prana

In Hindu philosophy, the cosmic life-energy, like the Taoist CH'I, that vitalizes physical bodies. A distinction is sometimes made between physical and psychic prana, the former associated with the gross mortal body, the latter with the 'subtle body' that is believed to survive the death of the physical. Gopi Krishna* sees in the BIOPLASMA[5] theory of Grischenko and Inyushin a parallel with prana. He writes:

In its cosmic form prana is a highly diffused intelligent energy spread everywhere. But in the individual it takes a specific form as the bioplasma or individual prana composed of an extremely subtle organic essence drawn from the elements and compounds forming the body ... The bioplasma, sustained by the cosmic ocean of prana, permeates each and every cell of an organism ... The nervous system with its countless extremely fine threads floats like a serpent on this pool of bioenergy, which is itself surrounded and permeated by the boundless ocean of universal life. [175]

Reincarnation

The belief that the soul is an entity independent of the physical body, which survives physical death and may be incarnated successively in a number of different bodies, is fundamental in most of the world's religions, and is found too in the great philosophers of the ancient world, Pythagoras, Socrates and Plato. Hindus and Buddhists, in particular, believe that a single human lifetime is only one stage in the development of a soul, which has to return to earth many times in many different bodies before it can attain perfection. They believe that a person's actions generate a force known as KARMA, which determines his destiny in the next existence. If the soul brings with it into life an accumulation of bad karma acquired through wrong action in a previous life, it will have to spend a lifetime expiating it in order to advance its process of growth. Such a belief accounts for the apparent injustices and inequalities of earthly life. It explains differences of personality and endowment, precocity in some children and special gifts in people of

genius. And it serves, as no other philosophical or religious concept does, to reconcile man to his fate while at the same time encouraging him to change himself.

The fact that the concept of reincarnation explains so much and is so useful does not, of course, argue for its truth. In a scientific sense, the hypothesis of reincarnation is neither falsifiable nor provable, but one psychic investigator, Dr Ian Stevenson*, has undertaken a careful and extended study of the evidence, and has accumulated over a thousand cases which he considers are 'suggestive of reincarnation'. In such cases a person, generally a child, appears to have memories and impressions of a previous life. Often these are quite detailed and specific and are confirmed by subsequent investigation.

A typical case was that of Jasbir Jat, a child born in the village of Rasulpur in Uttar Pradesh, India, in 1950. At the age of three the child had fallen ill with smallpox and nearly died. When he recovered he was strangely changed. He said his name was Sobha Ram and that he was the son of a Brahmin of the village of Vehedi, which is about 20 miles from Rasulpur. Some time later a Vehedi woman who had been born in Rasulpur paid a visit to her home village. She had not been back since 1952, when Jasbir was only 18 months old, but he recognized her. From others she learned the story of his strange claim and behaviour, which she repeated to her own family when she returned to Vehedi. When the family of the late Sobha Ram Tyagi heard about it, they paid a visit to Rasulpur to meet Jasbir. The child greeted them all by name, showing that he knew the relationship of each to Sobha Ram and many facts about their life in Vehedi. He also gave an exact account of how Sobha Ram had died, which was as a result of a fall from a carriage during a marriage procession.

When Dr Stevenson investigated the case he visited the two villages and talked to the people involved. He compiled a list of thirty-nine facts about Sobha Ram's life that Jasbir had mentioned before he met the Vehedi family. Of these, thirty-eight could be corroborated. The one that could not be corroborated was the most intriguing of all. Jasbir stated that Sobha Ram's fatal fall had been caused because he had been poisoned, and he even named the murderer. There was no way of proving this, but Stevenson discovered that the family had suspected that Sobha Ram had been murdered. Furthermore, he found that the time of Sobha Ram's death coincided with the time of Jasbir's smallpox illness, during which he too had almost died.

This is one of thousands of reported cases that are suggestive of reincarnation. The only alternative explanation of them would appear to be in terms of the operation of some kind of 'super ESP'. [312]

Ritual

Ritual may be regarded as the routine of religion, the mere observance of formalities according to custom, or as the very height of religion, the act in which the encounter with the divine is accomplished. It may serve to maintain the beliefs, usages and customs that give a social or cultural group its identity. On the other hand it may be a way of passing on certain basic cosmic or psychological principles that transcend any group interest and are of universal relevance. Of course, ritual actions can also be a symptom of mental illness, when they are simply repetitions divorced from meaning. It is the rituals that illustrate and elaborate a meaning that are a powerful means of working upon and elevating human emotions and thought. Rituals also serve to reconcile, to petition, or to initiate; they may be fertility rites, rites of passage from one stage of life to another, reenactments of actions of the gods; they may serve to bring about ALTERED STATES OF CONSCIOUSNESS[4]; they may release the basest urges of human nature or stimulate and aid its loftiest aspirations; they may be regarded as escapes from reality or as means of entering more deeply into it.

For the religious man ritual gives dramatic form to his worship; it is the means by which the sacred takes place in time. For him time itself is sharply distinguished into the sacred and the profane. Sacred time is preeminently the time of the great festivals of a religion. All religions have such festivals, which are not just commemorations of some past event but rather a reliving of it. There was a time when the gods were active on earth, and in the festival they become active again, coexistent with living man. It is by performing ritual actions that man enters sacred time. [79]

Samadhi
In Hinduism and Buddhism, an ecstatic state of ego-less and desire-less consciousness that is the goal of religious disciplines such as the various YOGAS.

Satori
In Japanese ZEN Buddhism, the word for ENLIGHTENMENT.

Scientology
A philosophy, a quasi-religious movement, and a system of psycho-dynamic techniques founded and developed by L. Ron Hubbard*. As a movement, scientology has had a bad press, charged with financial exploitation of gullible devotees, and alienating them from social and family ties and responsibilities. Hubbard is generally represented as a charlatan, and censured for claiming false academic qualifications and having started his career as a science fiction writer. Undeniably, scientology proposes some highly eccentric ideas, particularly about genetics and about the history of the universe, which have more in common with SF than with science proper. But its philosophy and psycho-dynamics are neither so eccentric nor so sinister as its critics maintain.

The philosophy has much in common with Buddhism and oriental philosophy, and also has affinities with GNOSTICISM. What Hubbard calls the MEST uni-

verse (the world of Matter, Energy, Space and Time) is regarded as a prison in which the individual's essential Self is confined and kept ignorant of its true immortal nature. Most people acquiesce in their confinement, they agree that the MEST universe is reality, and their consciousness is entirely bound up with MEST. The techniques of scientology are designed to enable people to break from this bondage, to expand their consciousness beyond MEST. What keeps people in bondage is what Hubbard calls 'the reactive mind'. Everyone has early experiences of the world that determine their reactions to future experiences and situations, so that, confronted with the new, the mind flips into an unconscious mode of reaction, it 'goes solid', entrapped in MEST. Hubbard likened these reactions to 'tape-loop' responses and called their determinants 'engrams'. In psychiatry they are called traumas. The psycho-dynamic techniques of scientology are designed to identify and eradicate these engrams, and thus liberate the individual from his collusion with the MEST universe. Where it departs from orthodox psychiatry is in maintaining that eradication is not achieved through mere recognition, through bringing unconscious determinants into the light of consciousness, but only through engaging the imagination and the will in an act of conscious duplication of the psychic determinants laid down in engrams.

There are psychological hazards in therapies that seek to reactivate

traumas, and some of the op-
probium heaped upon scientology
arose from the fact that some
people subjected to its techniques
were psychically destabilized by
them in ways that their therapists
were not competent to cope with.
An objective view of scientology
must concede the unattractiveness
of its cultic aspect and the preposterousness of some of its mar-
ginal ideas and teachings, but
should also acknowledge that, developed in the early 1950s, it was
in many respects the precursor of
the HUMANISTIC[4] and TRANS-
PERSONAL   PSYCHOLOGY[4]
movements of two decades later,
and of psycho-dynamic techniques
such as GESTALT THERAPY[4],
PSYCHOSYNTHESIS[4], PSYCHO-
DRAMA[4] and PRIMAL THER-
APY[4]. [84, 138]

Seth material

A body of writings produced by
the American trance medium Jane
Roberts* in the 1960s and 1970s
and allegedly dictated by a discarnate entity named Seth. Much
of the material is consistent with
other philosophical, religious or esoteric teachings, but the language
and imagery in which it is expressed is fresh and vital and the
material reads as quite un-
derivative. The insights it gives are
by turn philosophical, metaphysical, theological, cosmological, psychological and historical; and to be
able to generate fresh ideas in all
these areas is certainly the mark of
a very remarkable mind. Whether
that mind is the subconscious of
Jane Roberts, or what psychologists call a secondary or dis-

sociated personality, is a matter of
conjecture, although 'Seth' himself
specifically refutes these and other
psychological explanations, and describes himself as 'an energy essence personality, no longer materialized in physical form'. Both the
puzzle of its provenance and its
intellectual substance make the
Seth material fascinating reading.
[267, 268]

Shamanism

Shamans are the magician-priests
of tribal communities in Central
and North Asia and the Arctic.
Shamans are said to be able to
leave their body at will, and to
travel throughout the material
world or the regions of the dead.
They claim that there are spirits,
gods and demons that are responsive only to their powers.
Besides curing sickness, a shaman
directs communal ceremonies and
escorts the souls of the dead to the
other world. According to Mircea
Eliade*, the shaman is able to do
these things because he has
mastered the techniques of ecstasy:

that is, because his soul can safely ab-
andon his body and roam at vast distances, can penetrate the underworld
and rise to the sky. Through his own
ecstatic experience he knows the roads
of the extraterrestrial regions. He can
go below and above because he has
already been there. The danger of
losing the way in these forbidden regions is still great; but sanctified by his
initiation and furnished with his guardian spirits, the shaman is the only
human being able to challenge the
danger and venture into a mystical geography.

   The 'techniques of ecstasy' are in

fact techniques of out-of-the-body projection. The shaman achieves a trance-state through dance, music, fasting, meditation, drug-taking, or self-hypnosis. In some tribal societies the shaman not only accomplishes the healing of ailments believed to be caused by 'loss of soul', but also practises DIVINATION and CLAIRVOYANCE[5], and can travel out of his body to locate lost objects, people or animals. Shamans are reputed to be able to cover vast distances in an instant, to be in two places at the same time, and to visit places inaccessible to ordinary mortals. Buddhist legend tells of the miraculous lake Anavatapa, and Hindu legend of the mysterious northern land Svetadvipa. Both are places that can only be reached by those capable of magical flight. Legends of visits to the underworld, which are common in Nordic and Greek mythologies, are expressions of the shamanic tradition. Eskimo shamans claim to undertake fantastic journeys, remain out of the body for days, and return to tell of adventures in the depths of the sea or among the stars. During their 'flight' their physical bodies remain in a state of suspended animation, motionless and apparently lifeless. [80]

Spiritualism

Institutionalized spiritualism, with churches, accredited mediums, and services in which communications are held with the spirits of deceased persons, is little more than a century old. But the beliefs that spiritualists profess, the phenomena they construe as supportive of those beliefs, the purposes they congregate for and the means they employ to fulfil them, are ancient and found in virtually all human societies. That the deceased 'pass over' to another world, that certain gifted living individuals can hold converse with them, and that they can produce manifest effects in the material world, even transiently appear there in apparent physical form, are beliefs so transculturally common, and historically subscribed to by such a majority of mankind, including most of its revered spiritual teachers, that they can scarcely be put down to superstition.

If for many people spiritualism whiffs of crass superstition, craven gullibility, or frivolous dabbling with the supernatural, the impression is probably attributable to the reputation it and its devotees acquired in the late nineteenth and early twentieth centuries. It had against it both the orthodox churches and orthodox science, the former because it appeared a debasement of religion and served as a refuge for defectors from the true faith, the latter because the phenomena it dealt with and put forward as evidential of its truth were incompatible with the prevailing POSITIVIST[1] scientific worldview. Furthermore, many mediums were demonstrably bogus, their séance-room 'phenomena' – floating trumpets, levitating tables, rappings, 'apports', etc. – were preposterous, and the very idea of bamboozling the bereaved for profit was morally repugnant. But if institutional spiritualism and mindless ostensible trafficking with the dead in services or séances earned spiritualism a bad name, there were a number of distinguished philosophers, scientists and psychologists – for instance Henry Sidgwick*, Frederic W. H. Myers*, William James*, Sir Oliver Lodge*, William Crookes*, Henri Bergson* and Charles Richet* – who were convinced that not all the phenomena were bogus, and that controlled and systematic study of them might further the advancement of scientific and psychological knowledge. With the foundation of the Societies for Psychical Research, in England in 1882 and in the US in 1889, the foundations of modern PSI[5] research were laid. Though modern psi research has largely severed its links with institutional spiritualism – which, however, continues to flourish – and has repudiated the 'spirit' hypothesis for the cause of PARANORMAL PHENOMENA[5], it owes its origin to it.

See also CROSS-CORRESPONDENCES[5]. [60, 70, 229, 232]

Subud

A movement that developed around the Javanese Sufi mystic Bapak Mohammed Subuh*. As a young man, Subuh had experiences of divine illumination, and he later discovered that he was able to induce such experiences in others. All that was required was that a person should mentally and physically relax, so as to become empty and receptive, and then a simple touch by Subuh would spark the experience. This was referred to as 'the opening'. Subud, as a movement, has no doctrines, but consists simply of groups of people congregating to reexperience their 'opening' and the sense it confers of receiving and embodying divine power. This is done through a ritual known as the 'latihan'. The word is Indonesian for 'exercise', but when used by Subud members it appears to mean something more like 'divine grace'. A person can be 'in latihan' not only while participating in the ritual, but at any time in the circumstances of ordinary life. Bapak Subuh himself said he was always in latihan, even while watching TV. But he also warned that followers should not seek the latihan experience too often or for too long – too fervent a pursuit of spiritual experience negated the meaning of the experience. Two or three times a week for half an hour was sufficient by way of exercise to enable the soul to grow. Subud, like ZEN, seems to say that enlightenment can come easily, in a flash, when a person is properly prepared, and for the initiate the latihan is a process of purification, of clearing the mental and emotional dross that clutters the inner life and constricts the soul. In the latihan people behave as the spirit moves them; they may stand, sit, move about, dance, cry, laugh, chant, or whatever; nothing is prescribed, except submission and receptivity. And no particular result is looked for, no specific feedback into normal life. Some people have had seeming miraculous cures of illnesses, others have developed psychic faculties, many have ecstatic experiences and develop enhanced sensitivity to their environment and other people – sometimes to 'negative vibrations' which make the experience distressing. Openness to the divine power is not necessarily a comfortable or enjoyable condition. But it is a human potential and, as such, some human beings will always need to fulfil it. Subud ministers to this need, but it is unusual among neo-religious movements in that it does not particularly exalt it. Bapak Subuh himself made a point of being an ordinary man and engaging in the ordinary activities of life, and although he no doubt possessed unusual wisdom and insight he was loath to be regarded as a teacher or guru, preferring rather the status of 'helper'. If it seems an anomaly that such an unassuming man should allow a movement to be named after him, it should be pointed out that the word Subud is in fact a contraction of the three Sanskrit words, *Susila*, *Budhi* and *Dharma*, which mean 'right living', 'the inner divine force', and 'submission to divine power'. [234]

Sufism

A diffused, esoteric spiritual tradition, closely associated with the religion of Islam but not exclusive to it, which has no doctrines, institutions or scriptures, but has been claimed as the spiritual kernel from which the branches of religious orthodoxy have sprouted – only to lose, too often, their spiritual essence after becoming so formalized. There have been, throughout history, many schools of Sufism, for it is of the nature of the tradition that it should be transmitted through exemplars, and as no teacher is bound by any orthodoxy

he may imbue or embellish the tradition with a contribution uniquely his own, which, however, because he is a Sufi, will blend with and enrich the tradition as a whole. Such contributions have often been through the arts, particularly poetry, music and dance. Not only oriental classics such as the poems of Omar Khayyam and the *Thousand and One Nights*, but also Western ones such as Cervantes' *Don Quixote* and the poetry of the troubadours, are considered quintessential Sufi texts.

Sufism is frustratingly fugitive for anyone who would seek to pin down its meaning. Its spirit is better expressed in fables, jokes and paradoxes than in any philosophical formulations. It has to be experienced to be known. There are Sufi mystics, ecstatics, and devotional worshippers, but their transports take them only temporarily away from the mundane, and invariably they return to participate positively in the practical world. This practicality, and also the characteristic Sufi paradoxicality and humour, were exemplified by two channels of the Sufi tradition who have had a wide influence in the West in the present century, George Gurdjieff* and Bapak Subuh*. [291, 292]

Tantra

A relatively late development (third and fourth centuries AD) of an Indian school of YOGA, which rejected the asceticism of the traditional schools. Both Hindu and Buddhist schools of tantra developed, and they had in common the adoption of practical strategies for the attainment of liberation, or SAMADHI, through physical and sensory experience. While the ascetic school regarded the body and its desires as obstacles to liberation, the tantrics regarded them as potential vehicles, for they saw the body as a microcosm governed by the same principles as governed the macrocosm, the universe. In particular, they emphasized the principle of the right balancing and union of polar opposites, specifically of the male and female principles. In the tantric school known as that of the 'followers of the left-hand path' this took the form of ritual sexual union, or *maithuna*, an elaborate and prolonged ceremony directed not towards sexual release but towards the transcendence of ego-consciousness and union with the divine. As one of the tantric texts says, 'By the same acts that cause some men to burn in hell for thousands of years, the yogin gains his eternal salvation.' [105, 216]

Tao

In Chinese philosophy, the ultimate, all-embracing reality, the unitary principle that underlies all phenomena, that unites and activates the dynamic polarities of YIN AND YANG. The word means 'the Way', and it could be said that the Tao is the way things are and work, the natural order of things. Taoist philosophy emphasizes the futility of trying conceptually to formulate or say what the Tao is, and stresses that it can only be known by observation and experience. The Tao governs the universe and life in all their aspects, and the highest human wisdom is that which has learnt to conform with its governance. Such wisdom is only attained by observation of the processes of change and transformation in the natural order, which occur cyclically, governed by innate, not external, forces, and manifest spontaneously. Spontaneity, likewise, should govern human action, which should arise from intuitive knowledge of the right time and appropriate action to achieve effects in conformity with the Tao. Lao Tzu, author of the basic Taoist text, the *Tao te Ching*, even taught that 'by non-action everything can be done'. The Taoist view of life and the universe is the basis of the I CHING. [102, 180]

Tarot

A set of seventy-eight playing cards, widely used for DIVINATION, which incorporates a congeries of enigmatic mythic images that are variously interpreted by occultists as there is no consensus as to their origin and meaning. The tarot is said to have first appeared in Europe in the fourteenth century, and scholars have detected in it correspondences with Greek mystical philosophy, Jewish KABBALISM, and ancient Persian and Egyptian religion, but who created the amalgam remains a mystery. There is a tradition that the gypsies did, but as its appearance in Europe preceded theirs the theory is insupportable, although it is certainly true that the gypsies adopted it as a divinatory instrument. All that can be said is that the tarot appeared without an interpretative literature or a coherent philosophical context, and therefore lent itself to adaptation to various metaphysical, mystical and psychological schools of thought. The symbolism and iconography, even, are not sacrosanct, but have been adapted to the different interpretative systems to which the tarot has been co-opted. There are, therefore, several different tarots, and there have developed in recent times different ways of using them, not only for divination but also as what Carl Jung* called 'symbols of transformation', potent images which facilitate the conscious apprehension of unconscious material and may activate the higher intuitive faculties. [217, 253, 357]

Theosophy

A blend of Eastern and Western mysticism and esoteric teachings. The Theosophical Society, founded in 1875, was the creation of the extraordinary Helena Blavatsky*, a woman who combined indisputable mediumistic and psychic powers with an aptitude for unscrupulous chicanery. Her book *Isis Unveiled* (1877) was intended to be the theosophical bible, and she maintained that it was not her creation but that of spirits who used her as a channel for the communication of their teachings. It is a book of eclectic erudition, which amalgamates elements of Greek and Egyptian mystery religion, KABBALISM, and Hindu, Buddhist and Taoist scripture. Theosophy flourished, first in the US and then in India, helped by the remarkable mediumistic phenom-

ena that Madame Blavatsky manifested. Another massive volume, *The Secret Doctrine* (1888), was added to the theosophical literary corpus, and when Madame Blavatsky died in 1891 the movement had acquired a following that ensured its survival.

Theosophical literature was enlarged by the contributions of A. P. Sinnett*, Annie Besant*, and C. W. Leadbeater*. But far surpassing all these, in coherence, lucidity and comprehensiveness, was the series of books written by Alice Bailey* between 1919 and 1949, which allegedly were the telepathically communicated work of 'the Tibetan', a recluse residing in a monastery in the Himalayas. Whatever their provenance, in the body of modern 'revealed' crypto-spiritual writings, the Alice Bailey books stand out for their consistency and wisdom.

There runs through theosophy a strong element of messianism. Madame Blavatsky sometimes said that the main purpose of the Theosophical Society was to prepare mankind for the coming of the Maitreya, the World Teacher. In 1909 Leadbeater psychically identified a 14-year-old Indian boy as the Maitreya, and subsequently he and Annie Besant brought the boy up to fulfil the role. Which perhaps in a way he did, but not within the theosophical movement, for as the independent teacher Jiddu Krishnamurti* he acquired a devoted following worldwide. In 'the Tibetan's' books the messianic message survives (one of Alice Bailey's last scripts was *The Reappearance of the Christ*), elaborated with the teaching that the 'reappearance' will be preceded by 'the externalization of the Hierarchy', i.e. the appearance in the world of a number of great initiates who, while doing normal worldly jobs, will serve as guides and spiritual leaders.

Krishnamurti renounced theosophy because he saw it becoming institutionalized and a refuge for dissidents from the established religions, and there is no doubt that he was right to do so. But the body of theosophical literature, for all its eclecticism and sometimes seemingly wilful obscurantism, is not to be glibly dismissed. As Theodore Roszak* has written: 'if we search the strange mythological extrapolations of these occult evolutionists to discover the vision they offer of human potentiality, we may, at the very least, find them among the most innovative psychologists of our time'. [12, 28, 32, 33, 184, 278, 299, 357]

Vedanta

The philosophy, as distinct from the creed, of Hinduism. The name derives from the body of scriptures known as the Vedas, which are among the oldest texts in world sacred literature. Vedanta is the quintessence of the *Upanishads*, the *Bhagavad-Gita* and the *Mahabharata*, texts which relate in poetic or narrative form its basic teachings. These are: that there exists an enduring Reality beyond the changing appearances of the world and the flux of our experience of it, and this Reality is divine; that man belongs to this divine Reality, and the purpose of life is to attain union with it; that the individual soul

may go through many incarnations, acquiring in each either good or bad KARMA and correspondingly advancing or hindering its progress towards the ultimate goal of union; and that all religions, and all sects within them, are in agreement as to fundamentals, and their differences in detail, expression, ritual and symbolism are irrelevant. In addition to the ancient and classic texts, the corpus of Vedanta philosophy includes a wealth of exposition, teaching, commentary, and narrative and poetic literature which has been added to it down the ages. [148]

Wicca

Witchcraft, considered by its devotees to be 'the old religion' of worship of the Earth Mother and the ceremonial promotion of fertility. In Old English, the verb *wiccian* meant 'to practise sorcery', and the association of witchcraft with magic and the supernatural remains, as does its association with malevolence and concupiscence. These associations largely derive from the persecution of witchcraft in Europe from the Middle Ages into the eighteenth century, and the 'confessions' extracted from putative witches under torture which represented the projected fantasies of the torturers more than the experience or practices of their wretched victims. There is projection, too, in the fact that witchcraft is almost universally attributed to women: projection of male fear of and fascination with powers that subvert the achieved psychic and social equilibrium and the rationality that sustains it. A distinction between black and white witchcraft is often made, and when the Witchcraft Act was repealed in England in 1951 there followed a revival of the cult, with practitioners – now often male – of the white persuasion eloquent in promoting it as an innocuous nature religion. [214, 231, 356]

Work, the

The SUFI teacher George Gurdjieff* maintained that although the potential for spiritual evolution may be man's unique endowment it is not a natural thing, and to accomplish it requires unremitting effort and dedication. At his Institute for the Harmonious Development of Man at Fontainebleau in France he put disciples through a gruelling training which was referred to as 'the Work'. The Work involved submission to Gurdjieff's will and commands, and subjection sometimes to his insults, merciless interrogation and even shock physical chastisement. It sometimes involved actual work, for instance digging or building, in which the disciples were pushed to the point of exhaustion. In group sessions, one aspect of the Work was the performance of a sequence of exacting dances, or 'movements' as they were called, which demanded unnatural co-ordinations, and in the course of which students were required on command to freeze in position, as an exercise in 'mindfulness'.

Gurdjieff taught that most people go through life asleep and unconscious, and that the few who are going to advance human evolution must first be awakened. Although in the context of Eastern religions this is neither an unfamiliar nor a contentious proposition, the Gurdjieffian Work has an element of eccentricity and arbitrariness, and of elitism and authoritarianism, that jars with its alleged spiritual orientation, and indeed with the Sufi tradition from which it supposedly derived. Furthermore, it was allied with such a bewildering serio-comic metaphysic and sometimes engaging but often suspiciously cynical mystagogy that one cannot but wonder whether 'the Work' was designed to fulfil or to mock the aspirations of its devotees. [244]

Yin and yang

The polar opposite but complementary principles believed in traditional Chinese philosophy to constitute and govern all things. Evolved from the fundamental polar opposites of light and dark, above and below, male and female, and developed with the correlation of other complementarities such as active and passive, strong and weak, firm and yielding, the yin-yang dynamic became the basis not only of Chinese philosophy but also of medicine (see ACUPUNC-TURE[6]), culinary and dietary practice (see MACROBIOTICS[6]) and divination (see I CHING). The fact that such practical applications of the conceptual scheme could be seen to work has impressed many Western thinkers, among them the physicist Niels Bohr* (see COM-PLEMENTARITY[2]) and the psychologist Carl Jung*.

See SYNCHRONICITY[1]. [102]

Yoga

Sanskrit word for 'union', used to denote any discipline that has as its object the uniting of the individual soul with the divine. There are several distinct types of yoga, or more precisely 'yogic paths' because all are regarded as ways towards the experience of SAMADHI, the ultimate divine union. Karma yoga is the way of action and good works; hatha yoga is the way of physical discipline and exercise; bhakti yoga is the way of devotion and prayer; jnana yoga is the way of philosophical contemplation; raja yoga, the 'royal way', combines the other disciplines and seeks to synthesize physical, mental, emotional and spiritual development. TANTRA and KUNDALINI yoga, while they depart from the others in their attitude to sexuality, and obviously might attract devotees of dubiously spiritual motivation, also can open the way to the *samadhi* experience.

Incidental to the yogic aspiration towards union, practitioners of the disciplines sometimes acquire supernormal abilities, to endure pain or to manifest PSI[5] faculties at will. In the *Yoga Sutras* of Patanjali the acquisition of such abilities is considered unremarkable, and it is stressed that the yogi should not allow such inconsequential things to distract him from his purpose. [81, 221]

Zazen

The form of MEDITATION practised in ZEN training. It consists in just sitting, sometimes for hours on end, maintaining a prescribed posture and rhythm of breathing and a tranquil and non-active state of mind, so that the fundamental unity of mind and body is experienced.

Zen

A branch of Mahayana Buddhism strongly influenced by Chinese Taoism. Zen emphasizes the primacy of the experiential approach to knowledge and ENLIGHTENMENT, and the inadequacy of thought and intellect. Historically, it became a foundation of Japanese culture, and in this context enlightenment is known as *satori*. Zen does not require of its devotees assent to any body or doctrine, and it is not prescriptive as to principle or conduct, but it does demand a high degree of austerity and dedication. Although knowledge and enlightenment cannot be acquired or worked towards, because they are states of being and consciousness that in experience suddenly supervene over ordinary states, the mind and body can be trained to facilitate the onset of this essentially mystical experience. Zen training consists in cultivating the art of unencumbered and direct seeing (much Japanese and Chinese art derives its unique character from Zen influence), or intense mental concentration on insoluble riddles and paradoxes (see KOAN), or the cultivation of an effortless skill, for instance in archery, or the performance of complex rituals that are meaningless in themselves but demand a total absorption, such as the Japanese tea ceremony or flower arrangement. Zen is not exclusively a monastic discipline, but also one that can be practised in the context of everyday life and work. This, together with its un-dogmatic and non-institutional framework, and its emphasis on tranquillity and non-striving, has led many Westerners to embrace it as a more congenial religion than any that their own cultural tradi-tion has to offer, although the number who have practised it so diligently as to experience *satori* is probably small. [128, 222, 345]

4

PSYCHOLOGY

Altered states of consciousness

That human beings experience or are capable of a variety of states of consciousness is a fact recognized by all religions and that has been variously exploited by them, for instance in the use of psychoactive substances in ceremonial or ritualistic practices, or in the use of meditative techniques to facilitate religious or mystical experiences. Until comparatively recent times interest in non-ordinary states of consciousness seemed relevant only in religious contexts, or to poets and artists. Psychology, because of its POSITIVIST[1] and BEHAVIOURIST bias and its aspiration to be scientific, was slow to explore the subject, although William James* and F. W. H. Myers* laid the groundwork for such exploration, and Freud's* and Jung's* investigations of DREAMS enhanced understanding of the commonest altered state of consciousness. In recent years, however, psychologists, parapsychologists, and even some physicists have shown increasing interest in non-ordinary mental states, the experiences people have in them and the information or knowledge they may acquire through them.

States of consciousness may be altered, for experiential or experimental and research purposes, by a variety of means, such as HYPNOSIS, drugs, MEDITATION[3], BIOFEEDBACK[6], and various techniques of trance-induction. The employment of such means was long inhibited by two factors: a tendency to regard them as violations of normal consciousness or of the integrity of the person, and a belief that non-ordinary mental states were deviant and that therefore no relevant information could be gleaned from them, except about pathological conditions of the mind. These biases and inhibitions have now largely been superseded by the recognition that INNER SPACE[1] is a viable area for exploration, and that what we call normal consciousness may not be the necessary condition for our perception of reality but in some respects may even be an inhibitor of it. If the abilities people manifest in altered states, and the knowledge they acquire therein, are different from or even conflict with those of normal consciousness, this does not in itself invalidate them, and indeed the differences and conflicts may be pointers to new understandings. Many scientists have acknowledged that their important insights or discoveries have come in altered states of consciousness, and today there are many who would agree with Charles Tart's* proposal that consciousness should be considered a manipulable variable for the purposes of scientific research.

See STATE-SPECIFIC SCIENCE[2]. [247, 319]

Androgyny

A combination in an individual of male and female characteristics. Whether such characteristics as dominance, aggression and sexual promiscuity in the male, and passivity, caring and loyalty in the female, are biologically inherent or culturally conditioned is a matter of ongoing and unresolved controversy, probably because both factors are involved to varying degrees. Emphasis on the differences between men and women tend to be made by people disposed to explain and exculpate social and domestic inequalities. But it is indisputable that there are greater differences within the sexes than between them, that only one of our 23 pairs of chromosomes is different in male and female, and also that in the embryonic stage of life there are no sex differences before the age of about 8 weeks. There are many males in whom the supposedly typical female characteristics are highly developed and even dominant, and vice versa. Although social and politico-economic structures still tend to reinforce sex differences and role functions determined by them, the demarcations have become less rigid of recent years, and many psychologists now acknowledge that a common cause of neurosis is the repression of characteristics and behaviours considered inappropriate to a person's sex, and that psychic INDIVIDUATION and health often involves the recognition and fulfilment of the individual's androgyny.

Anima/animus
See JUNGIAN PSYCHOLOGY.

Antipsychiatry
A movement in psychological thought that was prominent in the 1960s and 1970s, and associated with Michel Foucault* in France, Ronald Laing* in England and Thomas S. Szasz* in the US. In its polemic against psychiatry it probably over-stated its case and

subsequently suffered from so doing, but it did contribute importantly to a revision of attitudes to MENTAL ILLNESS.

According to Foucault, the diagnosis of madness is a sinister kind of social labelling which creates a category of individuals that society can make scapegoats of. As in the Middle Ages lepers were the social outcasts, in modern times the so-called mad are, and psychiatry cannot properly diagnose or treat them because it colludes with society in labelling and segregating them. Laing and Szasz took up this conspiracy theory, particularly with reference to the diagnosis and treatment of SCHIZOPHRENIA, arguing that the illness so labelled was not exclusively a property of the individual in whom the symptoms primarily manifested but equally of his or her family and social environment. [40, 92, 179, 313]

Archetype
See JUNGIAN PSYCHOLOGY.

Authenticity
The condition of being SELF-ACTUALIZED, liberated from the psychic determinants of role and of expected or prescribed modes of 'being in the world'. The concept derives from EXISTENTIALISM[1], and is specifically applied in DASEINANALYSE and HUMANISTIC PSYCHOLOGY.

Behaviourism
The manifesto of the psychological school of Behaviourism was written by the psychologist J. B. Watson* in 1913. It declared that, 'the time

Body language

has come when psychology must discard all reference to consciousness ... Its sole task is the prediction and control of behaviour; and introspection can form no part of its method.' By thus rejecting subjectivist approaches in psychology, behaviourism was seeking to become rigorously scientific, to establish a data-base of unambiguous empirical and quantifiable fact. The model for this project was CLASSICAL PHYSICS[2], and it shared with nineteenth-century physics a MECHANIST[1] and POSITIVIST[1] bias. While these biases were eroded and found incompatible with theoretical and experimental developments in modern physics, in academic psychology in Britain and the US behaviourism remained the dominant orthodoxy for decades and exerts a powerful influence to this day, largely through the work of Watson's heir, B. F. Skinner*.

It was Skinner who coined the term 'operant conditioning' and developed the techniques of behaviour control that it designates. Pavlov had studied and developed 'respondant' conditioning, which involved eliciting from an animal a predictable response to a stimulus. In Skinner's technique the animal was enabled to 'operate' on its environment and rewarded for doing so in a specified way; for instance a rat would be dispensed a food pellet whenever it pressed down a lever with its paw, and thus the behaviour of lever-pressing would be 'reinforced' by the reward. Sophisticated developments of this technique have been employed effectively with human

beings, in education, in psychotherapy, in altering the behaviour patterns of recidivist prisoners, and, more sinisterly, in 'thought reform' projects. So successful, in fact, have such applications been, that Skinner has advocated large-scale behaviour modification, or 'the psycho-civilization of society', as the only means of establishing a humane, rational and peaceful world: a project which critics have designated a form of 'friendly fascism'.

Objective psychology and the study of behaviour have yielded relevant and valuable insights into human beings and societies, and also techniques that demonstrably work. But underlying behaviourism there is an image of man as a manipulable mechanism, as an 'empty organism' amenable to any kind of conditioning, which is surely as wrong as it is sinister. And the behaviourists' attempt to purge the language of psychology of such terms as consciousness, imagination, mind, purpose, and desire, was a form of ideological radicalism which imposed too restrictive limits upon psychological discussion and research. In recent years a reaction has set in in the form of the HUMANISTIC and TRANSPERSONAL PSYCHOLOGIES, developed by a 'reformed' Watsonian behaviourist, Abraham Maslow*. [170, 300, 302, 341, 342]

Body language
The expression or reflection of feelings, attitudes and mental states in involuntary gestural or postural behaviour. That such behaviour con-

stitutes a non-verbal language is a fact that most people would attest from their own experience, for instance in circumstances of sexual attraction or combative confrontation. Body language is not always congruent with what is expressed verbally, and an experienced or intuitive 'reader' may infer falsehood or insincerity from the incongruity. Body language is studied by psychologists by means of careful frame-by-frame analysis of filmed situations of human interaction, and such studies have led in recent years to the spread of general popular awareness of body language, and ability to interpret it, largely through the influence of Desmond Morris's* review of the research, *Manwatching* (1977). [86, 226]

Brain rhythms

Alternatively, brain waves, so called because of the wavy patterns which they produce when amplified to furnish a visual representation of the brain's electrical activity by an electroencephalographic (EEG) machine. EEG recording was developed in the 1930s as a tool of brain research and of diagnostic practice in psychiatry and neurology. Four kinds of brain wave were distinguished according to their frequency per second. The highest frequency is that of the beta wave, which is the normal waking rhythm of the brain, associated with activity, thinking and problem-solving. The slower alpha rhythm occurs when the eyes are closed and the mind inactive, and is associated with a relaxed, meditative state.

The still slower theta rhythm is an indicator of drowsiness, and delta waves appear when a person is deeply asleep. Early researchers observed that there are rough correlations between personality types and characteristic brain activity, for instance that under identical conditions some people will produce a lot of alpha waves and others none at all, and some enthusiasts foresaw the development of a character typology based on brain wave analysis, but such aspirations proved ill-founded because there turned out to be too many factors involved in the production of the various waves, and generally the brain's recorded chatter was too confusing a mix to enable the analyst to distinguish 'signal' from 'noise'. However, the idea that a person might be able to achieve more coherence and consistency in his EEG reading if he was kept informed about his brain rhythms led in the 1960s to the development, and use in therapy, of BIOFEEDBACK[6]. [37, 38]

Character armour

See REICHIAN THERAPY[6].

Co-counselling

With the recognition that at times people need help in understanding and confronting problems of life and relationships, and that psychotherapy does not cater to this need, for such people are in no sense sick, organizations offering counselling services have become increasingly popular in recent years. Some offer counsel to people confronting specific crises, such as job-loss, marital breakdown or suicidal tendencies, others offer more general help in enabling people to work out their problems in a context where they feel accepted and not judged. But many people who have problems find it difficult to put themselves in a situation where another person is assumed to be wiser or know better, and co-counselling, or re-evaluation counselling, has developed to serve the needs of such people. This is counselling on a peer basis, in which members of a group pair off and each in turn adopts the role of client and counsellor. The emphasis, however, is more upon listening and attending to the other, and encouraging the expression of problems and their attendant feelings, than upon giving advice or guidance.

Collective unconscious

See JUNGIAN PSYCHOLOGY.

Consciousness

Philosophers and psychologists in the West have traditionally been concerned with the subject of consciousness from the point of view of specifying it and its characteristics as uniquely human attributes, and have been little concerned with its modes, varieties and potentialities. Eastern and esoteric traditions, on the other hand, have been concerned not only with the varieties of consciousness but also with the development of psychological techniques for experiencing its modes and altering its functioning. In recent years Western psychology has benefited from an input from these latter sources.

The foundation of Western science upon Descartes'* radical doubt and Hume's* EMPIRICISM[1] precluded the development of a comprehensive psychology of consciousness. The CARTESIAN[1] dualism, the division of the world into 'thinking substance' and 'extended substance' was descriptive merely, and did not furnish a basis for the study of the nature of 'thinking substance'. Hume's assertion that introspection yielded no apprehension of a self but only 'a bundle of perceptions and ideas' has been influential down to the present time; its bias can be seen in BEHAVIOURISM's denial of the reality of mental states, in empiricist philosophers' delimitation of consciousness to the input of sense-data, and in neuroscientists' tendency to regard it as a phenomenon identical with and explicable in terms of the electro-chemical activity of the brain.

These have been the dominant and orthodox modes of thought in Western scientific culture. But in the nineteenth century a number of philosophers and psychologists adopted different attitudes and initiated a more comprehensive science of consciousness. William James* not only opposed Hume's metaphor of a bundle of sense-impressions with his own metaphor of 'the stream of thought, of consciousness, or of subjective life', thus endowing consciousness with a coherence and purpose that Hume denied it; he also wrote that: 'Our normal waking consciousness, rational consciousness as we call it, is but one special type of consciousness, whilst all about ... there lie potential forms of consciousness entirely different.' James's contemporary Henri Bergson* drew attention to an important characteristic of consciousness with his 'filter theory' (see below). And of course the nineteenth century was the century of the discovery, first by writers such as Goethe* and Hoffmann and later by psychologists such as Hartmann and Freud*, of the UNCONSCIOUS, which raised a multitude of problems for the empiricist and rationalist view.

Consciousness at the rudimentary level is clearly related to perception. To be conscious is to be conscious of something. But is perception exclusively a matter of the brain's response to sensory input, as empiricism maintains? When the philosopher A. N. Whitehead* distinguished between 'immediacy perception' and 'meaning perception', and when Edmund Husserl* proposed the principle of the INTENTIONALITY[1] of consciousness, both were contesting a naïve empiricism and arguing that consciousness is constituted not merely by response, but rather by an inherent ordering principle. The function of consciousness that makes a construct or shapes a meaning from the data mediated from external reality by our sense organs cannot itself be a part of that reality; it must be independent of it. To assert its independence on these grounds does not, however, endow consciousness with any spiritual properties. Bergson's argument that our senses are not so much receptors as filters, that they select and reduce inputs from

our environment to ensure that consciousness is not overwhelmed with more data than it needs or is competent to deal with, implies not only that consciousness is constructive but also that it is a construct, a thing defined and limited by the needs it serves, which may be no more than an organism's rudimentary biological or survival needs. Animals are conscious in this sense.

Awareness is perhaps the primary distinctive mode of human consciousness. And the primary datum of awareness is the self. Excepting perhaps some of the higher primates, animals do not have a self-image. Humans have not only a self-recognition image but also a self-ideal image, and this distinguishes them even from the higher primates. In humans, 'meaning perception' and 'intentionality' are not directed exclusively to data serving biological or survival needs. The need to consolidate a self-image, a sense of personal identity, and the need to fulfil an ideal self-image, are also active functions of consciousness. But the needs for consolidation and fulfilment are often in conflict. For the purposes of consolidation, consciousness still acts as a filtering and reducing mechanism, discarding information that seems irrelevant to or disruptive of the self-recognition image; although what it seeks to discard is not always discardable and may get lodged in the unconscious. Personal consciousness in this sense is still a functional construct, enabling a person to exist and act not only in a physical environment but also in a social environment. It may have its idiosyncrasies – more bias towards aesthetic awareness in one person, towards political awareness in another, for example – but it is limited by its determinants. In the individual it is what James referred to as 'normal consciousness', and in the collective it constitutes a consensus consciousness, a delimited awareness of what is real or relevant.

When consciousness entertains a self-image not for consolidation but for fulfilment of an ideal it has to open the 'reducing valve' to let more information in, and at the same time it has to develop its competence to cope with the increased input. It has to expand, both as a receptor and as a processor of information. That human beings need to experience expanded states of awareness, or higher states of consciousness, and that the frustration of this need has pathological consequences, is a basic principle of HUMANISTIC PSYCHOLOGY. Recognition of this fact has led modern psychologists to explore Eastern and esoteric teachings about consciousness and its modes. At the same time Western thought and science, putting off the empiricist and rationalist straitjacket, has made its own contributions to a broader comprehension of consciousness. The unconscious, originally regarded as a stratum of chaos, incoherence and uncontrolled urges underlying rational consciousness, has been found to possess powers, knowledge, capacities, even wisdom, that consciousness does not have, to be in some ways more aware.

When the philosopher Michael Polanyi* made a distinction between 'articulate' and 'tacit' knowledge he anticipated the finding of SPLIT-BRAIN research, that the two hemispheres of the brain function as two distinct modes of consciousness, processing information in quite different ways. PSI[5] research has not only demonstrated that consciousness is not necessarily bound by physical limitations, but also that it may even survive brain-death. Studies of BRAIN RHYTHMS and MEDITATION[3] have shown that consciousness is not identified with the 'chatter' of the neocortex, and indeed that when not invaded by this 'chatter' it may become 'transpersonal', 'oceanic', or 'cosmic', as mystics from all ages and cultures have attested. Today the 'potential forms of consciousness entirely different [from our normal, waking, rational consciousness]' that William James wrote about, are not only being acknowledged as real but also explored, comprehended, and assimilated to a new consensus reality. [149, 220, 241, 242, 250]

Daseinanalyse

Literally translated, the word means 'being there analysis'. The Swiss psychologist Ludwig Binswanger* was the leading figure in a school of EXISTENTIALIST[1] analytical psychology which derived from the philosophy of Martin Heidegger*. Heidegger held that human beings create for themselves modes of 'being in the world' that trap them in 'inauthentic existence', and Binswanger and his followers considered that the resultant sense of unfreedom is frequently a cause of neurosis. Existential analysis sought to bring into psychology the principles and methods of PHENOMENOLOGY[1], to obtain a total and objective view of an individual's 'world design' uninfluenced by the analyst's preconceptions or values. A person made aware of the structure of his world design by analysis may be brought to recognize it as inauthentic and constricting and seek to change or transcend it. In this way, *Daseinanalyse* may be therapeutic, although Binswanger and the 'Zurich school' always disclaimed the role of psychotherapists, preferring to be regarded exclusively as analytical psychologists. [29]

Depth psychology

The term refers to the work and ideas of those schools of psychology that seek to comprehend human behaviour and mental functions in terms of the contents and dynamics of the UNCONSCIOUS, in particular the FREUDIAN and JUNGIAN schools.

Double bind

A situation in which no available option is right. A person is in a position where he can't win, whatever he does. The term was coined by Gregory Bateson* in the context of a discussion of the causes of SCHIZOPHRENIA. Specifically, for a child a double bind situation would be when he received from one or both parents contradictory verbal and non-verbal messages such that if he acted upon either he would suffer punishment or disfavour. Frequent experience of double bind situations, Bateson maintained, may force a person to retreat into a world of private fantasy and to manifest the types of behaviour commonly designated schizophrenic. [16]

Dreams

Not only dreamers, but also dream researchers and theorists, seem to get the type of dream that they need. Freud* once wrote that his theories must be true, 'otherwise there would have to be two quite different kinds of dreaming, one of which has come only under my observation, and the other only under that of earlier authorities'. But what seemed preposterous to Freud is undoubtedly true. There are not only two but many different kinds of dreaming. A Dutch psychologist, Frederik van Eeden*, who had been independently studying dreams for many years when Freud's *Interpretation of Dreams* was published in 1901, clearly distinguished nine different types of dream, and rarely encountered in his studies the overt or disguised eroticism that Freud found everywhere he looked.

Freud considered dreams to be 'the royal road to the unconscious'. He showed that dreams are often elaborately symbolic, that they have different 'manifest' and 'latent' levels of meaning, and he established principles for analysing the mechanisms of the 'dream work' in which the unconscious converts unacceptable psychic contents into acceptable forms in order to express or gratify them. Freud assumed that the need that dreams fulfil is to give expression to repressed feelings of sexuality, guilt or deprivation. His sometime colleagues Alfred Adler* and Carl Jung* had different theories. Adler took the view that dreams are often a confrontation with the unconscious, and an attempt on its part to solve problems carried over from the waking life. Jung proposed that dreams are compensatory, that they fulfil a need 'to try to restore our psychological balance by producing dream-material that re-establishes, in a subtle way, the total psychic equilibrium'; and that they may convey a message from the unconscious regarding the ordering of the dreamer's life or psychic functioning, or indicating the direction he must follow. He also distinguished what he called 'great' dreams from ordinary ones, and illustrated the creative potentials of dreams with examples from the history of the arts and science of ideas, visions, and solutions to problems coming to people in dreams.

The dream phenomenon is so varied that no one theory can encompass it. Freud, Jung and Adler laid different emphases because they had conceptual biases, and their contributions to our understanding of dreams are invaluable. But they derived their data mostly from their experience as psychotherapists, and it is arguable that therefore it was atypical. The psychologist Calvin Hall* was of this opinion. Working with the evidence of a sample of 10,000 dreams which he collected from ordinary people, he found that most of them were concerned with everyday situations and problems. 'A dream

is a personal document, a letter to oneself', he wrote, and he maintained that dreams give us knowledge of ourselves and others and of our conception of our situation in the world, and that because they are basically visual representations, 'pictures of what the mind is thinking', they can be relied on to be more truthful than the verbal representations that the conscious mind formulates. He therefore proposed that people should deliberately work at the task of recalling and interpreting their dreams, as a means of self-knowledge and problem-solving, and in his book *The Meaning of Dreams* (1953) he lays down some useful working principles for people who undertake this task.

The basic problem for anyone who wished to study dreams in the past was the elusiveness of the data. Few people are able to remember their dreams in detail, and when they do a psychologist cannot be certain that the details have not been added and elaborated in a post-dream period; nor can he be sure that the recalled dream is typical, so until electrophysiological monitoring techniques were developed a psychologist had no way of systematically studying mental activity during sleep. The breakthrough discovery was made by Nathaniel Kleitman and a student assistant, Eugene Aserinsky, at the University of Chicago in 1953. They observed that during short periods while a person is asleep his eyes move about rapidly under his closed lids, and that EEG recording of the brain waves showed a particular type of activity during these periods of rapid eye movements (which became known as 'REM SLEEP'). They also found that if a person is awakened during a period of REM sleep he will be able to give a verbal account of a dream he has just had or that has just been interrupted. Further research showed that periods of REM sleep occur at approximately 90-minute intervals throughout the night, and that these periods are part of a regular sleep cycle comprising four distinct stages, which is repeated four or five times a night, so that there are this number of dream periods, although people normally remember only the last dream of the last period.

Electrophysiological monitoring has facilitated the study of types of unusual dream for which evidence was formerly scant and elusive, for instance various types of psychic dream. In addition to their work on DREAM TELEPATHY[5], researchers at the Maimonides Medical Center in Brooklyn contrived an ingenious method for testing subjects for dream PRECOGNITION[5], and their results seemed to show that dreams sometimes can be precognitive, as a mass of anecdotal evidence from all times and cultures indicates. What is known as the HYPNOGOGIC STATE of consciousness, i.e. the state intermediate between sleep and waking, also became accessible to study by means of the new techniques. The psychologist Lawrence Kubie had called the hypnogogic state 'a dream without distortion', and observed that in it memories are retrievable that are blocked from normal consciousness and distorted when they occur in full-scale dreams. The hypnogogic state is rich in imagery and potentials for creativity, and psychologist Charles Tart* has suggested that 'there are many times when we believe we are just "thinking deeply" or "concentrating" in which we momentarily slip into a hypnogogic state and perhaps utilise this altered state of consciousness for enhanced creativity'. [2, 94, 123, 160, 186]

Ego
See FREUDIAN PSYCHOLOGY.

Encounter therapy
A means of developing self-awareness and exploring interpersonal relationships in a social context (the encounter group). Developed by behavioural psychologist Will Schutz, encounter differs from other dynamic growth therapies such as PSYCHODRAMA and PSYCHOSYNTHESIS, in the stress it puts upon non-verbal communication and upon the importance of the body and the proper channelling of physical energy as essential to psychological and physical health. In an encounter group all the participants engage in turn in active expression of feelings about themselves and towards others, and are subjected to scrutiny and confrontations that force them to express such feelings honestly and to deal positively with any problems they may engender. Particular emphasis is placed upon making each participant aware of his 'self-concept', exploring feelings of inadequacy, willingness to ex-

Freudian psychology

press or accept control and authority, and ability to give and receive affection. Encounter, strictly speaking, is not a therapy, but a method of orientation towards life and relationships, and of enhancing awareness of them, that can be practically applied to many problems and situations. [288]

Engrams
Traumas.
See SCIENTOLOGY³.

Existential psychology
See DASEINANALYSE and LOGO-THERAPY.

Freudian psychology
The psychological concepts and theories developed by Sigmund Freud* constitute arguably the most profoundly and widely influential system of thought to have been developed in the past century. Although Freudian psychology can be faulted for its partiality, its underlying pessimism, its REDUCTIONISM¹ and DETER-MINISM¹, we cannot deny its enduring influence on the way we think about ourselves, our relationships and the world. Freud's biases and intransigence alienated many of his colleagues and followers, such as Jung*, Adler*, Reich* and Rank*, but his ideas remained reference points in relation to which they developed their own concepts and psychoanalytic methods.

Before Freud, the causes of mental illnesses and nervous disorders were generally assumed to be organic, and subject to medical treatment. One of his tutors, the French neurologist Jean-Martin Charcot*, questioned this assumption and achieved some remarkable cures of hysteria by employing HYPNOSIS, which suggested that both cause and cure lay in the mind, or in a part of it that was made manifest under hypnosis. Although Freud did not originate the concept of the UNCONSCIOUS, he did develop ideas about its nature and dynamics that were at once conceptually original and practically effective. In his own practice he at first employed hypnosis as a means of probing the unconscious, but soon abandoned it in favour of the psychoanalytic method that he developed, which involved encouraging patients to talk about their symptoms, childhood and other memories, and DREAMS (which he called 'the royal road to the unconscious'), and eliciting from them, by techniques such as that of 'free association', clues about psychic states and problems of which they were quite unaware. Almost invariably, the problems turned out to be sexual, to have their origin in some kind of childhood trauma, such as seeing parents copulating and feeling usurped from the mother's love, or being parentally admonished for some allegedly improper behaviour. The idea of infant sexuality was shocking and unacceptable to many of Freud's contemporaries, but he amassed from his clinical work evidence that made it undeniable. The universality that Freud claimed for the male 'Oedipus complex' – the subconscious desire to murder the father and sleep with the mother – and for female 'penis envy', is certainly disputable, but the fact that sexuality manifests in childhood and that some adult neuroses develop from its being punished and repressed then is not.

In Freudian theory, the mind is a hierarchical structure, and its component elements coexist governed not by laws of harmony and reciprocity but by impulses of conflict and antagonism. The main culprit in this intrapsychic imbroglio is the 'id', the pleasure-seeking, infantilely demanding, irresponsible component of the personality. The second component, the 'ego', is governed by the 'reality principle' (as opposed to the id's 'pleasure principle'), by reason, sanity and judgement. Then there is the 'superego', a higher level of the unconscious, the seat of ideals, principles and conscience. The ego looks up to the superego and tries to be governed by it, but its efforts are continually subverted by the intrusions of the id, which makes its equilibrium precarious. Disequilibrium results in mental breakdown, which requires the repair expertise of the psychotherapist.

The mechanical metaphor may be criticized as a crude simplification, but it emphasizes the fundamental bias of the Freudian system. To fault Freud for conceptualizing in terms of the science of his day is to presume upon the benefits of hindsight, but we can retrospectively criticize the system without belittling the man or his achievement. It was a system based upon a MECHANISTIC[1] model and which generated conceptual formulations that were metaphorical but

purported to be and were long accepted as being physical realities. Neither the id nor the energy that drives it, the 'libido', is a physical reality. Nor is it necessarily true, as strict adherence to the mechanistic model requires, that all adult psychic disequilibrium can be traced back along a chain of linked causes and effects to origins in childhood or infant trauma.

If bias disqualified Freud's ideas from the universality and scientific objectivity that he sought for them, it nevertheless vouchsafed him insights that an unbiased investigator would be unlikley to achieve. Human sexuality would not be so well understood as it is today but for Freud's bias. Nor would the psychic stratagem of repression, of the censoring and burying in the unconscious of experiences and behaviours too painful or shameful to live with. Nor would the interpretation of dreams. And furthermore, what is regarded as bias in a scientist is attributed vision in an artist, and it is arguable that Freud's contribution to culture is more in the latter mode than the former. Some of his case reports are as enthralling to read as novels, and it is understandable why the novelist Thomas Mann called him 'the poet of the unconscious'.

Freud himself would not have appreciated the compliment. Although he was well versed in literature in several languages, he invariably brought his psychoanalytic eye to bear upon it and its producers, seeing in it the 'sublimation' of psychic conflicts unresolved in the personality. His attitude to religion was equally reductionist. It belonged, he said, 'among the neuroses of mankind'. It is significant that for Freud the superego was not the spiritual, creative or aspiring component of the personality, not the 'higher self' in any positive ethical sense of the term, but was rather the censorious and constraining parental figure.

When he developed his psychological ideas in the context of a socio-political philosophy, Freud came to the conclusion that although men might suppress their fundamental urges towards self-gratification and pleasure in order to secure the benefits of civilization, the suppression would always be grudging and give rise to frustration, and from time to time would manifest as 'thanatos', the urge towards death and destruction. It was a pessimistic philosophy, but it was of its time, and when Freud died, on the eve of the Second World War, having escaped from Vienna to London the year before, it certainly seemed as if history was vindicating it. [94–9]

Gestalt therapy

The word 'Gestalt' means 'figure' or 'pattern'. A basic principle in gestalt psychology is that human beings need to shape their experience into patterns, and that they are uncomfortable with anything they perceive or conceive that does not fit into a pattern, or that they regard as an unfinished pattern. Gestalt psychotherapy uses DREAMS and their elucidation as its major tool because it regards them as 'unfinished business of the unconscious', and the object of its

methods is to enable a person to achieve wholeness and release blocked energies by using dream material as a guide to a therapy of action.

Whereas Freud* regarded dreams as 'the royal road to the unconscious', Fritz Perls*, the creator of gestalt therapy, regarded them as 'the royal road to integration'. His methods derived through Wilhelm Reich*, from Freud, but he had a fundamentally different idea of what constitutes therapy. For Freud dreams were a means of channelling off potentially disruptive forces of the psyche, and his therapy consisted in making the patient aware of what his dreams signified. This was consistent with his fundamental belief that the superego, the rational, cerebral and moral component of the personality, should dominate the more infantile and less worthy components, and that psychic health consisted in such domination. Perls did not set such store by the superego functions of understanding and control. He believed that the 'unfinished business' of the personality indicated by the dream had to be finished, to be lived or acted out, before therapy could be considered complete. A concept of mind and body unity informed his practice, whereas Freud's was informed by a dualist attitude. In psychiatric practice the therapist is a disembodied voice to the patient; he sits behind him and out of sight and adopts an authoritarian role. Gestalt therapy, by contrast, takes place in an 'eyeball to eyeball' situation, and it consists not in analysis and interpretation but in what

Perls called 'dreamwork'. He considered that there was too much verbalizing in orthodox psychiatry, and that such verbalizing was a block to real experience, through which alone the process of integration can be pursued, and his 'dreamwork' consisted in directing a subject, rather in the manner of a theatre director, to act out parts of his or her dream and thereby to probe their significance.

Informing Perls' therapeutic method was a theory of personality which he had formulated. It proposed that there are five personality layers that a person must work through before he begins to live authentically. These are:

1 The cliché layer or, as Perls sometimes alternatively called it, 'the chickenshit level', upon which people deal with life and with others in terms of meaningless formulae and clichés.

2 The games-playing layer, or 'bullshit level', upon which we play the role of parent, spouse, lover, boss, doctor or whatever, but really make little contact.

3 The impasse or neurotic layer, upon which clichés and role-playing no longer serve to insulate us from reality, and we are aware of ourselves, our real feelings and problems, but are stuck with them.

4 The implosive or death layer, which we reach when blocked feelings and psychic energy become contracted and knotted up.

5 The explosive or life layer, which is attained through the release of blocked energies, and results in a person feeling free and fulfilled and being able to live authentically. The explosion may take the form of grief, anger, orgasm, or joy.

In 'dreamwork' the therapist uses the material from a person's dreams to enable him or her to move through the layers and eventually reach the explosive layer, where authentic existence begins. The great contribution of Perls to psychotherapy was to evolve techniques to make dream experience part of the process of personal growth. Carl Jung* had realized that dreams are 'full of future psychic situations and ideas'. Perls, working with the insights of Reich, showed how these germs might be made to develop and nourish the evolving person. [182, 251]

Humanistic psychology

Modern psychological theory and practice has four distinct schools or trends. The first is that of BE-HAVIOURISM, the second the FREUDIAN and psychoanalytic school, the third and fourth are respectively the humanistic and TRANSPERSONAL psychologies and are closely linked. Humanistic psychology focuses on the nature, functions and characteristics of the psychologically healthy human being; it is concerned less with exploring the ramifications of the UNCONSCIOUS than with investigating the potentialities latent in the 'superconscious'. Its basic orientation and concepts were developed by the US psychologist Abraham Maslow*.

Fundamental to humanistic psychology is the belief that its concern is with all of human life and experience, and not merely with their pathological aspects. It regards the frustration of man's 'meta-needs' – life-enhancement as distinct from life-sustaining needs – as potentially the cause of as much distress as the frustration of his biological and basic instinctual needs, and it investigates the conditions pertaining to the fulfilment of these needs. Psychotherapy, it maintains, was primarily an adjustment therapy, which was concerned with integrating the individual into society and did not question the values, purposes and normative principles of that society. The concern of humanistic psychology, on the other hand, is with growth and SELF-ACTUALIZATION, in other words with integrating the individual with a norm not determined by society but by his own personality needs and potentials. In this psychology, therefore, needs that fulfil no obvious biological or social purpose are recognized as real and important and are catered for. Maslow called these 'B-needs' (being needs) as distinct from 'D-needs' (deficiency needs). Typical B-needs are the needs for personal growth, for creative expression, for PEAK EXPERIENCES, for ecstasy in the literal sense of transcendence of the self, and for playfulness. Humanistic psychologists maintain that not only psychological but also biological and social ills result from the frustration of these needs.

Humanistic psychology is so called because its primary concern is to specify what constitutes full human-ness, to define the conditions and psychodynamics that on the one hand enable people to attain it and that on the other hand prevent them doing so. As Maslow put it, for a cat there seems to be no problem about being a cat, but the human species seems to find it hard to discover and attain its specieshood. Humanistic therapies assist this discovery and attainment. They act on the premiss that there is an essential human nature, and on the principle of 'uncovering'. Although the focus upon growth, self-actualizing and the fulfilment of B-needs has been construed by critics as asocial and an engagement in selfish introspection, what in fact happens in humanistic therapies is that through discovering a self-identity, however idiosyncratic, people also discover their humanness, their identity with the whole human species.

A number of therapies have been developed based upon the principles of humanistic psychology, employing different strategies for 'uncovering', for instance: CO-COUNSELLING, ENCOUNTER THERAPY, GESTALT THERAPY, GUIDED FANTASY, PSYCHODRAMA, PRIMAL THERAPY, ROGERIAN THERAPY and TRANSACTIONAL ANALYSIS. [205, 206, 207]

Human potentials movement

A collective term for the several techniques of psycho-spiritual 'affective education' (such as BIOENERGETICS[6], GESTALT THERAPY, HUMANISTIC PSYCHOLOGY, TRANSACTIONAL ANALYSIS) which are concerned not with the psychological 'adjustment' of 'patients' but with facilitating personal development and the fulfilment of potentials in 'clients' who are functionally sane and normal individuals. These techniques consolidated as a movement in the 1970s with the appearance of 'Growth Centres' such as the Esalen Institute in California where their various therapies were practised in 'workshops' and seminars. The movement represented a new orientation in psychotherapy, a shift from emphasis on healing to emphasis on fulfilment, gratification and SELF-ACTUALIZATION. It extended the range and concept of therapy, and established a new standard of what constitutes psychic health. The fact that most of the Growth Centres did not last has been construed as a self-indictment of the human potentials movement, although in fact their closure was generally a result of their founders' repugnance to becoming institutionalized, which they regarded as contradictory to their basic objectives. A more relevant criticism of the movement is that it caters to a minority able to afford its therapies, but that does not gainsay the value and relevance of the therapies themselves, which are still widely practised and available. [230, 277]

Hypnogogic state

A borderline state of consciousness between wakefulness and sleep. In this state people are prone to experience remarkably vivid and real-seeming images or hallucinations, which are generally fragmentary and divorced from a coherent narrative context, and are also more accessible to recall than dreams normally are. When the hypnogogic state is prolonged – which some people claim can be accomplished at will with practice – LUCID DREAMS may be experienced.

Hypnosis

A parodoxical mental state which can be induced in one person by another, or alternatively self-induced, employing techniques that focus attention and suspend the operations of normal consciousness. It is paradoxical because a person under hypnosis is less self-aware and self-governed than normal, but may manifest abilities of mind, such as memory recall, or of body, such as tolerance of pain, that transcend the normal.

Nineteenth-century physicians, such as James Braid*, who coined the term 'hypnotism', employed hypnotic induction in therapy to alleviate non-organic disorders, and in surgery as an analgesic method. Freud's tutor, Jean-Martin Charcot*, used it psychotherapeutically to treat hysteria, a practice which Freud himself later abandoned because he considered that it merely alleviated symptoms and did not enable a patient to achieve a lasting cure by understanding the nature and causes of his symptoms. Today psychotherapists tend to follow Freud's example, and with the development of modern analgesics hypnotism is rarely used in surgery, except to a limited extent in dentistry, or indeed in therapy, except for such purposes as breaking addictive habits such as smoking. It has been and still is used as a tool in parapsychological research, where a good deal of experimental evidence has accrued indicating that hypnosis, whether self- or other-induced, enhances PSI[5] receptivity and performance.

Hypnosis *per se*, as a mental phenomenon, has been the subject of recent psychological research which has established some facts and discredited some myths. Although hypnosis does not facilitate superhuman mental or physical feats, it does enhance some abilities, such as vivid and detailed recall of the events and circumstances of a 'forgotten' past phase of life, and, on the physical level, muscular performance and the endurance of fatigue. Hypnosis also renders subjects highly susceptible to suggestion. Sensory illusions can be induced in or subsequent to the hypnotic state by suggestion, and corresponding involuntary behaviours can be elicited. The myth of the evil hypnotist using post-hypnotic suggestion to make someone commit a crime has, however, been discredited, for hypnotized subjects balk at doing things they find morally repugnant. [76, 131, 132]

Id
See FREUDIAN PSYCHOLOGY.

Individuation
See JUNGIAN PSYCHOLOGY.

Jungian psychology
Carl Gustav Jung* was originally a disciple of Freud*, but he disagreed with him about the primacy of sexuality in human motivation and the dynamics of the UNCONSCIOUS, and in 1913 he left the psychoanalytic movement. In his own 'analytical psychology' the constituents and dynamics of the human psyche are quite different from those emphasized by Freud. The unconscious, for Jung, was not exclusively a realm of conflict and unresolved personal

neuroses; it was also, and more importantly, the seat of human creativity, of spirituality and religious experience, and a rich repository of wisdom and symbolism. Jung introduced the term 'collective unconscious' to designate a stratum of psychic activity below the level of the personal unconscious. The past common experiences and the acquired wisdom of the human species are stored in the collective unconscious, and are sometimes projected from it, in dreams or in works of art. Symbolism is its language, and particularly the symbolism of 'archetypes'.

The 'archetype' was one of several Jungian concepts that crossed the frontier from specific academic to popular lay usage. An archetype, he wrote, is 'an irrepresentable, unconscious, pre-existent form that seems to be part of the inherited structure of the psyche' in the same way that instincts are part of its inherited structure. He originally used the term 'primordial image' for this component of the unconscious, but as the word 'image' implies something with a definite content he adopted the term 'archetype' to stand for an ordering or patterning principle in the psyche, a kind of field force determined only by its form. When specific contents were added by consciousness or by cultural influences, the archetype would become an archetypal image. The image might vary greatly from person to person or culture to culture, but the archetype, the underlying form, was part of the collective unconscious of mankind, a transpersonal and transcultural phenomenon.

Other Jungian terms that were adopted into the general vocabulary were 'extrovert' and 'introvert'. Jung introduced them in the context of his theory of 'psychological types'. The theory posited four psychological functions: thinking, feeling, sensation and intuition, and proposed a typology in which the basic characteristic of extroversion or introversion was linked with each of these four functions. The scheme yielded eight distinct types of human individual, e.g. the extroverted thinking type, the introverted intuitive type, etc. Ideally, an individual should have the four functions equally developed and in balance, but in practice, Jung found, people tended to orient themselves towards the world and experience by developing one function at the expense of the others. Carried to an extreme, the tendency resulted in neurosis.

The concept of balance, of psychic integration, is central to Jungian psychology. Jung departed from Freud, and anticipated HU- MANISTIC and TRANSPERSONAL PSYCHOLOGY, by recognizing spiritual growth as a human need as important as the sexual one. He called growth the 'individuation process'. It was a process of consciously bringing into balance the several components of the psyche, thus making them dynamically interactive and making the person whole. Jungian therapy is oriented towards this end. It seeks the alleviation of repressions, and has this in common with Freudian therapy, but it recognizes other re-

pressions than the sexual. If an extroverted thinking type represses his feeling function, the imbalance not only inhibits his growth but also may become manifest in behaviour prompted by the unconscious, or in the content of his dreams. Jung called the repressed components of personality the 'shadow'. When a person behaves apparently atypically, his conduct may be determined by his shadow. Shadow figures may appear in dreams, sometimes imbued with archetypal characteristics. In particular, the 'anima' and 'animus', respectively the feminine aspect of man's nature and the masculine aspect of woman's, may take on archetypal stature and force, demanding to be recognized by consciousness and integrated into the personality.

Jung had a lifelong interest in the esoteric and the paranormal which was rooted in personal experiences, many of which he recounts in his autobiography *Memories, Dreams and Reflections*. It was an interest that carried him far beyond the limits of acceptable scientific or psychological investigation, for instance into developing theories about ALCHEMY[3] and about UFOS[5]. His most influential and possibly most prescient theory in this area was that of SYNCHRONICITY[1]. [156–60]

Logotherapy

A form of existential psychoanalysis that has affinities with Binswanger's* DASEINANALYSE but is more oriented towards therapy. Its founder Victor Frankl* learnt from his experiences in concentration camps that mental and physical health in human beings largely depends upon their sense of purpose and meaning. In place of the Freudian will-to-pleasure and the Adlerian will-to-power, Frankl regarded the will-to-meaning as the primary human motivation, and its frustration as a fundamental cause of neurosis. Modern man, he observed, largely lives in an 'existential vacuum', lacking a sense of purpose and direction, the ability decisively to choose, and any conviction as to the meaning of existence, and as a result suffers boredom, anxiety, loss of energy and instinctual drives, and in chronic cases physical or mental breakdown. Logotherapy seeks through analysis to obviate or cure this condition, but the analysis does not focus upon subconscious conflicts, but rather upon discovering the subject's potential life purpose and meaning, which, Frankl emphasized, must refer to something beyond the self. To imbue lives with purpose and meaning is of course the concern of religion, and logotherapy may be regarded, as one writer has said, as a kind of 'pastoral psychology'. [93]

Lucid dreams

A type of dream experience which normally occurs in the HYPNO-GOGIC STATE between deep sleep and waking, and that differs from other dreams in that it is not so irrational or discontinuous with normal experience. The lucid dreamer is often fully aware that he is dreaming, and may even to an extent be able to control the development of his dream. The dream is usually very vivid, and

the dream world substantially like the world of waking experience. Sometimes it is preceded by a false awakening, which heightens the dreamer's confusion between the worlds of dream and reality. When the third-century Chinsese philosopher Chuang-Tzu dreamed that he was a butterfly and on awakening pondered the question, 'Who am I in reality, a butterfly dreaming that I am Chuang-Tzu, or Chuang-Tzu dreaming that he is a butterfly?' he expressed the sense of realism and ambiguity that the lucid dream experience typically brings. Such dreams are not explicable in terms of conventional psychological theories. They are not disguised expressions of unconscious mental processes, their subject matter is not bizarre or symbolic, and they do not appear to be compensatory or wish-fulfilling. They are perhaps more interesting to the philosopher than to the psychologist, for they emphasize the ambiguity of reality and the tenuousness of our hold upon it; and also to the parapsychologist, because they are similar to OUT-OF-THE-BODY EXPERIENCES[5] and some people who profess to be capable of voluntary ASTRAL TRAVEL[5] have described induction methods that take the lucid dream as a point of departure. [114]

Mental illness

Antisocial behaviours, uncontrolled rages, depressions or anxieties, feelings of dissociation from everyday reality, or conviction of association with non-ordinary realities, are some of the symptoms that cause psychiatrists to diagnose patients as mentally ill. But it is not clear precisely what mental illness is. Thomas S. Szasz* has argued that the very concept is a myth (see ANTIPSYCHIATRY). This is an extremist argument, but it is certainly true that the tendency to think of mental illness as analogous to physical illness has created diagnostic problems and also inappropriately influenced prescriptive approaches and treatments. Mental illness cannot be as precisely identified as physical diseases; the distinctions between the three broad categories of NEUROSIS, PSYCHOSIS and SCHIZOPHRENIA cannot be so clearly specified. And to treat mental illness on the assumption that it is an organic dysfunction, with a cause locatable in the brain or attributable to hormonal imbalance or genetic abnormality, and therefore seek remedies by administering drugs or electric shocks or even undertaking surgery, should be regarded as a disastrously irresponsible practical application of a false analogy. It has, however, been the common practice in mental health institutions, and generally remains so. In fact, the very practice of institutionalizing people diagnosed mentally ill is prejudicial to effective therapy. Such therapy must encourage and work with the self-healing potential of the patient, and this cannot be done in the depersonalizing environment of a psychiatric hospital. It should also be based on the assumption that, although some mental disorders may have a genetic component (there is some evidence that a ten-

dency to manic depression runs in families), episodes of mental illness are not generally symptomatic of genetic abnormality or brain dysfunction, but are critical stages on the patient's way back to mental balance and health, and that the therapist's function is to serve as companion, counsellor and guide on that journey. [40, 92, 313]

Neurosis

In psychoanalysis, the term designates certain mental states considered abnormal to the degree that they constitute a mental illness. Psychologists of different schools attribute neuroses and neurotic behaviours to different causes, and tend to propose different therapies. The commonest neuroses are anxiety states, compulsive states and hysterical states. Anxiety becomes neurotic when its intensity is disproportionate to the alleged cause; compulsive or obsessional behaviours are neurotic when a person cannot control or resist them even though he may find them repugnant; and hysteria generally manifests as a physical dysfunction or manifestation of symptoms for which there is no apparent physical cause.

Operant conditioning

See BEHAVIOURISM.

Peak experience

In the HUMANISTIC PSYCHOLOGY of Abraham Maslow*, the peak experience is a central concept. Maslow observed, both in his clinical practice and in his phenomenological studies, that psychologically healthy and humanly

Perinatal experiences

fully functioning people have more frequent and more intense peak experiences than others, and that such experiences are not a by-product of their health and full functioning but an essential condition of it.

The peak experience is an experience of joy, of extended consciousness, of affirmation, of a meaningful focusing of energy or attention. It may occur in a religious, aesthetic or creative context, but also in quite mundane, domestic situations; rapt attention to a landscape or a symphony on the one hand, and on the other feeling an upsurge of love for a partner or a child or a sense of satisfaction in something accomplished. Peak experiences are not uncommon, all human beings have or have had them, but many of the conditions and circumstances of life inhibit them, for instance routine, habit, worry, frustration, resentments, bias towards practicality, material considerations, a sense of onerous responsibility, competitiveness, feelings of the meaninglessness or purposelessness of life. Many people look back with nostalgia to childhood or to the beginnings of a love affair, because the peak experiences they had then have since diminished or proved elusive.

Maslow specified characteristics of the peak experience, both in itself and in respect of its psychological concomitants or consequences. It is, first of all, an identity experience, a sense of being whole, integrated, not split or in inner conflict, fully oneself, and at the same time a sense of being meaningfully identified with others or with the world. It is an experience of being on top form, able to accomplish things with ease, being unblocked, uninhibited, capable of spontaneity, expressiveness, creativity. It is a sense of 'being here now', of freedom from past and future, of one's responses to experience being uncontaminated by habit, expectation, hopes or fears. It often involves a sense of completeness, culmination, consummation, and sometimes of being lucky, graced, or blessed.

In humanistic psychology, the peak experience is not just a 'high', a *frisson*, but a necessary facilitator for the formulation of mature, positive values. Maslow found that 'peakers' are more responsible, more motivated, and have more physical and mental energy available for positive work in the world, than non-peakers. [205]

Perinatal experiences

Experiences that people may have in the course of PRIMAL THERAPY. The psychologist Stanislav Grof* has distinguished four levels of perinatal experience, each of which correlates with distinct stages of embryonic life and has both biological and spiritual components. At the first level, which corresponds with the blastospheric stage of the embryo and primal union with the mother, the experience is of cosmic unity and the 'oceanic' type of ecstasy; at the second level, corresponding to the experience of uterine contractions prior to birth, feelings of entrapment and oppression and of hopelessness and agony prevail; at the third level, corresponding to the stage of propulsion through the birth canal, a person has spiritual experiences of confrontation with death, of wild rapture and sometimes of intense sexuality; while at the fourth level, which biologically is that of separation from the mother and the formation of a new type of relationship, the predominant feelings are of liberation, redemption, rebirth, love, forgiveness, and expansion of consciousness. These correlations of biological experiences and spiritual experiences are, Grof says in his *Realms of the Human Unconscious*, 'vital elements in the dynamic of the unconscious', and are 'a very important intersection between individual psychology and TRANS-PERSONAL PSYCHOLOGY'. [121]

Primal therapy

A method of psychotherapy that dispenses with analysis and seeks the resolution of neuroses through a process of painful catharsis. Its creator, Arthur Janov*, maintained that no therapy could be effective that did not uncover 'primal pains', i.e. hurtful experiences undergone not only in childhood and infancy, but ever further back, in the foetal and embryonic stage of life. Primal pains determine adult neuroses and also neurotic behaviours such as smoking and alcohol- or drug-addiction. They can only be dispelled by being re-experienced, not only recalled but actually gone through again, but now with the pain not suppressed but given vent to in the act of screaming. Primal therapy is a harrowing experience, requiring an initial three weeks of intensive

work accompanied by the renunciation of any neurotic habits, followed by several months of regular work in a primal therapy group.

See also PERINATAL EXPERIENCES, REBIRTH EXPERIENCE. [151]

Psychedelic experience

The word psychedelic means 'mind-manifesting'. Coined in 1957 by the psychologist Humphry Osmond, and first used in the context of psychological research with psychoactive drugs, the term was later more loosely used to designate bizarre drug-induced mental states and their representation in works of art characterized by distorted figuration and lurid and dissonant colour. Osmond coined the term psychedelic because the terms formerly used for psychoactive chemical substances, 'psychotomimetic' and 'hallucinogens', implied that what they did was mimic psychoses or induce hallucinations. The new term stressed their capacity to catalyse unusual mental processes and to make unconscious material available to experience and consciousness.

In the late 1960s and early 1970s, before the use of LSD and mescaline even in psychological research was banned, a number of psychologists conducted extensive phenomenological studies of psychedelic experience. Dr Stanislav Grof* used LSD in both research and clinical contexts. He observed that when people underwent a series of LSD psychotherapy sessions they tended to go through different stages, as if different levels of the unconscious were being opened up and integrated with the personality in sequence. The first category of experience was that of abstract and aesthetic visions, of delightful intensifications and bizarre distortions of sensory experience. This type of experience is the one most commonly reported by people who take LSD once or twice for the sake of experiment, and if a person is unprepared or if the 'set and setting' are adverse these intense visionary experiences can be harrowing. People who have emotional problems or are psychologically unbalanced are likely, under the influence of LSD, to find what Grof calls the psycho-dynamic level of the unconscious activated next in their early sessions. At this level, he found, the Freudian concepts of the UN-CONSCIOUS and of psycho-sexual dynamics are helpful as interpretative frameworks, and up to a point their validity is confirmed. Many personal life experiences, going back to childhood, may be relived, and these experiences tend to cluster around a primary trauma, so that when the switch is thrown by the action of the drug the uprush of memories constellated about a particular problem or experience can be quite overwhelming. Below the psycho-dynamic level, Gros found a stratum of the unconscious that psychoanalytic theory had not divined. He called it the level of PERINATAL EXPERIENCES, and he observed that 'everyone who has reached these levels develops convincing insights into the utmost relevance of the spiritual and religious dimensions in the universal

scheme of things'. Further, when subjects had worked through and integrated the material from the psycho-dynamic and perinatal levels, Grof found, TRANS-PERSONAL experiences would dominate all subsequent sessions. In these experiences ego boundaries are loosened and consciousness may expand to encompass other people and other aspects of the world, and in some cases the very limitations of time and space are apparently transcended. Grof said that he had difficulty reconciling these experiences with the conventional scientific philosophy that he had formerly believed in.

Robert Masters* and Jean Houston* reached conclusions similar to Grof's as a result of their extensive research. Comparing drug-induced mystical experiences with those obtained by the traditional arduous disciplinary methods, they observe that whereas the latter methods involve a process of emptying the mind of all its empirical content and making consciousness virtually a vacuum, the opposite happens in the drug experience: 'Consciousness expands and reaches outward to encompass a wealth of phenomena unprecedented in the subject's experience'. On the basis of their own research with six subjects who had mystical experiences under drugs, Masters and Houston reached the conclusion that:

The beneficial effect of the psychedelic experience was to take the subject through a process of experiencing Essence in such a way that it illuminated all of existence, making him more interested in and more responsive to the phenomena of existence than he had been before. Thus, instead of retreating from the phenomenal world, as often occurs with the traditional mystic, the psychedelic subject was inspired by the process of his experience to a kind of flight *towards* reality.

[121, 208]

Psychocybernetics

A system of self-development devised by Dr Maxwell Maltz*, a plastic surgeon who had observed in his work the importance of the self-image in determining human personality and behaviour. Maltz sought to apply the principles of CYBERNETICS[7], the science of effective organization and control, to psychology. In cybernetics, mechanical and organic systems are seen as goal-oriented, optimally effective only when all aspects of their functioning are governed by their particular goal-orientation. Analogously, in human beings the self-image functions as a goal, and governs behaviour and information-processing. A negative self-image attracts negative information input, a positive one the reverse. Maltz developed a practical programme of exercises designed to enable people to create a positive and realistic self-image by means of autosuggestion, goal-seeking and behaviour modification. [201]

Psychodrama

A method of psychotherapy that seeks through the objectification of feelings in a dramatic context to make a person aware of such feelings and able to resolve problems arising from them or from their suppression. It was developed by the Romanian psychiatrist Jacob L. Moreno*. Moreno rejected Freudian psychoanalysis for substituting a system of 'unreal transactions' between a patient and the world for the vital discovery of truth that alone makes change and growth possible. The psychodrama theatre designed by Moreno consisted of a circular stage with different levels which he called 'levels of aspiration'. Upon this stage the patient/protagonist, assisted by a therapist/director, would be encouraged spontaneously to express, verbally, gesturally or emotionally, suppressed feelings or aspirations. Actor/therapists might play other roles in the psychodrama, to focus the subject's feelings and prompt reactions, and a subject too inhibited to engage directly in the psychodrama may be represented by an 'auxiliary ego' while he watches from the audience. Family, friends, and other patients comprise the audience, and may also benefit from the experience. Subsequent to the action, the psychodrama is reviewed and analysed by the therapist, sometimes with the help of video recordings. Moreno conceived psychodrama not only as therapy but also as a means of enabling people to achieve 'a level of existentiality and depth', an authenticity and fulfilment in their lives and relationships, that could not be attained through orthodox psychotherapy. Psychodrama has affinities with PSYCHOSYNTHESIS, ENCOUNTER THERAPY and GESTALT THERAPY. [116, 224]

Psychosynthesis

Psychometry (or psychometrics)

The testing, measuring and assessment of intelligence. More highly regarded and credited in the 1950s and 1960s than in recent years, it has fallen into disrepute partly because its supposed objectivity is questionable and prejudice against certain human, particularly racial, groups has been shown to be built into its methodology, and partly because of the lack of consensus among psychologists as to the nature and characteristics of the faculty being tested. The question 'What is intelligence' has been aptly answered by one critic of psychometry as: 'What intelligence tests measure.'

Psychosis

In psychiatry, a class of severe mental illness characterized by personality derangement, misapprehension of reality, lack of awareness of being ill, and sometimes the occurrence of delusions or hallucinations. Morbid or degenerate brain functions are generally held to be accountable for the so-called organic psychoses, which include the senile, the alcoholic and the arteriosclerotic, but there is no medical or psychiatric consensus as to the causes of the so-called functional psychoses, which include paranoia, schizophrenia and manic-depression. Patients suffering from functional psychoses have been known to respond, on the one hand, to treatment with drugs, which suggests that the disorders are biochemical, and on the other hand to orthodox psychiatric treatments, which suggests that they are psychogenic. They have also been known to recover without any treatment at all, or apparently as a result of changes in their environmental or personal circumstances, which lends some credence to the arguments of ANTIPSYCHIATRY.

Psychosynthesis

A congeries of analytical and active techniques designed to bring about the integration and growth of the self and to release and direct the psychic energies generated by the process of integration and growth. Its creator, the Italian psychologist Roberto Assagioli*, was early influenced by FREUDIAN PSYCHOLOGY, but soon became dissatisfied with its partiality and limitations, both in its conceptual model of the dynamics of the psyche and in the orientation of its therapeutic methods towards adjustment rather than towards individual development and growth. Assagioli sought to bring spiritual needs and aspirations within the scope of a systematic psychology of man which was at once theoretical and practical. It could be said that he sought to complement Freudian 'depth psychology', with its emphasis upon the pathology of the unconscious, with a 'height psychology' which emphasized the creative and integrative powers of the 'superconscious' or 'higher self'.

The first objective of psychosynthesis is to enable an individual to discover, activate and harmonize all the characteristics and abilities that constitute his or her unique self. This involves a preliminary therapy to specify and de-activate psychic components that are not fundamental to the self or that positively inhibit its fulfilment. Psychoanalytical techniques may be used at this stage, but psychosynthesis goes far beyond psychoanalysis in then seeking to engage consciousness and the will in the task of harmonizing into an actively functioning whole all the liberated energies, both physical and spiritual, of the individual personality, and channelling those energies into creative work or expression.

The principles of psychosynthesis may be extended beyond the individual and towards creating integration and harmony in interpersonal relationships and in social groups. Assagioli's description of the techniques he developed over several decades of therapeutic practice and experiment were published in his book *Psychosynthesis* (1965). [7]

Rebirth experience

A psychological therapy which seeks to regress subjects to re-experience the birth trauma and conditions of life antecedent to it in order to confront and resolve any problems that may have arisen therefrom. While a majority of psychologists today acknowledge the fact that immediate post-natal experiences such as delay in rebonding to the mother may have profound influence upon a person's later life and personality development, only a minority accept that the birth trauma and PERINATAL EXPERIENCES from as early as the first three months after conception may exert a like influence.

The rebirth experience is the core of PRIMAL THERAPY. [151]

Regression

A return to a former psychic state, generally an infantile one, which is regarded by psychiatrists as a defence stratagem of neurotic patients. However, in therapy patients may be deliberately regressed in order to afford the therapist access to fixation points in the personality or traumatic episodes in the patient's past which may then be subjected to treatment. In PRIMAL THERAPY regressions even to the foetal stage of life are pursued. HYPNOSIS is a powerful instrument for effecting regressions, and under it some patients have even apparently regressed to activate memories of past lives, although the extent to which PSI[5] faculties are involved in the material gleaned from such regressions is not clear.

REM sleep

See DREAMS.

Rogerian therapy

Alternatively 'client-centred therapy', this was developed and practised by psychotherapist Carl Rogers* as a method for enabling people to achieve SELF-ACTUALIZATION. Rogers emphasized the necessity that a therapist should have a positive attitude towards his client's personality, values and goals, and not seek to govern or judge them, and conceived his function as that of the understanding helper. He laid down for therapists a programme for assisting the growth process, describing strategies for guiding clients through seven successive stages of self-awareness, self-acceptance and self-expression, towards a mature attitude of responsibility and an ability to interact effectively with others. [269, 270]

Schizophrenia

The most commonly diagnosed kind of serious MENTAL ILLNESS, although there is no clear psychiatric consensus as to its symptomology and treatment. Literally the word means 'split mind', and typically people whose utterances and behaviours are paradoxical, or who obstinately split themselves off from their family, social or cultural environment and contravene its behavioural norms, are diagnosed schizophrenic. The term is sometimes cynically used to discredit what is considered deviant social behaviour, even political nonconformity, and as a pretext for institutionalizing dissidents. In the view of ANTIPSYCHIATRY, schizophrenia cannot be regarded or treated as an ailment of an individual, but is a condition inherent in a community, be it a family or an entire society. Ronald Laing* has carried this argument further, maintaining that the putative schizophrenic may be the sanest member of such a community, whose behaviours are quite rational stratagems for maintaining his or her integrity within it and coping with its pressures. This view has some truth in it, or is true in some cases, and of course it appeals to that species of romantic idealism that regards the world as mad and only those it victimizes

as sane, but it does not lead to a therapy capable of alleviating the distress of many people who suffer from the mental disorders grouped under the catch-all rubric of schizophrenia. [40, 179]

Self-actualization

A key concept in the HUMANISTIC PSYCHOLOGY of Abraham Maslow*, meaning the discovery of one's authentic self and authentic life. Discovery in the literal sense, for in Maslow's view the essential, authentic life is covered over and stifled by extra-psychic determinants, such as culture, family, education, role conformity, environment. To enable it to grow, to become actual in the world, a person has to understand and neutralize these determinants, to learn how to listen to and be willing to act upon the promptings of the 'inner voice', which for most human beings is a weak signal which is generally distorted or drowned by environmental noise.

Despite the difficulties involved, many people do accomplish self-actualization, for the need to do so is one of the human 'meta-needs' which are distinct from but as powerful as the basic instinctual and biological needs. The accomplishment is often facilitated by a PEAK EXPERIENCE, which is a transient moment of self-actualization. Maslow observed and specified a number of common characteristics of self-actualizers. They are invariably energetically involved in causes or problems external to themselves; they are 'good choosers' in the sense that when confronted with a situation that comprises an alternative between a regressive or fear choice and a progressive or growth choice, they will unhesitatingly choose the latter, regardless of any difficulties involved; they are honest in their relationships and responses, clear in their own minds as to what they think and feel and not inhibited in expression; they are creative, open to new experience, spontaneous, capable of playfulness, humour and relaxation, but capable too of devoted and sustained work in their chosen area, and of carrying through their projects despite difficulties or problems.

The object of humanistic 'therapies' is to assist the process of self-actualization. They are not therapies in the sense of cures for psychological ills or deviations, although they do assume that self-actualization is such a fundamental human need that its frustration can result in such ills. [206]

Sensory deprivation

Experiments in depriving human beings of sensory inputs, by isolating them in chambers specially designed to give the minimum visual, auditory and tactile stimulation, have established two things: first, that sensory systems depend upon regular input to maintain their equilibrium; and second, that when deprived of such input the mind tends to compensate by generating hallucinations and fantasies. Sensory deprivation experiments have been employed by parapsychologists to test the hypothesis that when the distractions of sensory experience are minimized, the capacity for extra-sensory percep-

tions and experiences is heightened, and results have suggested that there is some truth in the hypothesis. As a method of self-exploration and -discovery, sensory deprivation, facilitated by special isolation tanks, had a vogue in the 1970s, largely owing to John C. Lilly's* reports of sensory deprivation experiments on himself. [190, 191, 257]

Split-brain hypothesis

That the two distinct hemispheres of the human brain have different characteristics and functions was a hypothesis proposed by the neurologist Hughlings Jackson* in 1864. It was not until a century later that the hypothesis became a subject of systematic research. In the 1950s Roger Sperry* and Ronald Myers of the University of Chicago discovered in an experiment with a cat that when the cable of nerve tissue between the two brain hemispheres known as the corpus callosum was severed, each hemisphere functioned separately as if it were a complete brain. If the cat was trained to perform a task dependent on visual input with one eye covered, it could learn to do so, but when the other eye was covered it had to learn all over again and showed no recognition of the problem.

In human beings the cutting of the corpus callosum is an operation sometimes performed in chronic epileptics, on the principle that the epileptic focus is on one side of the brain and the surgery prevents it spreading to the other hemisphere, which is therefore able to bring the seizure under control. In the

1960s Roger Sperry and Michael Gazzaniga made a study of patients who had undergone brain-splitting operations, and observed some curious side-effects. They found that subjects could carry out verbal commands like 'Raise your hand' only with the right side of the body, which is controlled by the left-brain. If a spoon was put in a subject's right hand, or a picture of a spoon was presented to the right eye only, he could name it, but if the left hand or eye was engaged he was unable to do so. These and similar observations led Sperry and Gazzaniga to conclude that the two hemispheres receive information in different ways and transfer it across the corpus callosum to enable the activities of the two sides of the body to be coordinated. It seemed that the left hemisphere controlled speaking, reading, and the performance of tasks requiring judgement or interpretation based on language or calculation, and that the right hemisphere was mute.

Later researches showed that although the right hemisphere may be mute it is far from imbecilic, and indeed that its abilities excel those of the left in some specialized functions. For instance, subjects proved adept at arranging blocks to match a pictured design or at drawing a cube in three dimensions with the left hand, but could not do so with the right hand. Artistic abilities, it seems, are right-brain functions. A Russian psychologist, A. D. Luria*, observed that a composer who suffered a stroke which affected his left hemisphere was subsequently unable to write musical notation, but he could compose better than before. The right hemisphere, it appears, is superior to the left in relational and integrative modes of thought and the recognition of gestalts, or wholes. The distinction between the promptings of head and heart, or between knowledge acquired by reason or by intuition, is a commonplace, but split-brain research has indicated that there is a neurophysiological basis for it. The distinction between the conscious and the UNCONSCIOUS can also be construed in terms of hemispheric duality. The right-brain is the seat of the unconscious, and maybe of functions, such as TELEPATHY[5] and PSYCHOKINESIS[5], which at present science and psychology consider paranormal.

The two hemispheres clearly complement each other. Scientific discoveries often come in a flash – a right-brain intuition – but they then have to be formulated, tested, intellectually considered as to their implications, and all these are left-brain functions. But functional complementarity is not easily established, and most human beings appear to have a hemispheric imbalance or bias. This is variable in different cultures and societies, but in ours the left-brain bias has long been dominant. The psychologist Robert Ornstein* has proposed that Western education should be changed and more emphasis put on the cultivation of the distinctive attributes of the right-brain, and that both man and his world would be improved thereby. That is as may be, but undoubtedly the new understanding of the different hemisphere functions has given aware people a valuable insight into their mental processes, and the opportunity to recognize and redress imbalances. [108, 242]

Thanatology

The study of the psychology of death and dying. The psychiatrist Elisabeth Kübler-Ross* has pioneered the study as a branch of HUMANISTIC PSYCHOLOGY, and as a result of her work both many terminally ill patients and people responsible for their care have learnt to regard dying as 'the final stage of growth', and to encounter it with greater understanding and acceptance.

Kübler-Ross has identified five distinct psychological phases that dying patients generally go through. The first is an experience of shock and an attitude of denial, accompanied by feelings of loneliness and isolation. Then follows a phase of anger and resentment, and envy of the living, when the concern and attentions of helpers and family are rejected. With the eventual subsidence of this rage comes a third phase when hopes of delaying death may be entertained, on the grounds that it is a punishment for conduct that may yet be amended. In the fourth phase death can no longer be denied, the patient becomes deeply depressed dwelling upon feelings of loss and unfulfilment, and this is often accompanied by a severe deterioration in his or her medical condition. The final phase is of acceptance, a turning from contemplation of the past to an awareness of what is and what must be,

and a peaceful spiritual accommodation to the inevitable.

Although it is not everyone who goes through these phases, and for many death occurs more abruptly, thanatology has a general relevance in making death a less taboo subject than it generally has been in secularized Western societies, as well as a quite specific relevance to the helping of the terminally ill to work through the process that will ultimately enable them to experience a good death. [176, 177]

Transactional analysis

A conceptual tool for describing and comprehending human behaviour. Transactional analysis was developed by the psychiatrist Eric Berne* and popularized in his book *Games People Play*. Berne proposed that every human personality has three distinct states of being and modes of interacting in the world, which he called the child, the parent, and the adult states. Expressed emotions and interpersonal behaviours can be regarded and analysed as transactions between these personality states. Subjective experiences in childhood constitute the child state, external and particularly parental influences in childhood constitute the parent state, and the adult state, which also begins in childhood and is consolidated throughout life, is constituted of experiences of learning, deciding, judging, taking responsibility, etc. In psychotherapy, transactional analysis seeks to develop and strengthen the adult state of being, by facilitating awareness of transactions governed by the child and parent states. In a given situation, transitions between the three states may occur frequently in the personalities involved, yielding a range of transactional combinations for the analyst to draw attention to. Such interplays of transactions can be construed as games, hence the title of Berne's book. Transactional analysis is a development of BEHAVIOURIST psychology, and as such has inherent limitations as a means of exploring and comprehending the individual psyche, but it is an effective tool for the understanding and development of interpersonal and group relations. [23, 25]

Transpersonal psychology

A development from and extension of HUMANISTIC PSYCHOLOGY. Both schools consolidated around the work of Abraham Maslow*. The various therapies associated with humanistic psychology tended to concentrate on enabling people to attain psychological health and SELF-ACTUALIZATION by expressing and experiencing their feelings and their bodies, but did not explore the transcendent experiences and transpersonal dimensions of the psyche that Maslow found were transiently revealed in the PEAK EXPERIENCE. It was to refocus psychological study and facilitating practice upon these experiences and dimensions that Maslow and his colleague Anthony Sutich founded, in 1970, the Association for Transpersonal Psychology.

Precursors whose work had had the same thrust and bias, notably Carl Jung* and Roberto Assagiolo*, were assimilated to the new movement, which became known as 'fourth force' psychology. Jung had pioneered the concept of a transpersonal 'collective unconscious', and had stressed the importance of spiritual and religious experiences in the process of 'individuation' (see JUNGIAN PSYCHOLOGY). Assagioli, the founder of PSYCHOSYNTHESIS, had developed his 'height psychology', a systematic mapping of higher states of consciousness and a specification of techniques for attaining them. In addition to these modern European precursors, transpersonal psychology found contributory material in ancient Eastern and esoteric psychologies and disciplines, such as ZEN[3], SUFISM[3], TAOISM[3] and YOGA[3]. With such antecedents, it can hardly be said that transpersonal psychology was new. What was innovative about it, what constituted it a 'fourth force', was its orientation, its being not an adjustment psychology but a fulfilment psychology, being concerned with 'the farther reaches of human nature' (Maslow's term) and their practical realization.

The Association for Transpersonal Psychology gives the following definition:

Transpersonal psychology is the title given to an emerging force in psychology and other fields by a group of men and women who are interested in ultimate states. The emerging transpersonal orientation is concerned with the empirical scientific study and responsible implementation of the findings relevant to: spiritual paths, becoming, meta-needs (individual and species-wide), ultimate values, unitive consciousness, peak experiences, B-values, compassion, ecstasy, mystical experience, awe, being, self-actualization, essence, bliss, wonder, ultimate meaning, transcendence of the self, spirit, oneness, cosmic awareness, individual and species wide synergy, theories and practices of meditation, sacralization of everyday life, transcendental phenomena, cosmic self-humour and playfulness, and related concepts, experiences, and activities.

[8, 206, 207]

Unconscious

An area of the mind not normally accessible to direct awareness but which often governs people's behaviour and mental activity. In his historical study, *The Unconscious Before Freud*, Lancelot Law Whyte* has illustrated how the concept of the unconscious evolved over a period of some two centuries from about 1750, and how in the course of its evolution it was subject to interpretations determined by temperamental, doctrinaire and ideological factors.

Goethe wrote: 'Man cannot persist long in a conscious state, he must throw himself back into the Unconscious, for his root lives there.' Whyte comments:

The discovery of the unconscious is the recognition of a Goethean order, as much as of a Freudian disorder, in the depths of the mind. But for two centuries, say from 1750 to 1950, many rationalists tended to regard the unconscious as the realm of irrational forces threatening the social and intellectual order which the rational consciousness, they imagined, had built up over generations . . . For others who saw deeper the unconscious was not a realm merely of chaos, conflict and destructive passions, but the source also of all the forms of order created by the human imagination.

This emphasis, on the unconscious as a creative and ordering function of the mind, is central to JUNGIAN PSYCHOLOGY, in which, too, was developed the concept of the 'collective unconscious', as a transpersonal pool of experience, knowledge, and imagery.

If Freud was not the discoverer of the unconscious, as is often popularly supposed, he was certainly the most thorough and intuitive diagnostician of its pathology. To him we owe the understanding of repression, and of the many ways in which thoughts and feelings that the conscious mind rejects or refuses to acknowledge may surface from the unconscious as determinants of behaviour, attitudes and mental constructs, often with dire consequences for individuals, relationships, or societies. From him, too, we have learned to look with a degree of scepticism upon human rationality and its constructs, upon the self-images that people entertain and project, the motives and beliefs they profess, for we know that often rationality is thin ice covering the deep pool of the unconscious.

The contents and capacities of the unconscious are still not fully understood. In particular, the phenomena with which PSI[5] research is concerned present a challenge to the scientific understanding of the human mind, although modern SPLIT-BRAIN research appears to have thrown some light on the outstanding problems. [121, 352]

Will therapy

Otto Rank* was a prominent Freudian psychologist who departed from orthodoxy first by emphasizing the primacy of the birth trauma as distinct from the Oedipal situation as the origin of neurosis, and secondly by developing, in his own practice, what he called will therapy. Rank maintained that what a neurotic patient required of a psychotherapist was a clash that would serve to galvanize his will to health. He believed that the will to health is innate in human beings, but in neurosis it becomes deflated and passive, and that no psychoanalysis that neglected to revive the will could be effective. Rankian will therapy is an orientation within psychoanalytic therapy rather than a distinct method, and was influential in shaping modern practice by diminishing the authoritarian role of the therapist and emphasizing the self-healing capacities of the patient. [258]

5
THE PARANORMAL

Astral travel

Alternatively, astral projection: OUT - OF - THE - BODY EXPERI-ENCES in the course of which the subject apparently travels to other locations, which may or may not be known to him. Such experiences may occur spontaneously or they may be voluntarily induced, or after an initial spontaneous experience a person may learn to induce them. If the person has not previously conceived of the reality of a non-physical component of himself, and of transmundane planes of existence, the experience generally carries the conviction of these realities, which in the occult tradition are known as the ASTRAL BODY[3] and the astral plane. That the experience is not hallucinatory or a kind of vivid dream is suggested by the concurrence of details in numerous accounts, and also by the fact that some astral travellers have returned from their journeys to give subsequently confirmable accounts of events they have witnessed. [223]

Aura

A kind of luminous mist said to surround the human body. It was independently depicted in the art of virtually every ancient culture – the best-known examples being of course the haloes shown around the heads of Christian saints. The tradition suggests that sanctity intensifies the aura, and indeed psychics, many of whom claim to be able to see people's auras, agree that their luminosity and colour are variable and correspond with inner states, both physical and spiritual. Psychic healers maintain that they can diagnose a person's state of health from the aura. Some even massage or otherwise operate upon the aura, holding that effects upon what they call the 'etheric body' can directly benefit the physical body.

There have been a number of scientific investigations of the human aura. In 1911 Dr Walter Kilner* described a technique he had developed for viewing it. This involved standing a subject before a dark screen and viewing the body through a glass stained with dicyanine, a coal-tar dye. Characteristics of the aura thus manifested, Kilner maintained, could be interpreted to facilitate medical diagnosis. Harold Saxton Burr's* study of LIFE-FIELDS[2], V. S. Grischenko* and Victor Inyushin's* investigations of BIO-PLASMA, and the phenomenon known as KIRLIAN PHOTO-GRAPHY, all testify to the existence of a kind of energy envelope that surrounds the human body and that manifests characteristics which correlate with states of the body. There is nothing necessarily supernatural about this, and to take it as evidence of the existence of the ASTRAL BODY[3] as an entity distinct and separable from the physical body is unwarranted, but it does suggestively correspond with esoteric traditions and beliefs concerning man's dual somatic constitution. [165, 173, 259]

Bilocation

Some recorded OUT-OF-THE-BODY EXPERIENCES have been verified by witnesses testifying to seeing the experient in a different location from where he actually was. Bilocation, or the phenomenon of a person being in two places at the same time, can only be comprehended in the context of belief in the existence of an ASTRAL BODY[3] capable of separation from the physical body and of travel independently of it. Religions, of course, maintain the existence of such an entity, a spiritual body which survives the death of the physical. There are legends of bilocation in the lives of the saints, and in modern times a Capuchin monk named Padre Pio, who scarcely ever left his monastery near Poggia, is said to have been capable of appearing to people in times of stress or danger in order to heal or help. The anecdotal evidence for Padre Pio's bilocations is substantial, but to the sceptic its association with religion and miracle will render it suspect. More puzzling are accounts of 'false arrival' cases, when a person is allegedly seen at a place before he actually arrives there. Tolstoy* related how he had this experience with an English visitor, Daniel Dunglas Home*, whom he saw arrive at St Petersburg station some hours before he actually did so, and in Scandinavia such cases are said to be so common that the term *Verdøger* (forerunner) is used to designate a 'false arrival' experience.

See also DOPPELGÄNGER. [192, 295]

Biogravitation

A term coined by Russian biophysicist Alexander Dubrov* to designate 'a new and previously unknown property of living systems and of man'. Dubrov hypothesized the existence of the property as a result of observing certain paranormal (his term) effects in the process of cell-division, for instance the movement of chromosomes towards the poles 'in a manner that is incompatible with the effects of all known physical forces except gravitation', the emission of high-frequency ultrasonic waves, and the formation of energy fields. These biogravitational forces, he further observed, have properties consistent with observed PSI phenomena, such as a capacity to carry information, to act at close or long range, to convert the energy of a field into matter, and to endure in the absence of the source that originally gave rise to them. 'The recognition of biogravitation', writes Dubrov, 'frees PSYCHO-TRONICS from many unnecessary and unscientific accretions and from mysticism and makes it a genuine scientific discipline, a science of the future.' [72]

Bioplasma

The existence of a counterpart to the physical body, an AURA, etheric or ASTRAL BODY[3], has been postulated in various systems of occult anatomy. In 1967 two Russian scientists, V. S. Grischenko* and Victor Inyushin*, reported research in which they coined the terms 'bioplasma' and 'bioplasmic body'. 'Our experiments indicate', wrote Inyushin, 'that bioplasma consists of ions, free electrons and free protons – in other words, sub-

Clairvoyance

atomic particles that exist independently of a nucleus.' Physical
bodies, he went on to say, have
'biofields' constituted by bioplasmic particles that emanate
from the body, forming a kind of
envelope surrounding the physical
body. Energy radiates from the
body, he maintained, in the form
of 'bioplasmoids' or 'micro-
streamers', and these emissions
'may be involved in TELEPATHY,
PSYCHOKINESIS, and other in-
stances of distant interaction between organisms'. He hypothesized
that there was a bioplasmic con-
ductive energy system within the
body, and said that his and his
colleagues' experiments indicated
that bioplasma is concentrated in
the nerve cells and that the main
centres of bioplasmic activity in
the body are the brain and the
centre of the spinal cord in the
region of the solar plexus. These
centres correspond with the major
CHAKRAS[3] of Indian occult anatomy.

Psychics have always claimed
that they could see a colourful aura
around the human body, and that
they could infer from the colours
and vibrancy of the aura facts
about the condition of the physical
organism. Inyushin maintained
that states of health, and even
moods, were reflected in the am-
plitude of energy in the bioplasmic
body, and that the intensity and
flow of this energy could be
observed and recorded by the techniques of KIRLIAN PHOTO-
GRAPHY.

There are clear correspondences
between bioplasma theory and Wilhelm Reich's* Orgone theory.
The existence of an atmospheric
and organismic energy continuum
is a recurrent concept both in esoteric philosophies and in modern
'fringe' science. [146, 175]

Clairvoyance
The ability to receive extra-sensory
knowledge of a thing or event that
is not known to any other human
being at the time. If an experimenter in a parapsychology laboratory shuffles a deck of cards and
gives the deck to the subject, and
the subject succeeds in guessing correctly the order of the cards in the
shuffled deck, the feat may be
called clairvoyant. Examples of
pure clairvoyance are fairly rare,
for usually some person – however
distant – knows the information,
and in such cases the knowledge
may be attributed to TELE-
PATHY. When a person consults
a 'clairvoyant', the information
given is as a rule already known to
that person – in which case it may
be telepathically mediated or
regarded as an exercise in retro-
cognition on the part of the clairvoyant. If it is predictive, it is ostensibly a form of PRECOGNITION.
It may also, certainly, be elicited
from the person by subtle stratagems that are in no way paranormal.

Despite the ill-repute of commercial 'clairvoyants' and the difficulty of specifying the conditions
for the operation of pure clairvoyance as distinct from other PSI
faculties, the evidence, both anecdotal and experimental, for the
fact that clairvoyance occurs is substantial. Anecdotal evidence in the
public domain includes the feats of

'psychic sleuths' who have helped police in murder and missing person cases, and the engagement of dowsers, who sometimes work exclusively from maps, in locating missing objects, faults in underground electricity, gas or water conduits, or mineral deposits. Among a wealth of experimental evidence in parapsychological literature are the REMOTE VIEWING experiments of Puthoff* and Targ*, and the results of card-guessing experiments conducted by numerous researchers.

In the nineteenth century Anton Mesmer* and his followers recorded many incidents in which people in the condition then known as mesmeric sleep gave descriptions of contemporary distant events that were later verified. Modern controlled experiments employing hypnosis have also demonstrated that on average one person in ten is able to exhibit clairvoyant abilities in trance. In particular, experiments in PSYCHOMETRY have often produced impressive results with subjects under hypnosis. [256, 307, 316, 359]

Clairvoyant reality

Lawrence LeShan* argues that there exist two distinct orders of reality, 'sensory reality' and 'clairvoyant reality'. Paranormal faculties develop, he says, when a person moves out of the sensory and into the clairvoyant reality. The difference between the two is largely a difference of thought and attitude, of ways of looking at the world. Most of us live most of the time on the level of sensory reality,

basing our thoughts on the information conveyed through our senses. We see people and things as separate entities, and we consider the most important things about them to be the properties that make them individual. From the other point of view, that of clairvoyant reality, the important thing about an individual is his or her relation to the rest of the universe. All beings – and even inanimate things like rock, water and earth – are seen as parts of a whole. Time, also, is perceived differently; it does not necessarily flow in one direction or at an even pace. Our everyday concepts of past, present and future are seen as illusions.

In distinguishing and describing these two kinds of reality, LeShan quotes several modern physicists. The atomic physicist J. Robert Oppenheimer, for example, acknowledged the existence of two realities in these words:

These two ways of thinking, the way of time and history and the way of eternity and timelessness, are both part of man's efforts to comprehend the world in which he lives. Neither is comprehended in the other nor reducible to it. They are, as we have learned to say in physics, complementary views, each supplementing the other, neither telling the whole story.

[188]

Cross-correspondences

After the death, in 1901, of Frederick W. H. Myers*, one of the founders of psychical research, three mediums began to produce automatic writings which appeared to constitute an ingenious demonstration devised by the discarnate

Myers to prove his survival. Mrs Verrall, Mrs Holland and Mrs Willett, who lived respectively in Cambridge, England, in India and in New York, did not know each other or have any contact, but over a period of fifteen years they produced automatic scripts which contained intriguing correspondences. Normally, 'spirit writings' may be plausibly explained as originating in the unconscious of the medium, or being picked up telepathically from the minds of other living persons, rather than as communications with the spirit world. But what if a message is communicated fragmentarily, some bits of it through one medium, others through a second, and the key that relates these otherwise meaningless communications is given to a third? This is the scheme that Myers is alleged to have posthumously devised, and both the ingenuity of its conception and the erudition manifested in its content would appear to be characteristic of him. Other deceased psychic researchers later apparently participated in the scheme, and the Society for Psychical Research in London amassed a great deal of material manifesting cross-correspondences which researchers have been puzzling over for decades without coming up with any explanation other than that it constitutes strong *prima facie* evidence for survival. [229, 281]

Cryptozoology

The study of unclassified animals and hominids. Reports of sightings of such creatures as giant sea- and lake-serpents, relict dinosaur-type reptiles, and in particular giant hirsute hominids such as the Yeti of the Himalayas and the Sasquatch and Bigfoot of North America, are numerous and persistent. Like other areas of the paranormal, scientific study is beset with the problems of the restricted accessibility of the data, dependence on anecdotal evidence, the possible perpetration of frauds and hoaxes, and the association of the subject with superstition and the sensational. However, there exists an International Society for Cryptozoology dedicated to a rigorous scientific approach, and its President, Bernard Heuvelmans, is the author of the main book on the subject, *On the Track of Unknown Animals.* [129]

Doppelgänger

What the early psychical researchers called a 'phantasm of the living'. The Societies for Psychical Research have on record many reports of 'crisis apparitions', visual or auditory experiences of communication from a distant person that were later found to coincide with the time that person died or underwent some other crisis experience. An SPR survey of 17,000 people who were asked if they had ever had a paranormal experience of another's presence produced 2,272 affirmative replies. On further investigation most of these were ruled out as attributable to dream or delirium, but there remained 32 cases supported by solid evidence and corroboration, of people who had seen or heard another person within twelve hours either way of the latter's death, which they were unaware of at the time of the experience.

The doppelgänger is not always or necessarily associated with a crisis, however. There are many recorded cases of BILOCATION, and of what are known as autoscopic phenomena, in which a person sees his or her own double or sees himself as if through the eyes of the double. This is one of the several kinds of OUT-OF-THE-BODY EXPERIENCE. [295]

Dowsing

Dowsing is sometimes called 'water witching', but its scope can extend to the locating of many other subterranean objects and substances, and the implication that it is some kind of supernatural faculty is denied by dowsers, who are generally – and appropriately – 'down to earth' people who consider their gift no stranger than any other uncommon human endowment.

'Radiesthesia' is another alternative name, but not all dowsers would agree that their faculty is a 'sensitivity to radiations' emanating from the substance or object they are dowsing. The theory is that the dowsing instrument – usually a forked twig or a pendulum comprising a bit of wood or stone suspended on a string – amplifies tiny muscular movements that the dowser unconsciously makes in response to the signal emitted by the buried substance or object. It has been suggested that the human body contains traces of all the elements, and that if a dowser is prospecting for gold, for instance, the radiation from any gold present at the site where he is dowsing will cause the traces of gold naturally present in his body to vibrate in resonance, and these vibrations will be amplified to move the twig or pendulum. This may be an explanation of the phenomenon, and it is true that some dowsers find it helps to carry a specimen of whatever they are trying to locate, but the radiation theory doesn't account, for instance, for the dowsing of a network of underground tunnels, and in particular it fails to account for the enigmatic but well-attested phenomenon of map-dowsing, when the dowser is not physically present at the site. At this level dowsing shades into CLAIRVOYANCE, and it seems that some kind of psychic as distinct from physical faculty must be engaged. [133, 187, 204]

Dream telepathy

The hypothesis that dreams may incorporate material generated by other minds than the dreamer's has been widely tested experimentally over recent decades, with apparently positive results. Dream telepathy experiments are one of several experimental strategies based on the idea that PSI is a function of the unconscious that is normally censored by the conscious mind, or that goes unnoticed in the normal circumstances of life because the psi-signal is a weak one and is generally smothered by the 'noise' of conscious mental activity.

In experiments devised and conducted by Montagu Ullman* and Stanley Krippner* in the 1960s and 1970s, subjects were ordinary people who volunteered to spend a night in a 'dream laboratory' wired to an EEG which would indicate when they were dreaming, and to be awakened to give a report of the dream while it was still vivid. In another room was an agent or 'sender', who at the beginning of the session randomly selected an envelope from a pile, each of which contained a postcard reproduction of a painting. The agent had to concentrate on this picture throughout the night and attempt to transmit his impressions of it to the sleeping subject. In the morning the tapes of the subject's dream reports and the target picture were given to independent judges who assessed the dreams for their correspondence, if any, to the picture.

What emerged strongly from hundreds of such experiments – and from the many spontaneous cases of dream telepathy collected by Ullman and Krippner – is that telepathic communication to a sleeping subject is a fairly frequent occurrence. However, the process is more of an infiltration of the dreamer's consciousness than a complete invasion of it. The target picture was never transmitted whole, as an image, but was broken up, and elements from it were interwoven with the sleeper's ongoing dream. Sometimes these elements were translated by the dreamer into an analogous form, just as in dreams we normally express material from real life in symbolic forms. [329]

ESP

The term 'extra-sensory percep-tion' was coined by J. B. Rhine in his book of that title (1934) to designate perception which does not involve known sensory functions, such as occurs in TELE-PATHY and CLAIRVOYANCE. These and PRECOGNITION are the primary ESP phenomena, and in the 1930s and 1940s Rhine and others, concerned to put research into them on a scientific basis, developed a method, based on card-guessing experiments and sophisticated mathematical evaluation of results, which appeared to demonstrate that ESP occurs although it is not a reliably reproducible phenomenon. The fugitiveness of positive results, the semantic problems posed by the term 'extra-sensory perception', and the fact that the ESP hypothesis could not satisfy the scientific criterion of FALSIFIABILITY[2], combined to make a majority of scientists sceptical of Rhine's work and ideas. As parapsychological research today covers a wider spectrum of phenomena than paranormal perceptual or cognitive functions, the term 'PSI' is generally preferred to ESP. [262, 316]

Ganzfeld

An experimental procedure in parapsychology designed by Charles Honorton* in the early 1970s. It consists in blanketing out sensory input in order to create a state conducive to extra-sensory perception. Experimental subjects sit or lie in a soundproof room, eyes covered with cotton wool and halved ping-pong balls, wearing a headset through which comes only the uniform low hiss of 'white noise'. With environmental distractions thus eliminated, Honorton proposed, subjects would be more acutely aware of their internal mental processes, and possibly more receptive to the 'psi-signal'. In Ganzfeld experiments a 'sender' located elsewhere in the laboratory area focuses attention on a visual image or upon a thought, the subject gives a continuous report of his or her mental thoughts and images, and the parapsychologist later assesses the recorded reports for ostensible correspondences with the 'target' material.

Ganzfeld experiments have produced results suggestive of the occurrence of TELEPATHY, CLAIRVOYANCE and PRECOGNITION. Honorton initially claimed a high success rate, but not all researchers who repeated his experiments were so successful, and critics who have reviewed the extensive experimental literature have not on the whole been convinced that it constitutes proof. As in other areas of psi research, there seems to be an EXPERIMENTER EFFECT[2], with some researchers getting highly positive results but others getting negative results, so that the overall statistical picture turns out to be null or ambiguous. [257]

Kirlian photography

The method of electrophotography developed by the Russian researchers Semyon and Valentina Kirlian* in 1939 and subsequently, which involved placing an object between two oscillator plates, one of them photosensitized, and then passing a high voltage current, produced some remarkable pictures which appeared to show a colourful energetic emanation from organic subjects. When the phenomenon was first publicized, enthusiasts declared that the Kirlians had succeeded in photographing the human AURA, but sceptics were quick to point out that the effects could be attributable to humidity or quite normal electrical artefacts of the photographic process. Subsequent attempts to replicate the Kirlians' work have left the interpretation of the phenomenon unresolved. Although the sceptical view prevails, it cannot satisfactorily explain the facts that the intensity of the 'emanations' manifested in the Kirlian photographs correlates with the physical state of the subject. For instance, photographs of the fingertips of a tired man showed a sudden remarkable change after he had taken a drink of vodka, and pictures of a healer's and a healee's fingertips before, during and after a healing session of the 'laying-on of hands' type seemed to show an energy-exchange process taking place. Furthermore, a correspondence has been observed between the points of the body where the apparent energy discharges are most intense and the points and meridians of Chinese ACUPUNCTURE[6] therapy. The occurrence of such correspondences suggests that the 'Kirlian effect' is more than merely artefactual. [173, 227]

Levitation

The ability to rise in the air and float about, like Peter Pan but without any mechanical or theatrical facilitators. Also the ability to make material objects, such as tables, act in defiance of gravity. The ability is often associated with holy men. The religious raptures of St Joseph of Copertino caused him regularly to levitate in front of numerous witnesses. Accounts of Indian holy men doing likewise are numerous. The most celebrated performance on record is that of the medium D. D. Home*, who astonished an assembly of guests by floating out through one window and in through another three storeys up above Victoria Street. The phenomenon may be put down to hallucination and group hypnosis, but on the other hand it is clearly akin to POLTERGEIST effects, which are not so accountable. The levitation of physical objects by PSYCHOKINESIS is more reliably attested than volitional or ecstatic bodily levitation, as for instance by the Toronto 'sitter group' that levitated a table in front of TV cameras. [245]

Medium

The word suggests an intermediary, and the assumption underlying it is that the medium is a go-between relating the human and spirit, or material and immaterial, worlds. Having relinquished this assumption, parapsychologists today prefer the term 'psychic' or 'sensitive', used substantively.

A distinction is made between 'physical' and 'mental' mediums. The middle period of psychical research, roughly the first three decades of the present century, was primarily occupied by the investigation of physical paranormal

phenomena produced by mediums. It is amusing to visualize distinguished and dignified gentlemen sitting in darkened séance rooms, engaging in a tug-of-war with a spirit over a wastepaper basket, listening to unearthly hands tap out a message on a typewriter or splash about in a bucket of paraffin wax in order to make 'spirit gloves', fending off the attentions of a materialized hairy ape-like creature with a penchant for licking everyone, or engaging in a half-hearted sing-song as directed by a spirit voice. These and numerous other absurdities are to be found in the records of séances that literary and scientific luminaries held with the famous physical mediums of the early twentieth century. Many parapsychologists today write off the entire episode as one in which a group of exceptionally talented charlatans and conjurors managed consistently to fool assemblies of naïve and credulous men of science, or alternatively allege complicity between the mediums and the scientists and writers. Undoubtedly there was a lot of fraud practised by the mediums, but a thorough study of the records will leave any reader with little doubt that at least some of the effects they produced were genuine PSI phenomena. One medium could, in full daylight conditions, make any one of a number of pendulums suspended in a sealed glass case at a distance from her move in any required direction. Another could produce a similar PSYCHOKINETIC effect: bring together two electrical contacts to complete a circuit though they were protected from physical interference by a cage, a glass case and a delicate soap bubble which would have been burst if the contact had been effected by normal means. Such evidence cannot easily be dismissed as fraud or delusion. Nor can the fact, automatically recorded by a thermograph during several independent sittings with various mediums, that the temperature in the séance room dropped by as much as 20°F and that the sharper drops coincided with the more violent physical manifestations of the séance. When all the fraud, delusion and absurdity of the middle period of psychical research is allowed for, there remains a residue of hard paranormal fact which is well-evidenced and cannot be explained away.

This is true, also, in respect of the phenomena produced by the great 'mental' mediums, such as Mrs Piper of Boston, Massachusetts, who convinced tough-minded researchers such as Ralph Hodgson and William James* that her paranormal abilities were genuine and constituted a *prima facie* case for survival. If the survival hypothesis is rejected, the paranormality of mediumistic phenomena is incontestable, and an explanation in terms of 'super-ESP' abilities has to be conceded, even by those who would concede it grudgingly as the less repugnant of two absurdities. [70, 188, 229, 232]

Near-death experiences

In his autobiography, Carl Jung* tells how, when he 'hung on the edge of death' after a heart attack, he had a kind of mystical experience:

I found myself in an utterly transformed state. It was as if I were in an ecstasy. I felt as though I were floating in space, as though I were safe in the womb of the universe – in a tremendous void, but filled with the highest possible feeling of happiness ... I can describe the experience only as the ecstasy of a non-temporal state in which present, past and future are one. Everything that happens in time had been brought together in a concrete whole. I was interwoven into an indescribable whole and yet observed it with complete objectivity.

He goes on to describe a sensation of floating away from the earth, seeing it from a distance, then standing at the door of a temple wreathed in flames, and experiencing as he approached it 'the whole phantasmagoria of earthly existence' being stripped from him, then entering a room and meeting 'people to whom I belong in reality', and then finally finding himself at peace in a beautiful garden.

Spiritualists believe that death is a transition, a rebirthing, a passing-over into a different stage of existence. The spiritualist writer and researcher Robert Crookall* has called it 'the Supreme Adventure'. The recorded experiences of people who have nearly died, in accidents, with heart attacks, or under anaesthetized surgery, often seem to confirm the spiritualist belief. Typically, a person experiences the separation of a component of himself or herself from the physical body, sometimes observing the relinquished body quite objectively, followed by a sense of travelling, sometimes in the familiar world, where events or people at a distance may be witnessed, and sometimes in a quite unfamiliar world, as in Jung's case. In many cases, the return to physical life and normal consciousness is experienced as more painful and less welcome than the death experience.

The utterances of MEDIUMS, allegedly channelling communications from people who have died, show an overall consistency in detail, both in themselves and with pseudo-death reports. In addition to the above-mentioned characteristics, they commonly report encountering discarnate 'helpers', generally relatives or friends who have predeceased them. There have been cases where dying people have named a 'helper' whom neither they nor anyone else present at the death-bed knew was already dead. Other common characteristics are reports of passing through a doorway or tunnel, experiencing a great expansion of consciousness, then a coma or sleep, followed by an awakening. Crookall has published exhaustive studies of such reports, correlating material from diverse sources and cultures, and persuasively arguing that its coherence constitutes strong evidence for survival.

Spiritualist belief aside, reports of near-death experiences must be of interest to psychologists for what they reveal of the human mind in a confrontational situation that is unique for everyone but common to all. The psychiatrist Elisabeth Kübler-Ross* titled one of her books *Death: The Final Stage of Growth*. The emphasis is consistent with the orientation of HUMANISTIC[4] and TRANSPERSONAL PSYCHOLOGY[4] towards facilitating and valuing spiritual experiences for their psychic growth potentials. Depression, fear and anger are understandable responses to the prospect of imminent extinction, but in death as in life they are spiritually nullifying. If reports such as Jung's can help assuage them, and prepare people to approach death with anticipation of the experience of an altered and enhanced state of consciousness, they are of inestimable value, particularly in a time when the conventional solaces of religion are for many people beyond belief. [60, 160, 177, 243]

Out-of-the-body experiences

An experience of separation of a component of the conscious self from the physical body. Such experiences have been recorded in all cultures throughout history, and reports from widely different and unconnected sources have so many similarities that the phenomenon cannot be attributed to superstition or hysteria. Statistical surveys suggest that OBEs occur to as many as one person in five. Usually the experience comes at a time of crisis, but sometimes it happens spontaneously and for no apparent reason.

Celia Green* has undertaken a study of OBEs based on the testimonies of 326 experients who completed a questionnaire. Over 60 per cent of the group reported having had one experience, 18 per cent had had between two and five, and the remaining 22 per cent had had six or more. The group consisted of people of all ages, and showed that the incidence of OBEs diminished in later life, was common in childhood among subjects who had had more than one experience, and tended to cluster between the ages of 15 and 35 for those who had had only one. About 32 per cent reported that their OBEs had occurred as a result of an accident or under anaesthetic, 12 per cent reported them occurring during sleep, 25 per cent under conditions of psychological stress, and the rest while awake and active and going about their normal routine.

Recently Charles Tart* has conducted controlled experiments with subjects who commonly experience OBEs. His first subject was a young woman who told him that since childhood she had quite regularly woken up briefly in the night and felt that she was floating near the ceiling of her bedroom and could look down on her body lying on the bed. She volunteered as a subject for research and slept under observation in a psychophysiological laboratory on four different occasions. Tart wrote a five-digit random number on a card which was placed on a shelf near the ceiling. On all four nights the woman said that she had had OBEs, but only on one occasion did she feel that her 'second body' had floated to a position from which she could observe the target number, which she correctly said was 25132. This is one example of numerous experiments by Tart and other parapsychologists which have yielded positive results.

A considerable number of psychically gifted people have developed in themselves the ability to have OBEs at will. Some years ago a famous experiment was conducted with Eileen Garrett, a medium highly respected by scientists for her intelligence and willingness to participate in research. Mrs Garrett was able to project out of her body in a trance state, and to report on what she saw. In this particular experiment she was in her apartment in New York with her secretary and a psychiatrist. The target point for her projection was the office of a doctor in Reykjavik, Iceland. The doctor had assembled a number of objects on a table in his office, which the medium was to attempt to describe. She not only described the objects correctly, but also repeated word for word a passage from a book he was reading at the moment, and reported that the doctor's head was bandaged. Both the passage from the book and the fact that he had had a head injury just before the experiment took place were later confirmed by the doctor, who also said that he had sensed the presence of Mrs Garrett in his office during the experiment.

The fact tht OBEs occur suggests to some people that human beings possess a second body or double that is not subject to the limitations of the physical body. The concept of the ASTRAL[3] or subtle body is common to Eastern and esoteric philosophies. In SHAMANISM[3] there are what Mircea Eliade* has called 'techniques of ecstasy' which enable the shaman to leave his physical body. Shamans have been observed in a cata-leptic state of suspended animation for days at a time while allegedly travelling out of the body, and to return to normal consciousness possessed of correct information about distant events. [113, 117, 223, 318]

Paranormal phenomena

Events that baffle scientific under-standing or confound scientific bias. The prefix 'para' means beyond or beside, but the term paranormal is not generally used descriptively but pejoratively, with the implication that the phenom-ena so categorized are delusory or irrelevant. Phenomena so regarded today, at least by orthodox science, are all the PSI phenomena, some unorthodox medical and healing phenomena, and a host of reported strange events, such as UFO sight-ings, unexplained appearances or disappearances of people or ob-jects, sightings of unclassified an-imals, anomalous archaeological findings, and causally inexplicable meteorological events. Phenomena regarded as paranormal in the past but now accepted by most sci-entists were magnetism, meteor-ites (stones cannot fall from the sky because there are no stones in the sky, said the great French scientist Laplace, with then irrefu-table logic), HYPNOSIS[4], PSYCHO-SOMATIC[6] illnesses and effects, and some animal behaviours, such as apparent advance awareness of volcanic events, and the infal-lible 'homing' capabilities of some birds and fish.

Some phenomena are para-normal in the sense that their oc-currence is infrequent or outside the normal experience of the major-ity of people. Other phenomena, however, such as TELEPATHY and SYNCHRONICITY[1], are so commonly experienced and so widely believed in that their nor-mality can scarcely be questioned. They would be more appropri-ately called paraconceptual or transgressive phenomena, with the understanding that what they transgress is not normality but the known laws of science.

Poltergeist

Although the word suggests the existence of a supernatural entity, parapsychologists do not consider the poltergeist phenomenon to be attributable to 'boisterous spirits'. They prefer to speak of 'recurrent spontaneous PSYCHOKINESIS' (RSPK). Poltergeist effects have been reported down the ages and from all parts of the world, and the correspondences within the anec-dotal records clearly point to the fact that the phenomenon is genu-ine, recurrent, and tends to develop and abate according to a pattern. It was Frank Podmore, one of the nineteenth-century founders of psy-chical research, who first observed that when 'poltergeists' are active there is usually an adolescent in the vicinity. He did not draw the modern conclusion, that RSPK is an unconscious expression of re-pressed hostility, frustration or sexuality, but suggested rather that naughty children faked the pheno-mena to deceive, mock, and avenge themselves upon the adult world.

Poltergeist phenomena are often too massively energetic and too bizarre to be easily dismissable as trickery. For instance, in a case that occurred in 1967-8 in a lawyer's office in the Bavarian town of Rosenheim, the 'poltergeist' manifested remarkable technical expertise. Electric light bulbs exploded, neon lights kept going out and were found to be unscrewed from their sockets, automatic fuses blew without cause, four telephones rang simultaneously, conversations were abruptly cut off and the firm's telephone bills rose astronomically, for the counter at the post office registered numerous calls. When parapsychologist Hans Bender investigated the case, it turned out that the phenomena were RSPK effects connected with a 19-year-old female employee. A physicist from the Max Planck Institute in Munich who participated in the investigation wrote about the phenomena: 'We came to the conclusion that they cannot be explained by means of today's theoretical physics ... I cannot offer any model which seems to fit these phenomena. That they really do exist could be established with the utmost certainty.'

'Poltergeist' phenomena constitute good and well-authenticated evidence that mind can interact with matter in quite powerful and dramatic ways, but as they are always unconscious and involuntary effects and appear to be related to unstable and transient mental states, it is difficult to investigate them scientifically. [19, 358]

Precognition

Of all the PSI functions, precognition – the ability to obtain knowledge of future events – seems to the common-sense point of view the most preposterous. However, physicists have rather less difficulty with it than they have with TELEPATHY or CLAIRVOYANCE. It is quite consistent with RELATIVITY[2] and QUANTUM THEORY[2] to propose that significant events cause a perturbation in the space-time in which they occur, and, like a stone thrown in a pond, send out waves in all directions, backwards as well as forwards in time, so that memory traces may be created in a person's brain by the precursor wave of a future event. Before the Aberfan disaster in Wales in 1966 – in which 116 children were killed when a mountain of coal waste slipped and engulfed the village school – scores of people all over Britain had dreams of the event, and a subsequent investigation showed that the dream premonitions went back over several weeks but had become more frequent in the days just prior to the disaster; a pattern that would be consistent with the idea of a precursor wave diminishing in power as it propagated outwards.

At a parapsychology conference, the physicist Gerald Feinberg* gave a talk titled 'Precognition – a Memory of Things Future', and in the subsequent discussion he was asked to explain how the remarkably numerous Aberfan precognitions could have occurred according to his theory. Feinberg replied that if someone read a newspaper report after the disaster, this could have 'produced a trace in his brain which went back before it happened, so that he could remember it before it took place'. One reason why such propagation of information backwards in time does not seem so preposterous to physicists is that one of their number, Richard Feynman, was awarded a Nobel prize for demonstrating that subatomic particles must, for short durations, move backwards in time.

Physics aside, it may be reasoned that when we speak of the present moment we do not speak of a point in time but of a duration of awareness, and that in different states of consciousness this duration may be extended or contracted. People of acknowledged psychic ability have expressed this sense of extended awareness. Alan Vaughan*, a psychic who predicted Robert Kennedy's assassination, has written: 'As I become highly activated, sufficiently to lose my sense of ego-identity, then conventional time loses its meaning, as I get caught up with extradimensional adventures in the future.'

The concurring testimony of poets, mystics and psychics, supported by the findings of modern brain research, leaves no doubt that there are other modes of temporal experiences than the linear, sequential mode. As Robert Ornstein* has said:

For us, an event is considered 'paranormal' if it does not fit within the coordinates of ordinary linear time. But if linear time is but one possibility, these unusual events, unusual communications, may in fact occur, even though they cannot be charted in the coordinates of linearity.

[13, 87, 241, 333]

PSI

An umbrella term used to designate a range of PARANORMAL PHENOMENA, both mental and physical, in particular TELEPATHY, CLAIRVOYANCE, PRECOGNITION and PSYCHOKINESIS.

There is a school of thought which holds that psi is a vestigial function in human beings, a throw-back to an earlier stage of evolution, and there is another school which maintains that it is an evolutionary function, a throw-forward to a more developed stage. Both schools can marshal facts to support their views.

The vestigial function argument gains support from the observable fact that people with psi abilities are not on the whole conspicuously evolved people in any generally acknowledged sense. They are not as a group notable for their wisdom or morality. They are, in fact, as diverse as people with any other rare gift, such as for art or poetry; and there is some evidence that a certain naïvety favours psi functioning and that the higher cortical activities of the brain inhibit it. Also, people in hysterical or psychotic states more often exhibit psi abilities than do well-integrated and balanced people, and if normally balanced people do manifest them it is usually in situations of crisis when, it may be argued, a latent archaic mode of communication has been temporarily seized upon by the unconscious to cope with a problem of vital information transfer which the normally more reliable modes developed by *Homo sapiens* in the course of evolution are not in the circumstances able to accomplish.

In support of the alternative view of psi as an advanced and evolutionary function there is evidence from various sources that psi abilities manifest in people who practise disciplines of self-development, or whose personalities are integrated in psychotherapy. In yogic teachings, the emergence of *siddhis*, or psi abilities, in the course of the yogi's training, is an acknowledged fact, and the trainee is warned not be be allured or wonderstruck by the powers he acquires. As the purpose of yogic training is to enable an individual to attain SAMADHI[3] and liberation from the wheel of birth and death, the exercise of psi powers for their own sake, and attachment to them and pride in them, are regarded as regressive tendencies.

The vestigial- or evolutionary-function debate about psi is not resolved by opting for one view or the other. The evidence is that there is truth in the esoteric teachings that hold that there are higher and lower forms of psi. There is no necessary psychological connection between psi ability and spirituality or evolutionary development, although the very existence of non-material realities and interactions lends support to the view that the world accessible to us through our normal senses is not all that there is, and that different experiential realities are accessible to different states of consciousness.

From the point of view of GENERAL SYSTEMS THEORY[1], natural systems are regarded as being more or less highly evolved depending on the number of functions or the amount of information they can contain while maintaining a state of structural organization. As psi is an extension of the effective information-gathering capability of the organism, it may be regarded according to this viewpoint as a function of a highly evolved system, but only provided that the system remains stable. According to the Bergsonian filter theory of CONSCIOUSNESS[4], sensory systems are designed to filter and reduce information input in order not to overload the processing system, and a person who seeks to stop the filtering process and let more information into consciousness by cultivating psi abilities should be aware of the danger of overloading. The fact that people in psychotic and hysterical states more often manifest psi than more balanced people may be taken to signify that such states are favourable to the emergence of psi, but on the other hand it could be that psi abilities prematurely developed and not accommodated to the overall psychological condition of the individual actually cause the psychosis or hysteria.

Clearly, psi is not normally essential to survival or to the provision of primary needs, and it may even put these in jeopardy. So why all the interest that has been manifest in it in recent years? Two different reasons may be suggested. First, it has the fascination of the unexplained, the mysterious, for some people perhaps the heady whiff of the supernatural. Second, it constitutes a challenge to science. Although science has not explained or incorporated psi, the phenomena are less dissonant to minds grown used to contemplating the marvels of modern subatomic physics and of cosmology than they were to earlier scientists entrenched in a materialist-rationalist worldview. [316, 343]

Psychic healing

Healing by means of the 'laying-on of hands' is a phenomenon as old as recorded history and attested in most of the world's religions. That such healings occur is undeniable, but they are generally attributed to suggestion and categorized as 'faith cures'. However, some experiments with healers indicate that there is more to it than this. A Canadian healer, Oscar Estebany, co-operated with researchers in two series of experiments in which strict scientific protocols and controls were observed. In the first series, his handling of a group of mice from which small areas of skin had been removed resulted in their healing more quickly than those in control groups handled by non-healers or not handled at all. In the second series, Estebany 'healed' enzymes, in solution in a flask, which had been damaged by exposure to ultra-violet light. The experiments seemed to indicate that some kind of energy had emanated from or been channelled by the healer's hands. However, when a sensitive gaussmeter was placed between Estebany's hands, no magnetic field

effect registered, so it appeared that the energy involved was not electromagnetic. It has been suggested that there may be some correspondence between psychic healing and PSYCHOKINESIS. [112, 304]

Psychic surgery

If the idea that the physical body is enveloped by an 'etheric' or energy-body taxes credulity, the proposition that operations performed on this non-physical entity can alleviate chronic conditions of the physical body is even more difficult to credit. In some psychic surgery operations the patient lies fully clothed on a medical couch and the physical body is not touched at all. The celebrated English practitioner George Chapman operates in a trance state, moving his hands an inch or so above the body, and maintains that the healings thus accomplished – the effectiveness of which hundreds of grateful patients attest – are the 'spirit work' of a distinguished surgeon named William Lang, who died in 1937. Reports of the work of psychic surgeons in the Philippines and Brazil are more sensational, involving bloody incisions into the physical body made without surgical instruments, the removal of diseased tissue or tumours, followed by instant healing of the wound. Observers such as Lyall Watson* have vouched for the genuineness of the phenomenon, and one psychic investigator, Guy Playfair*, who was initially highly dubious of reports of such healings, was persuaded of their effectiveness by undergoing an operation himself. Such testimonies notwithstanding, the reported phenomena of psychic surgery remain more difficult than other PSI phenomena to accommodate to any conceptual framework, except that of SPIRITUALISM[3]. [49, 252, 344)

Psychokinesis

An effect of mind upon matter without the mediation of motor mechanisms, i.e. the muscles and nerves of the body.

The fact that mind can act directly upon the material world was clearly demonstrated by the neurophysiologist Dr W. Grey Walter*, who reported his researches to the scientific world in 1969. Walter situated his subjects in front of a TV screen on which they were told that, when they pressed a certain button, an 'interesting scene' would appear. Attached to the subject's frontal cortex were electrodes which transmitted electrical impulses from the brain through an amplifier to the TV set. Walter found that the brain produced a small 'expectancy wave' about one second before the subject pressed the button, and that, amplified by his circuitry, this wave would itself change the scene on the TV screen. Some subjects learnt to change the picture literally at will, without even bothering to reach for the button. Grey Walter's data were not ridiculed, for they were not obtained in the pursuit of parapsychological research, but his experiments clearly demonstrated that thought is a kind of energy and that PK is not theoretically implausible.

PK was much in the news some years ago on account of the metal-bending feats of the Israeli psychic Uri Geller* and others. Geller's flamboyant manner of demonstrating his powers, combined with the acrimony of his critics, particularly the stage 'magicians' who sought to show how he might have cheated, served to discredit both Geller and PK in many people's eyes. Yet there were many scientific experiments with Geller, which were not much publicized, the results of which were difficult to explain away. Eldon Byrd, a naval scientist, reported that Geller had succeeded in distorting a piece of nitinol, a metal alloy that cannot normally be distorted unless it is heated above a temperature of 900° F. Ronald Hawke of the Lawrence Livermore Laboratory of the University of California told how Geller had succeeded in altering or erasing the magnetic programmes stored on cards used to feed information into computers. Professor John Hasted of Birkbeck College, London, reported a dematerialization event that occurred when Geller visited his laboratory, and also an experiment in which the psychic had accelerated the pulse rate of a Geiger counter.

Other evidence for the occurrence of PK is afforded by the phenomena of POLTERGEISTS and PSYCHIC HEALING.

In the early years of psychical research, PK effects were reported in séance sessions, when groups of people assembled, usually with a 'physical' MEDIUM, to consort with putative spirits, whose favoured means of demonstrating their presence was by making tables and other objects move or levitate. Recent 'sitter group' experiments, conducted under séance-like conditions but with more sophisticated methods of control and of registering results, and without necessarily working with the 'spirit' hypothesis, have demonstrated that substantial PK effects can be produced by a 'group mind'. One group working in Toronto even demonstrated the phenomenon on TV. [119, 245, 246, 263, 316]

Psychometry

A form of CLAIRVOYANCE in which impressions and information are ostensibly elicited from a physical object. Alternatively, and preferably, if only to avoid confusion with the other meaning of the term (see entry in the Psychology section), the phenomenon is known as 'object reading'. Some psychics manifest a remarkable ability, when holding or handling an object, to obtain from or through it information about its history or about persons previously associated with it.

A convincing example is given by Lawrence LeShan* in his book *The Medium, the Mystic and the Physicist*. LeShan designed an experiment with Mrs Eileen Garrett*, one of the most respected of modern mediums or 'sensitives'. He packaged a number of small objects in envelopes, giving each a code number, and these envelopes were in turn put in larger coded envelopes by someone else to ensure that when Mrs Garrett handled the envelopes not even he would know what was in them (in order to rule out the possibility of telepathic 'leakage'). One of the objects was a clay tablet, and it happened that this was handled before it was packed by a secretary from an office neighbouring LeShan's but who had no connection with his work. In the experiment, Mrs Garrett picked up the envelopes in turn, read the code numbers, and proceeded to give the impressions she received from the objects they contained. Her utterances were recorded, and they included a detailed physical description of the secretary, an account of her job history and her relationship with her daughter. When the 'readings' were later matched with the code numbers on the envelopes, it was found that the object she had handled when she gave the commentary was the clay tablet that the secretary had picked up in LeShan's office.

This would appear to be an example of pure clairvoyance, for the information Mrs Garrett obtained was unknown to anyone at the time, except the secretary, who was then 1,500 miles away and did not know the experiment was taking place. Was the clay tablet somehow charged with information by the last person who had handled it before it was packed, or did it function as a link or 'relay station' for telepathic communication between the secretary and the sensitive? The two explanations are equally unacceptable to reason and science, and neither offers any clue as to why Mrs Garrett picked up the particular information that she

did, which had only a superficial
and tenuous relation to the history
of the clay tablet. Contemplating
such 'evidence', one can appreciate
why scientists and psychologists on
the whole eschew parapsychology
and regard its alleged phenomena
as probably fraudulent or artefactual and anyway so fugitive and
unpredictable as to be irrelevant.
[188, 359]

Psychotronics

The term generally used by Russian and Eastern European scientists to designate the multidisciplinary study of PSI phenomena.
The field of research is co-extensive
with that of parapsychology, but
the term psychotronics is preferred
because it does not suggest that it
is a fringe or maverick science (the
prefix 'para' meaning 'beside'),
and also because it emphasizes the
orientation of the research towards
establishing physical rather than
psychological explanations of the
phenomena.

Remote viewing

The phenomenon used to be
known as 'travelling clairvoyance',
but in modern parapsychological
research the term 'remote viewing'
or 'remote perceptual ability' is preferred. These terms were coined by
the physicists Harold Puthoff* and
Russell Targ*, who conducted experiments at the Stanford Research Institute in California to
test whether people possess the ability paranormally to obtain information about remote events or
locations.

Over a period of three years,
Puthoff and Targ conducted an

experimental project using many
different subjects, including sceptical ones. Subjects were required
to sit in a room with one member
of the experimental team while
another member drove to a
randomly selected location within
the San Francisco Bay area. After
allowing him half an hour to get
to the target location, the subject
would start to attempt to use his
psi ability to view the scene, and
would describe his impressions to
the team-member with him.

Puthoff and Targ's most surpris-
ing finding was that the majority
of people, given guidance as to how
to exercise their 'remote perceptual
ability' and how to learn to distinguish the parasensory 'signal' from
sensory 'noise', soon developed the
ability to describe features of
remote target locations. Other researchers have tried to replicate
their experiments, though not
always with such impressive results. There are reported results,
however, which imply that Puthoff
and Targ have been researching a
genuine phenomenon. For instance
Charles Tart* has conducted
remote viewing experiments and
obtained results which he declares
'support Puthoff and Targ's work',
and two scientists at the University
of Chicago, J. P. Bisaha and B. J.
Dunne, have obtained positive results in intercontinental remote
viewing tests and have written:
'The significant results lend further
support to the hypothesis that the
extrasensory channel of communication and/or perception
utilized in remote viewing is a widespread and relatively common
faculty.' [256, 316]

Telepathy

The generally accepted definition of the term is that of its creator Frederic Myers*, who defined it as 'transmission of thought independently of the recognised channels of sense'. In the nineteenth century, the term 'thought transference' was frequently used as synonymous with telepathy, and the phenomenon investigated was mind-to-mind communication. Experiments were designed in which an agent tried to 'send' a thought or mental image to a subject situated in another room, and results were obtained that appeared to confirm the hypothesis that there existed a parasensory channel of communication between minds which certain particularly gifted people were able to use. The hypothesis also seemed to be confirmed by the vast amount of anecdotal evidence, collected by the Societies for Psychical Research in England and the US, of spontaneous thought-transference, particularly in circumstances of crisis. All the evidence seemed to point to the conclusion that by means of deliberate concentration, or in circumstances that spontaneously produce such concentration, the mind can generate a kind of thought-energy that can be picked up by another mind with which it is attuned; i.e. that telepathy is a kind of 'mental radio'.

This is a view still commonly held, but no parapsychologist accepts it as proven as an explanation of what occurs when the form of paranormal communication that we call telepathy takes place. That it does take place is a fact attested by a great deal of both anecdotal and experimental evidence, as well as by popular belief (a survey by sociologist Andrew Greeley in the US in 1975 revealed that 58 per cent of his sample believed they had had some kind of telepathic experience). The fact that the evidence is not widely accepted by scientists is partly attributable to the prevalence of the radio analogy, which assumes that in telepathy transmission occurs by means of a channel and that the process necessitates the generation of some kind of electromagnetic energy. The fact that proponents of the telepathy hypothesis have been unable to specify the nature of the channel or the energy involved has made the occurrence of the phenomenon highly dubious to orthodox scientists.

If we modify Myers's definition to 'inter-psychic communication or interaction independent of the recognized channels of sense', the hypothesis takes on a different complexion, for the assumptions that telepathy is something deliberately accomplished and that some kind of energy is involved in the process are removed. That telepathy is a function of the unconscious, that its occurrence is in the nature of an involuntary 'uprush from the unconscious', is suggested by most of the anecdotal evidence, and modern parapsychological research has generally been conducted on this premiss.

There are two predominant trends in modern research. Researchers on the one hand have sought the induction of PSI-conducive states, through hypnosis, meditation, sensory deprivation, or sleep (see DREAM TELEPATHY), on the assumption that in such states mental 'noise' is minimized and the unconscious 'signal' can be heard. On the other hand researchers have employed sensitive electronic equipment to monitor subtle physiological responses to remote stimuli.

In a typical experiment of the latter kind, conducted by Charles Tart*, a subject was 'wired up' to physiological recording devices, and was required to guess when electric shocks were administered to a second subject in another room. The second subject was given shocks at random intervals, and when this happened significant physiological reactions in the first subject were registered by the recording devices. His conscious guesses, however, did not correlate with the physiological information.

Both research of this kind, and of the kind that seeks to enhance telepathy by inducing mental states favourable to its occurrence, has demonstrated beyond reasonable doubt that telepathic communication or interaction is a reality. What kind of reality it is, how it relates to other realities, what it implies in the context of our understanding of nature and human nature, and what it implies for science, which on the whole continues to reject it as an unaccountable anomaly, remain contentious questions. [232, 262, 316]

UFOs

Unidentified flying objects, sometimes supposed to be alien spacecraft. Reports of sightings of UFOs, and sometimes of encounters with their occupants, are numerous and widespread. They have tended to come in waves since the late 1940s: a fact that may be attributable to collective hysteria or to periodicity in the supposed aliens' activities. Scientists accustomed to dealing with data that might be elusive but are not entirely preposterous and inconsistent with each other have been disposed to dismiss the whole phenomenon as nonsense, on the basis that the one thing they know to be capable of producing preposterousness and inconsistency is the human mind. Much reported UFO behaviour is mischievous or simply silly, and difficult to reconcile with the idea that UFOs are spacecraft from another world accomplishing a mission on earth. But to dismiss it all as delusory, or as unscrupulous hoax or opportunism, is too complacent and easy.

Carl Jung*, the first man of intellectual eminence to write on the subject (in *Flying Saucers*, 1958), came to the conclusion that UFOs were not a totally psychological phenomenon but must be real material objects, presumably from outer space, which had long been around and which man tended to invest with significances that said more about his unconscious needs and apprehensions than about their real nature. The subsequent prolific UFO literature certainly bears out the second part of his conclusion. In the widely read books of Erich von Daniken*, artefacts of ancient cultures, myths and scriptures, and technologically sophisticated ancient structures throughout the world, are taken as evidence of extraterrestrial visitation by UFOs in ancient times. People with a more scientific cast of mind have tended to interpret UFO activity in terms of exploration or surveillance of the earth by aliens, although this theory has become less plausible with our own development of means of surveillance from great distances with a single automated vehicle. And anyway, to what purpose this surveillance? Is it preparatory to an invasion by beings forced to leave a dying world? Or preparatory to a more beneficent intervention, an attempt to save mankind from the worst consequences of its own folly, or to raise human consciousness by forcing it to embrace a sense of the cosmic? These are some of the theories, and they and others have been argued with conviction, if not convincingly, in the UFO literature. [159, 279, 332]

Xenoglossy

The ability to speak an unknown language. In the biblical story, the 'gift of tongues' to the apostles came from God and had the purpose of getting the Good News disseminated. But when a person under a hypnosis or in a trance speaks a language he or she has no conscious knowledge of, the phenomenon tends to be taken as evidence of possession by, or the channelling of intelligence from, a discarnate entity. There are several cases on record, one even involving communication in ancient Egyptian. The psychic researcher Ian Stevenson* has reported a recent one. The subject was the wife of a Philadelphia doctor who occasionally used hypnosis on his patients. One day he hypnotized his wife, and in her trance she had the alarming sensation of being struck on the head and drowned. Then she said, 'I am a man', and gave the name 'Jensen Jacobi'. She spoke in broken English and a language that was unfamiliar to her husband, but which he later learned was Swedish. In all, eight sessions were held in which 'Jensen' communicated. In the later ones, Swedish people were present and received answers to questions they put in Swedish. Stevenson carefully studied the tapes of the sessions, and discovered that although the replies the entranced wife gave to the questions were brief, some 60 words were introduced into them that had not been previously used by any of the interviewers. Moreover, although 'Jensen' lacked words for many familiar twentieth-century objects, he was able to give the correct old Swedish names for museum objects from the seventeenth century. [312]

6

MEDICINE AND HEALTH

Acupuncture

An ancient Chinese medical art based upon a system of human physiology that to Western science seems occult, although evidence for the practical effectiveness of acupuncture therapy is undeniable. The body is alleged to possess a network of pathways – known as 'meridians' – along which flows a life-energy called CH'I[3] that has two balanced components, YIN AND YANG[3]. When these components get out of balance, or when the energy flow along a meridian becomes blocked, illness or organic disorder occurs, and the art of healing consists in restoring the balance or removing the blockage. This is done by inserting needles at specific points on the meridians. There are about 800 such 'acupuncture points'. Depending on whether a stimulating or a sedating effect is sought, needles of different metals are used. In addition to remedial therapy, acupuncture is used as a means of anaesthetizing, and quite major surgery can be performed upon fully conscious patients locally anaesthetized by strategically placed needles. Acupuncturists maintain that the primary meridians of the body can be felt in the pulse at the wrist, and treatment is always preceded by a pulse diagnosis, which to an expert practitioner can reveal incipient ailments that have not yet manifested physical symptoms. Acupuncture may then be used as preventive therapy. [145, 203, 327]

Aikido

Like other of the Japanese martial arts, aikido is at once a method of self-defence and a training designed to integrate mind and body. Developed in Japan in the 1920s by Morihei Uyeshiba, it enjoins upon its practitioners the responsibility to achieve and maintain optimum levels of physical and mental functioning, and also to employ the power thus conferred in observance of the basic ethical principle of inflicting the minimum injury possible upon an adversary. [348]

Alexander technique

Developed by and named after F. M. Alexander*, the technique is designed to re-educate the body and in particular to correct bad habits of posture, muscular tension and breathing, which Alexander maintained gave rise to a wide variety of ailments. In his original career as an actor, Alexander suffered a critical experience of loss of voice which doctors were unable to explain or help him with, and through self-observation in a mirror he found that the cause lay in postural habits he tended to adopt when acting, the correction of which resulted in the elimination of his voice problems. He proceeded to study all aspects of the use and misuse of the body, eventually giving up acting to practise as a therapist and to teach his technique to others.

Particular emphasis is put upon the harmonious structural integration of the head, neck and torso. Alexander technique practitioners use their hands to make postural corrections, and specify exercises to form new habit patterns. At first these postural changes may feel wrong, but this is because the body has accommodated to its habitual misuse and come to accept it as right and normal. Specific ailments that may be alleviated by the Alexander technique are back pains and disc trouble, migraine, asthma, hypertension, certain gastric and gynaecological disorders, and muscular cramps and palsies, to mention but a few. The technique also confers a general health benefit, enhancing vitality, self-awareness and self-confidence, and as preventive therapy is effective against many troubles that age in particular is prone to. [3, 14, 145]

Allopathy

Allopathy, or allopathic medicine, is the prevailing orthodoxy in Western societies regarding the understanding and treatment of DIS-EASE. Its characteristics are a heavy reliance upon drugs and surgery, a rigid demarcation of types of disease, and an approach concerned primarily with the alleviation of symptoms. In contrast to HOMOEOPATHY (Greek: *like* treatment of disease), allopathy (Greek: *other* treatment of disease) is interventionist medicine. Underlying its practice is a concept of the body as an assembly of parts all susceptible to their distinct kinds of malfunction and corresponding distinct kinds of treatment, from which follows the reliance on specifically targeted powerful drugs or in the last resort upon surgical excision or replacement of the diseased part. Since powerful drugs often create dependence and have pathological side-effects, and since the effectiveness of surgery is often of short duration, alternatives to al-

lopathic medicines have in recent times become increasingly recognized and sought. Such alternatives regard the body as a total organism and localized malfunction as symptomatic of the dis-ease of the organism, and in practice they seek to diagnose fundamental causes rather than symptoms and to treat them by non-interventionist methods. When disease is chronic, allopathic methods may be the only effective mode of treatment, but it is arguable that it is the biases of allopathy – towards symptom-alleviation and towards rigid demarcation of disease types – that enable it to become chronic in the first place. [122, 144]

Aromatherapy

The medicinal use of essential oils derived from plants, flowers and some wood resins. The therapeutic use of such oils and essences is recorded in Middle and Far Eastern medical history, and was revived in the 1960s by the French homoeopaths Dr and Mme Maury. In therapy, the aromatic oils are massaged into or applied to the skin, but alleviation of skin ailments is not their only function, although they are very effective in this respect and also for cosmetic purposes. The Maurys maintained that when their essential oils penetrated the skin they were rapidly dispersed around the body and could beneficially affect physiological functions. Scientifically, they explained these effects as due to the activity of free electrons which 'the odoriferous molecule' possesses in greater abundance than other organic molecules. [210, 324]

Autogenics

The development of mental control over biological and physiological functions that are generally considered involuntary and not susceptible to such control. The term was coined by a German physician, Johannes H. Schultz, who developed the principles and methods of autogenic training in his clinical practice in the 1920s. Schultz had originally employed hypnosis in his therapy, and had found that under hypnotic suggestion patients could be made to control supposedly AUTONOMIC functions such as temperature, heartbeat and blood pressure, and that such control alleviated distress and facilitated healing processes. But many patients could not be hypnotized, often because they had a resistance to surrendering control to the hypnotist. Schultz had the idea of working with such patients' desire for self-control and seeking means to extend it. The means he developed were simple autosuggestive techniques for inducing first deep relaxation and then controlled changes of specific physiological processes. Many PSYCHOSOMATIC disorders responded to autogenic training. Schultz's methods are still used by therapists today, sometimes without but more generally with the aid of electrophysiological monitoring equipment (see BIOFEEDBACK). [286]

Autonomic nervous system

The system that governs body functions not normally under conscious control, such as the circulation of the blood, respiration, heart rate, sweating and temperature regulation. It has two distinct components, the sympathetic and the parasympathetic systems, the former of which controls the abovementioned functions, and the latter the fundamental functions of digestion, defecation, micturition and sexuality. Although the autonomic nervous system is generally involuntary in its functioning, BIOFEEDBACK research has shown that it is possible for people to learn to control some of its processes, and that such voluntary control can in some circumstances be an effective mode of self-therapy.

Ayuraveda

Classical Indian medicine, a complex body of medical principles and practices developed and handed down over millennia. Like other traditional oriental systems, ayuraveda is HOLISTIC, comprising co-ordinated therapies for body, mind and spirit. It is also, on the theoretical level, highly schematized, regarding the body as constituted of five elements (earth, fire, air, water, and ether), which by preponderance determine five distinct human types, each prone to specific ailments accountable to humoral deficiency or excess and treatable by corrective dietary or medicinal therapy. [122]

Bach flower remedies

Edward Bach, originally an orthodox physician who practised in London early in the century, became a convert to HOMOEOPATHY, and developed his own range of remedies based upon the healing properties of thirty-seven different wild flowers. The system is one of vitalistic medicine, i.e. the derived healing properties are not conceived as to any degree chemical, but rather as essential energies. Nor are the conditions that the remedies treat physical ones, but rather are emotional disturbances, which Bach believed to be the fundamental cause of disease. [11, 48]

Bates eye method

The methods of 'visual re-education' developed by Dr William Bates* at the beginning of the present century are designed to enable people with problems of vision to correct them without recourse to wearing glasses, which Bates considered often do more harm than good. The fact that the Bates method of eye exercising can cure even quite chronic conditions is attested by Aldous Huxley*, whose account of his own experience, *The Art of Seeing*, supplements Bates's own practical book, *Better Eyesight Without Glasses*. [15, 142]

Bioenergetics

A therapeutic technique developed by Alexander Lowen* with the declared objective of helping a person 'get back together with his body and enjoy to the fullest degree possible the life of the body'. Greatly influenced by REICHIAN THERAPY, bioenergetics likewise seeks to break down the muscular tensions in the body that decrease the level of its energy.

Pointing out a fundamental difference between Western and Eastern systems of physical exercise, Lowen said that whereas the former aim at power and control,

the latter aim at 'coordination and grace and the attainment of spiritual feeling through an identification with the body'. Bioenergetics seeks to integrate Western and Eastern approaches, to seek grace and co-ordination and eschew power and control, but also to develop self-expression and sexuality, which are the body's means of extending itself and positively discharging its energy into the world. Another basic principle is that the energy in our bodies 'interacts with the energy around us in the world and in the universe', and that the degree of this interaction determines the degree of aliveness of the person. 'The more alive your body is, the more you are in the world', Lowen writes, and he stresses repeatedly that aliveness depends on the flow of energy, which in turn depends on its release from behind the ego defences and the removal of muscular blockages to its free flow.

The flow should be from the centre outward to the peripheries which are in contact with the external world. The human body has six main points of contact, the head, two hands, two feet, and the genitals, and ideally there should be a strong flow of energy from the centre to all six points, but in most people the flow is attenuated, and in some it is completely blocked, while in others it is uneven, for instance with the upper half of the body overcharged and the lower half undercharged. Asymmetry between the upper and lower halves of the body is a condition that Lowen observed in many people, and which he found so pronounced in some that the two halves did not look as if they belonged to the same person. And in all such cases there were corresponding psychological traits. The actual physical development of the respective halves, together with other signs such as the colour of the skin, indicates how much energy has been getting through to them, and an experienced bioenergetic therapist can read a great deal about a person's character simply by studying his body. There are two main areas of blockage, the 'narrows' of the neck and waist, and these are the two main points of focus in bioenergetic therapy, which employs breathing and physical exercises to open these 'narrows' and facilitate the energy flow. [195]

Biofeedback

A means of enabling human beings to control internal processes generally considered to be involuntary, by using instrumental devices for 'feeding back' information about those processes.

In the 1920s the Swiss psychiatrist Hans Berger invented a device, the electroencephalograph (EEG), for recording the brain's electrical activity by amplifying impulses picked up by electrodes attached to the scalp. He also distinguished different types of BRAIN RHYTHM[4] according to their frequency per second, and found broad correlations with specific states of mind. In the 1960s, the idea that a person might be able to influence his EEG reading if he were kept informed about his brain rhythms occurred to a number of researchers independently. A

neuro-physiologist, Dr Barbara Brown*, devised instruments in which coloured lights were turned on and off by specific brain frequencies, and found that when people were motivated to keep on a light of a particular colour, which meant maintaining a particular brain wave, they could learn to do so. A psychologist, Dr Joseph Kamiya, achieved similar results, adding to an EEG a relay circuit which turned on an auditory signal whenever the subject was producing the alpha brain rhythm. Most subjects were able to learn quickly to keep on the signal tone most of the time, and also to turn it off at will, which meant that they were controlling their brain states with the help of information feedback.

Kamiya also observed that the reports many of his subjects gave him of their mental state when they were producing alpha, a state that combined alertness with tranquillity, were like descriptions of what ZEN[3] meditation is like. The observation led to him and other researchers conducting EEG studies of meditators and yogis, and finding correlations between the coherence and consistency of the EEG readings and the subjects' proficiency as meditators. Drs Elmer and Alyce Green* took a mobile psychophysiology laboratory to India in 1973 and studied many yogis and their abilities to control not only brain rhythms but also such processes as heartbeat, body temperature, bleeding, and pain. Their findings led to important contributions to the study of how biofeedback can be used in healing and how it may enhance creativity.

Biofeedback devices have been demonstrated to be effective means of enhancing self-awareness and assisting processes of self-healing. The evidence that people can learn to control internal processes that have hitherto been thought to be involuntary is incontrovertible, but the question how this control is achieved and mediated remains a mystery, and carries implications for the MIND-BODY PROBLEM[1] that perturb the assumptions of conventional biology and neuro-physiology. [38, 115, 163]

Biorhythms

In addition to CIRCADIAN RHYTHMS, there are three fundamental biological cycles, or biorhythms, which influence human health and behaviour. There is a physical cycle of 23 days, an emotional or sensitivity cycle of 28 days, and an intellectual cycle of 33 days. We all have peaks and troughs in our respective cycles in the course of about a month, and there are transition points between the peaks and troughs which are critical points, particularly with regard to activities associated with the faculty that is in transition. The most remarkable thing about these three cycles is that they are so regular that the levels of a person's biorhythms can be ascertained for any day of his life on the basis of no other information than the date of his birth.

Death often occurs on a critical day in a person's biorhythm cycle. Accident proneness, too, has been found to relate to biorhythms. A Swiss researcher, Hans Schwing, analysed 700 accidents and found that 401 of them had occurred on critical days in the biorhythm cycle of the person responsible. As this is some 60 per cent of the accidents, and only 20 per cent of the days in a person's life are critical, the statistics clearly indicate that there is a higher susceptibility to accident on the critical days. Some firms in industries where there is a high element of risk have had biorhythm charts made for their employees, so that they can lay them off the more hazardous tasks on critical days or at least urge them to be extra cautious; one such firm, a Japanese transportation company, reported a reduction in their accident rate of between 35 and 40 per cent. Similar reductions have been achieved by many other companies in Japan and the US, and the cumulative success of practical applications of biorhythm theory leaves no room for doubt that the phenomenon is real and reliable.

Some sports team managers who are familiar with biorhythm studies are reported to take biorhythm calculations into account when selecting teams and allocating the positions of their players. And some psychologists have considered whether they might be applicable in improving that most common and turbulent team activity of mankind, marriage, although whether an ideal partnership would be between people who are biorhythmically in or out of synchrony is a debatable point. [147, 322]

Bodymind

A term recently adopted by therapists and diagnosticians concerned to emphasize the fact that mind and body constitute an integral system and interact in ways that conventional medical science either denies or neglects. The fact that mental stress, trauma or neurosis manifest not only in organic or physiological dysfunction but also in muscular rigidities and structural imbalance in the body is a basic principle of REICHIAN THERAPY and the various other therapies that have derived from it. Such therapies have demonstrated that not only do mental states affect the body but also that a therapist's work upon the body can alleviate inimical mental states (see ROLFING). BIOFEEDBACK research has also demonstrated bodymind integrality. The bodymind concept has evolved from and has helped consolidate HOLISTIC approaches to health and healing. [73]

Cancer therapy

Orthodox medicine generally employs the intrusive therapies of surgery and radiation treatment to combat cancer, but a number of alternative non-intrusive therapies have been successfully practised, in some cases with patients considered incurable by orthodox methods. Such therapies tend to be based upon the view that cancer is a stress-induced disease or that it is attributable to dietary imbalance or deficiency.

Effective nutritional approaches were developed in the early decades of the present century by the English physicians Robert Bell and F. W. Forbes Ross. Bell advocated a vegetarian diet, a regimen of exercise and deep breathing, and medication with a thyroid extract. Forbes Ross identified deficiency of potassium salts as a cause of cancer and achieved cures by boosting the potassium content of patients' diets, which he argued tended to be destroyed by prevailing methods of food production and preparation. A South African naturopath, Joanna Brandt, independently of Forbes Ross, achieved a self-cure of a large cancer by following a diet exclusively of grapes, which are rich in potassium, iron, organic sugar and proteins. Other and more recent nutritional approaches are the lactic acid fermentation diet of the German doctor Johannes Kuhl, and the red-beet-juice therapy of the Hungarian Nobel laureate Dr A. Ferenczi, both of which are based on the view that cancer is caused by impaired cell-respiration.

As stress produces biochemical effects and stressful living is generally accompanied by bad dietary habits, stress-reducing therapies may be regarded as complementary to nutritional ones. In the US, Carl Simonton and Ann Wooley-Hart have achieved cancer regressions in patients diagnosed as terminal, employing such unorthodox methods as training in meditation, relaxation and VISUALIZATION, and submission to spiritual healing and the laying-on of hands. Their work has shown that mental attitude and will play a part in both the genesis and the cure of cancer, and that much can be achieved by making patients aware of their own responsibilities and abilities in respect of their disease. [297, 298]

Chiropractic

A therapeutic technique of spinal manipulation which has much in common with OSTEOPATHY. It was developed by an Iowa practitioner, Daniel David Palmer*, in the 1890s. Palmer was undoubedly influenced by the creator of osteopathy, Andrew Still, but he did not share Still's belief in the role of the circulatory system. He maintained that disease is caused by pressures on the nervous system brought about by dislocated or misaligned bones and vertebrae; these pressures, he said, interfere with the functioning of the internal organs. Palmer started his career as a chiropractor with a sensational cure of his janitor, who apparently had gone deaf as a result of straining his back. When Palmer located a displaced vertebra in the janitor's back and manipulated it back into the correct position, his patient soon recovered his hearing.

The fundamental principle of modern chiropractic is that pathology originates in disordered physiology, which has its origin in aberrations in the functioning of the nervous system. These aberrations can be controlled by manipulation of the spine, which is an extension of the central nervous system and, ultimately, the brain. The basic difference between chiropractors and osteopaths is that the former tend to work on particular vertebrae, sometimes rather vigorously, while the latter prefer rotation and levering movements. Most practitioners today are familiar with the techniques of both therapies and will use whichever seems appropriate. Although chiropractors claim to be able to alleviate a wide spectrum of conditions, they are generally specialists in back trouble.

Professional societies in Europe and the US have established standards of practice and criteria for professional qualification in chiropractic, and in many places today chiropractic techniques are recognized as a valuable adjunct to conventional therapy. [68, 74, 289]

Circadian rhythms

We all have within us a number of 'biological clocks' which control different processes, and which in a healthy body should work in a complex synchrony. In what is known as the circadian rhythm of the body, there are regular cycles of changes in temperature, blood pressure, rate of respiration and of cell division, levels of sugar, haemoglobin and amino acids in the blood, and production of urine, of enzymes and of hormones. These changes are triggered by a complex interlinkage of internal and external synchronizers. The most potent external synchronizer is the light of the sun, and in experiments where people have been deprived of sunlight, for instance by spending weeks or months underground, they have tended to settle into a circadian physiological cycle of 25 hours rather than the 24 hours of the normal day. Psychological tests have established that people with regular cycles of about 25 hours are more stable than people whose cycles deviate significantly from this duration, and observations of people whose circadian rhythms have been disrupted, for instance by long-distance jet flights, have shown that such disruptions produce symptoms of stress and result in impairment of co-ordination and increased vulnerability to infection.

As the chemistry of the body changes by the hour in the circadian cycle, the administration of drugs should ideally be timed to take account of these changes. Surgery, too, could benefit by taking into account the biological time schedules of the patient, for susceptibility to anaesthetics and to infection, the rate of tissue repair and the reaction of the nervous system to trauma all vary in circadian cycles. Some surgeons working in the area of transplant surgery believe that a factor of success in their work may be the synchronization of the donor's and the recipient's circadian rhythms, and that a cause of rejection in some cases may be that the rhythms are out of phase. Medical science has not yet assimilated in practice all the knowledge about biological rhythmicity that research science has gained in the last two or three decades. [197]

Complementary medicine
So long as the practitioners of orthodox medicine regarded alternative therapists as quacks, and were themselves regarded as complacent bigots by those they so denigrated, accommodation between the two approaches was impossible. In recent years such an

accommodation has begun to take place, and one of the signs of it has been the replacement in many contexts of the term 'alternative medicine' with 'complementary medicine'. The term is reconciliatory, implying at least recognition of the alternatives when used by those of the orthodox persuasion, and when used by the erstwhile maligned 'quacks' conceding the primacy of the orthodox approaches. But more importantly, the term disposes people to recognize that no school of practitioners has a monopoly over effective techniques of healing, and to seek the complementarities most appropriate to their own condition – a search which can itself be an inception of healing.

Disease
Orthodox ALLOPATHY and alternative medicine are characterized by their quite distinct attitudes to disease. For the former it is a morbid condition of the organism attributable to a specific cause and that has to be attacked or expunged, whereas for the latter it is a symptom of the disruption of the total well-being of the organism that signals the need for therapy, but not necessarily therapy specific to the manifest focus of the disease. On the one hand disease is something to be fought, on the other it is something to be worked with and through. The allopath regards disease as a biological puzzle to be solved, seeks to pin down its causes and then to develop an effective remedy. From the point of view of alternative medicine such an approach and

strategy is doomed to ultimate failure even though it may initially appear to be successful, because its effect is to displace disease within the organism, so that eventually it manifests in another way, which for the allopath becomes another and unrelated disease. Allopathy regards disease as invasive, coming from outside the organism, and tends to employ invasive techniques such as drugs or surgery, to fight it. Alternative medicine acknowledges external factors in the causation of disease, but regards the susceptibility of an organism to those factors as the more fundamental cause, and seeks to direct therapy towards the removal of the susceptibility, which may be regarded itself as a dis-ease of the organism. [69, 122]

Drug

Any substance that can chemically affect somatic processes. Man has always used such substances both for medicinal purposes and to procure psychological effects such as alterations of CONSCIOUSNESS[4] and enhancement of physical and mental functioning. Today the psycho-social problems engendered by drug addiction and dependence have become matters of wide and profound public concern, with primary emphasis on the abuse of psycho-active drugs such as heroin, cocaine and cannabis, but also increasing awareness of the inimical effects of socially accepted drugs such as alcohol and nicotine. Modern medical pharmacology has achieved notable successes in synthesizing drugs targeted to affect specific bodily organs and

functions, but not always with complete understanding of their side-effects, which can give rise to IATROGENIC disorders as serious as the conditions they were designed to alleviate; and as medical pharmacology has given rise to a drug industry with an immense financial turnover, the problem of drug abuse has become one of wider implication than is generally realized.

See also PSYCHEDELIC EX-PERIENCE[4].

Eurythmy
See ANTHROPOSOPHY[3].

Fasting

People fast for a number of reasons, the commonest of which are to achieve weight loss and general health improvement, or to practise asceticism in order to achieve an enhanced spirituality or induce a religious experience. Fasting can serve these purposes, but there are provisos and problems that fasters do not always take into account.

Obviously weight can be lost by fasting, but it is generally quickly put back on afterwards unless the fast initiates a permanent alteration of dietary habits. In the interests of general health, the weekly or fortnightly one- or two-day fast, which gets the intestines cleared out and makes energy normally used by the digestive system available for internal regenerative work, is an excellent idea.

'Spiritual' fasting is beset with dangers and physiological misconceptions. For instance, foul breath is not a venting of bodily poisons, but a result of metabolic change to consumption of stored fat, which makes the liver produce more acetone. And the 'highs' that people experience when they fast, and which they may endow with spiritual significance, are accountable to the brain's switch-over from externally derived glucose as the source of the oxygen it needs, to internally produced ketone bodies. In a prolonged fast, the loss of muscle tissue and lean tissue can be irreversible, depletion of sodium and potassium can cause impairment of the kidneys, and permanent brain damage can be sustained. Prospective fasters should not neglect to read Kafka's story *The Hunger Artist*. [274]

Guided imagery
See VISUALIZATION.

Herbalism
The prescription and use of plants and their derivatives for medication. Until about a century ago all medicines were derived from plants, but then chemists learnt first to isolate the active ingredients in proven plant remedies, then to synthesize them, and today most medicines and drugs are synthetic. However, with the developing interest in forms of alternative medicine, the prescriptions of herbalists are now increasingly in demand. Synthesized drugs have sometimes produced disastrous and unforeseen side-effects; the number and variety of them is bewildering even to doctors, and often they induce a dependence which is as inimical to health as the condition they are supposed to alleviate, whereas herbal remedies, administered in

accordance with traditional precepts, do not have these disadvantages.

Although it is entirely rational to use herbs for health and healing instead of synthesized drugs, what puts a lot of people off herbalism is certain elements of seeming irrationalism and superstition which make the relation between a herb and its alleged function appear quite arbitrary. The old herbalists had an elaborate system of correspondences between stars, herbs and parts of the body, and a magical methodology which required herbs to be gathered and administered at times that were considered to be astrologically propitious. They also tended to specify a plant's medicinal properties according to its colour or shape. Thus a plant with flowers the colour of dried blood would be applied for staunching wounds, and the mandragora (mandrake) and ginseng plants were attributed with many properties because their roots are shaped rather like human figures. People who can accept the idea that herbal remedies are as efficacious as and less harmful than chemical drugs are inclined to be deterred from trying them by herbalism's traditional association with sympathetic magic.

Modern herbalists generally disown such associations and present themselves as custodians of traditional folk wisdom, and many of them have enhanced their qualifications with a knowledge of pharmacology, which helps allay patients' suspicions that their knowledge may be the residual mumbo-jumbo rather than the residual wisdom of a species that used to live in closer SYMBIOSIS[1] with nature. The modern herbalist has a persuasive argument that on account of the disruption of this symbiosis, and the fact that people today live largely on a diet of processed, packaged and preserved foods that are deficient in some essential natural elements, herbalism's prescriptions for health and healing are more important than ever. [58, 74, 145, 216]

Holistic medicine

It would be difficult today to find a doctor or therapist who would admit to not being holistic in his approach. To consider the overall health profile of a patient, and to treat specific ailments not only as conditions to be alleviated but also as symptoms of more fundamental dis-ease, is simply good medical practice. But holistic medicine (or 'wholistic', as it is sometimes spelt to emphasize the fact that it is the whole person that is the subject of therapy) is more honoured in name than in observance by many medical practitioners, mainly because it demands a dedication to the patient and an investment of time that they cannot afford, and because modern medical technology and pharmacology have empowered them to alleviate symptoms more effectively. Holistic methods still tend to be confined to practitioners of the alternative or complementary therapies, who not only are dedicated to them in principle but also generally are able to devote more time and attention to their patients.

Homoeopathy

Homoeopathy was the creation of a German physician, Samuel Hahnemann*. While translating a medical textbook, Hahnemann came across an account of the effects of a drug derived from a Peruvian bark, which was said to relieve malaria and other fevers. Curious, he experimented with the substance on himself, and found after several days that he developed the symptoms of malaria. It seemed that a substance that would cure a condition in a sick person would induce it in a healthy one. Working on this hypothesis, Hahnemann went on to lay the foundations of homoeopathy by trying out a variety of substances on healthy people and studying the symptoms they induced, then prescribing them as cures for conditions manifesting the same symptoms in ill people. Invariably the remedies worked. Hahnemann conjectured that the conventional medical attitude to symptoms was wrong, that symptoms were the body's way of combating disease, and that therefore a doctor's function was to help the body in its fight by inducing the appropriate symptoms rather than attacking them.

The drug with which Hahnemann first experimented was quinine. As this drug produces unpleasant side-effects, Hahnemann tried to determine the minimum dose that would be effective. This led him to another startling discovery. He found that the smaller the dose, the greater its curative effect. Taking one measure of the drug, he would mix it with nine measures of water or alcohol, then shake the mixture vigorously, producing a medicine with a potency of 1X. If one measure of this mixture was then mixed with nine measures of water or alcohol, the result would have a potency of 2X. Hahnemann used dilutions of 12X, i.e. one part in a billion, and found them to be effective. G. O. Barnard of the National Physical Laboratory has suggested that 'what Hahnemann found quite by accident was a means of separating the structural informational content of a chemical from its associated chemical mass'. Dr Barnard has further expounded a theoretical explanation of how water molecules, when shaken with a substance dissolved in them, might form polymers, or long chains of molecules, in the same shape as the molecules of the dissolved substance, and how this 'message' could pass on through a series of dilutions.

Whatever the explanation, many people testify to the efficacy of homoeopathic medicine. Sceptics point out that many also respond to PLACEBOS. Some clinical tests, however, indicate that homoeopathic treatments are more effective and long-lasting than placebos. [31, 122, 145]

Hydrotherapy
'Partaking of the waters', both externally and internally, has long been recognized as therapeutic, as the abundance of spas in many countries testifies. Practical hydrotherapy is primarily concerned with external applications, and may consist in cold or hot applications or in their alternation. Cold water therapy, which constricts blood vessels, helps alleviate pain and inflammation. Hot applications or immersions that raise body-temperature stimulate the immune response, increase the white-cell count and decrease the red, and have anti-bacterial effects. The benefits of stimulation of the circulation are secured by 'contrast bathing' – i.e. alternating from hot to cold. In what is known as the 'Sitz bath', a patient's feet are in cold water and the rest of the body up to the waist in hot: a treatment which is said to benefit sufferers from piles, some gynaecological conditions, and prolapse.

Hypnotherapy
HYPNOSIS[4] is not widely used in psychotherapy, because most practitioners believe, as Freud did, that it is preferable to engage a patient's fully conscious self in the comprehension and alleviation of his symptoms. With deep-seated neuroses this is undoubtedly true, and few hypnotherapists today would consider it adequate treatment merely to relieve such a condition by administering post-hypnotic suggestions. Hypnotherapy can, however, be usefully and effectively employed in treating mild neurotic conditions that manifest in such habits as heavy smoking, over-eating or -drinking, or nail-biting, and in relieving STRESS-related conditions such as insomnia, migraine, stammering, and hypertension. [132]

Iatrogenic illness
The term (derived from the Greek: *iatros* – physician, *genesis* – origin)

used to designate illnesses caused by medical treatment itself. The idea that doctors actually cause illnesses was turned to dramatic effect by Molière and Bernard Shaw, but today it is not an outlandish theatrical irony but a statistically proven and disturbing fact. One research study showed that one in every five patients admitted to a typical research hospital acquires an iatrogenic illness, and one in thirty of these dies as a result. To attribute iatrogenic illnesses to medical incompetence, to the inadequacies of large medical institutions to provide adequate health care and an appropriate psychological environment for ill individuals, partially explains the phenomenon. Other factors are the unpredictability of the side-effects of powerful modern drugs and invasive therapies, and, at a more fundamental level, conventional medicine's underlying assumptions about the nature of disease and the human organism, and its bias towards specialist treatments, which both precludes a HOLISTIC approach and fosters in the patient the psychologically undermining attitude that his disease is an affliction unaccountably visited upon him and which he is powerless to combat. [122, 144]

Ionization therapy

The general health benefit of air composed predominantly of molecules with a negative electrical charge is acknowledged beyond dispute, and in recent years air ionizers, which increase the supply of negative ions in the air, have become available and widely used.

Negative ions are destroyed by atmospheric pollution, and positive ions are created by central heating, and the combination of these two factors in many homes and workplaces makes the atmosphere generally unhealthy and people subjected to it prone to depression, lethargy and respiratory disorders. Air ionization combats these tendencies, and when intensified for purposes of therapy it is beneficial for sufferers from bronchitis, sinusitis, asthma, hay fever and catarrh.

Iridology

To examine the eyes for signs of organic disorder is a part of orthodox medical practice, but few doctors credit the claimed diagnostic scope of iridology, or iris diagnosis. Discovered over a century ago, independently by a Hungarian and a Swedish physician, iridology was later developed in the US by Dr Bernard Jensen, who devised an 'iris chart' that showed correspondences between bodily organs and functions and specific areas of the iris. Iridologists claim not only to be able to diagnose present ailments and pathogenic conditions, but also to be able to obtain information about past illnesses. Degrees of toxic accumulation in various parts of the body can be detected by iris diagnosis, and a person's general well-being can be ascertained. Iridology, however, cannot be as specific as to the extent and nature of organic disorders as more orthodox diagnostic techniques, but as an initial screening technique it has the advantage of being at once general and non-invasive. [152, 170]

Macrobiotics

An oriental system of dietary NATUROPATHY based on the principle that foods are broadly divisible into those having YIN or YANG³ characteristics, and that health is maintained by properly balancing these complementarities. Cereal grains are said to contain the best natural balance of yin and yang, and therefore constitute the basis of a macrobiotic diet, generally comprising at least 50 per cent of the food intake. Organically grown foods are used whenever possible, and processed foods are avoided, as are sugar, salt and refined carbohydrates. Animal and dairy foods may be incorporated in a macrobiotic diet, though in small and controlled proportions. Avoidance of excess is fundamental, particularly with regard to liquids. Sometimes a ten-day brown rice diet is recommended for people making the transition from an ordinary to a macrobiotic diet, in order to purge the body of accumulated toxins. [282]

Megavitamin therapy

Certain mental and physical disorders are commonly accompanied by specific kinds of vitamin deficiency, and may be alleviated by administering the appropriate vitamin in megadoses. Schizophrenics, alcoholics, manic depressives, and drug addicts often respond positively to megavitamin therapy, particularly when it is administered in a controlled situation and accommodated within an overall therapeutic programme. [1]

Naturopathy

The facilitating of the natural self-healing capacities of the body. Naturopaths maintain that physical organisms have an innate self-balancing and self-regulating capacity, a 'body wisdom', that disease occurs as a result of inhibiting this capacity, and that a 'nature cure' allied to an educated awareness of the body's needs and signals can enable a person to achieve and maintain a state of optimum health. Naturopaths generally prescribe FASTING as an initial means of eliminating fundamental causes of disease, and sometimes assist this process with HYDROTHERAPY. Naturopaths do not generally claim to be able to cure chronic states, but rather conceive their therapy as preventive and educative, as the encouraging of dietary habits and mental attitudes conducive to maintaining health and vitality. [145, 236]

Osteopathy

The founder of osteopathy (literally 'bone disease'), the American doctor Andrew Taylor Still*, said that it was revealed to him by God in 1874. The basic premise of osteopathy – which is used to treat all illnesses, not just bone disorders – is that bone dislocations are the fundamental cause of disease, by blocking blood vessels and nerve pathways, and thus the flow of vital energies through the body.

'Whenever the circulation of the blood is normal, disease cannot develop because our blood is capable of manufacturing all the necessary substances to maintain natural immunity against disease', wrote Still. The theoretical purpose of his osteopathic practice was to remove circulatory system blockages by means of spinal manipulation, thus enabling the body to marshal its natural defence mechanisms against disease. Although his idea of the function of the blood in the immune system does not accord with modern thought, his emphasis on the body's capacity for self-regulation and self-repair fits well with current HOLISTIC beliefs. Subsequent research has confirmed the importance that Still placed upon the spine, including the fact that all bodily organs and functions are connected to the spine.

Osteopaths claim to be able to treat a wide variety of conditions, including asthma, gastric ulcers, bronchitis, sinusitis, and migraine. There is no doubt that osteopathy can be an effective therapy, although perhaps not for the reasons proposed by Still. The key may lie in the effect of spinal manipulation in reducing tensions and increasing energy flow in the musculature of the body. In any case, osteopaths do not hold that spinal manipulation is a panacea which renders other therapy unnecessary, and many recommend complementary psychological or biochemical remedies. [134, 145]

Pain

Pain as an organism's warning system, a neurological response that alerts it to danger, is clearly a good and necessary thing. And viewed rather metaphysically, pain or suffering may be regarded as the goad of growth and achievement. But pain is also sometimes a non-functional concomitant of disease, or a crippling thing in itself, as in back pain and migraine headaches, and as such its alleviation is a responsibility of medical science. Drugs have long been used for this purpose, particularly opium and its derivatives, but their consistent use is beset by the problem of addiction and dependence. ACUPUNCTURE has proved an effective alternative for the control of some kinds of pain, and so has electrical nerve stimulation, a counterpart technique of Western medicine. Psychological methods have also recently been developed, based upon the understanding that the intensity of the pain response has no constant ratio to the stimulus but is affected by such factors as attention, anxiety, expectation and suggestion. HYPNOSIS[4] is a particularly effective pain alleviator, and techniques of auto-hypnosis can be practised by people afflicted with a pain-conducive condition. The potentials of BIOFEEDBACK and VISUALIZATION for the relief of pain have also become widely recognized and exploited recently. [213]

Placebo

An inert substance administered as a medication to a patient under the impression that he is taking a genuine medicine. It has often been observed that patients respond to such treatment, and this response is commonly known as 'the placebo effect', and ascribed to the fact that the ailment was merely imaginary. But alternatively viewed, the placebo effect may be regarded as evidence that consciousness can play an active part in the healing process. To argue from the fact that a placebo can affect only the mind, to the conclusion that any condition it alleviates must have been *only* in the mind and therefore not real, is to confess to an uncompromising materialist bias that medical evidence does not support, for quite chronic ailments have been known to respond to placebos.

Psionics
See RADIONICS.

Psychosomatic illness
The fact that physical and mental conditions are correlated, that an ailment manifest in the body may have its cause in a state of mind, is acknowledged in orthodox medical theory, but the processes involved in psychosomatic illness, the precise ways in which pathological states of the mind translate into pathological states of the body, are little understood. The term 'psychosomatic illness' was formerly used with the implication that manifest physical symptoms attributable to mental causes were less chronic and more easily curable than disorders of purely physical origin. If the term has a less wide currency today it is not only because this naïve misconception has discredited it, but also because no class of specifically psychosomatic illnesses can be designated, and also because a complex interaction of mental and physical factors is now acknowledged as being involved in virtually all disease causation.

Radionics
The Radionics Association defines radionics as:

a method of healing at a distance through the medium of an instrument or other means using the ESP faculty. In this way, a trained and competent practitioner can discover the cause of disease within any living system, be it a human being, an animal, a plant, or the soil itself. Suitable therapeutic energies can then be made available to the patient to help restore optimum health ... Basic to radionic theory and practice is the concept that man and all life forms share a common ground in that they are submerged in the electromagnetic field which, if sufficiently distorted, will ultimately result in disease of the organism.

The term 'radionics', then, is a new word for the ancient medical practice of PSYCHIC HEALING[5]. It differs in that it purports to be based on an understanding of how such healing works. Radionics was developed by a San Francisco physician, Albert Abrams. In 1910, while examining a patient with a growth on his lip, Abrams discovered that when he percussed a certain spot on the patient's abdomen with his fingers, it gave out a dull note. Further investigation revealed that different physical ailments were connected with the emission of dull notes from different spots on the abdomen, and Abrams surmised that disease emitted electromagnetic radiation. He conducted some highly original experiments and made some strange findings, such as that when a diseased person was connected to a healthy one by a wire, the latter's abdomen yielded the appropriate dull note. Even connection to a sample of the patient's blood produced the same effect. Reasoning that if disease consisted in an alteration in the radiation emitted by part of the body it should be curable by treatment with appropriate electromagnetic radiations, Abrams developed an apparatus for producing such radiations. He apparently had considerable success in healing patients with this apparatus, although others to whom he sold it had less happy results.

Abrams himself did not suggest that it was the operator, not the apparatus, that was responsible for the cure. After his death, one of his followers, Ruth Drown, introduced a series of modifications in his equipment and methods, such as eliminating much of the crypto-electrical circuitry from the controversial 'black box', and treating patients at a distance. Today many practitioners prefer the term 'psionics' to radionics, asserting that the analogy to radio broadcasting is misleading since diagnosis and healing are achieved through the human PSI[5] faculty. [183, 315]

Reflexology

A manipulation technique that focuses upon the feet and is employed by expert practitioners both diagnostically and therapeutically. It is alternatively known as zone therapy. Established by a US doctor, William Fitzgerald, early in the century, and subsequently developed by a number of practitioners, notably Eunice Ingham in the 1930s, the method has affinities with ACU-PUNCTURE although no direct derivation has been acknowledged. Fitzgerald discovered in practice that specific organic and physiological functions respond to pressure and massage applied to parts of the body remote from and apparently unconnected with them. He divided the body in ten zones, and sought to map the patterns of relations between them. In practice, however, the zone of the feet, where nerve endings are close to the surface, proved the most effective to work upon. All the organs and parts of the body have a reflex point on the feet, and dysfunctions are signalled by pain when pressure is applied to the related reflex point. Therapy consists in massaging the appropriate point, and reflexologists claim that many conditions can be alleviated by such treatment, for instance gallstones, migraine, sinus trouble, arthritis, constipation, and liver and heart problems. Massage is believed to disperse congestions and to facilitate the healthy flow of blood and energy throughout the body, and regular foot massage is said to contribute to health maintenance and to prevent illness becoming established. [21]

Reichian therapy

Originally a Freudian therapist, Wilhelm Reich* developed in the 1920s and 1930s ideas and practices that were scorned at the time but have become increasingly influential since the 1960s. BIOENERGETICS, PRIMAL THERAPY[4] and ROLFING all derive from Reich's pioneering work. Fundamental to this work was the idea that functional and organic illnesses are attributable to the blockage of the natural processes of intake and outflow of biological energies in the body, and the various Reichian therapies seek to break down these blockages, either with manipulative techniques or by encouraging the release of suppressed emotions. In a healthy organism, Reich believed, energy flows without impediment, but psychological trauma or neurosis can become locked into the body, causing rigidities which impede the flow. In the complete sexual orgasm, which proceeds through the four stages of tension, charge, discharge and relaxation, the energetic process essential to health is seen at work. But many people, Reich found, are not orgastically potent, even though they may be sexually active. Orgastic impotence, he maintained, occurs because the body becomes 'armoured', i.e. the musculature becomes habituated to tensions which constrict the flow of energy.

Reich used the term 'character armour' to designate a rigidity which results not from trauma or psychosis but from ego-consciousness, a person's consolidating an individual personality or character which is really a shell, a front, a stratagem for being or seeming to be someone in the world. The protective shell of character inhibits spontaneity and the natural flow of feeling, and a person so 'armoured' does not live life intensely and is likely eventually to manifest physical symptoms of energy blockage, so that dis-ease becomes disease. The spontaneous

person, the 'genital personality', does not have this kind of inhibiting ego-consciousness and is less likely to succumb to disease.

The emphasis that Reich put upon energy led him to investigate its nature. He devoted much of his life, particularly in the later years, to performing experiments and developing theories about what he called 'orgone' energy. This energy, he maintained, flowed through the atmosphere and through biological organisms; it was the fundamental life-energy. Reich developed a device for accumulating and concentrating atmospheric orgone which he called the orgone box, and he claimed that it could be used for many therapeutic purposes, and could even cause some cancers to regress. Reich's later work is generally regarded as cranky and misconceived, but although he may have made exaggerated claims, the nature and direction of his research was neither so preposterous nor so discreditable as his detractors maintained. The existence and flow of an energy with the characteristics that Reich attributed to orgone was taught in ancient Chinese and Hindu philosophy, where it was called respectively CH'I[3] energy and PRANA[3]. In the West, Paracelsus in the sixteenth century wrote about a life-energy which he called 'munia', and more recently Galvani, Mesmer, von Reichenbach, Kilner, H. S. Burr (see LIFE-FIELDS[2]), Paul Kammerer, Semyon Kirlian (see KIRLIAN PHOTOGRAPHY[5]) and numerous other scientists and philosophers have put forward theories similar to Reich's. Research into the healing properties of atmospheres with enhanced negative ion content has been conducted worldwide recently with positive results, and some neo-Reichians have argued that the orgone box was therapeutically effective because it accumulated negative ions.

Whether or not the conceptual foundations of his work hold good in the light of ongoing scientific research, the effectiveness of Reichian therapy and its derivations cannot be denied. [195, 202, 260, 261]

Rolfing

A technique of deep muscular manipulation developed by the physiologist Ira Rolf*. Properly called 'structural integration', the technique is designed to correct gravitational imbalance in body postures and movements, and relieve rigidities and inflexibilities in the musculature caused by psychological trauma and consolidated by habit. The relation of psychological trauma to physical states, its permanent effect upon posture and muscular tension, was discovered by Wilhelm Reich*, and Rolfing is a variant of REICH-IAN THERAPY. In the ten sessions of a Rolfing course, subjects often vividly recall experiences, sometimes forgotten ones, which are later found to account for the tension locked into the part of the body being worked on at the time of recall. The therapy does not involve psychoanalysis, but it does sometimes make manifest psychic material which the subject can then deal with. By restructuring

body postures so that they make use of gravitational forces instead of involving the body in continual combat with them, Rolfing is said to enhance energy. Other benefits attested by people who have undergone Rolfing are alleviation of psychosomatic ailments and anxiety states, increased sensitivity and receptivity, positive attitude changes and enhancement of self-esteem and confidence, weight loss, and increase of stamina and ease in the performance of physical tasks and exercises. [73, 271]

Self-healing

Physical systems are by their very nature endowed with self-repair and self-healing properties, and traditionally medicine's primary concern was with comprehending the processes involved and facilitating their operation. With the development of medical technology a majority of physicians departed from this tradition, believing that medical science had developed more powerful or quickly effective tools for healing or combating disease. This attitude not only disregarded the natural self-healing properties of organisms, but also invested the medical specialist with a status that discouraged the patient from conceiving that he could himself participate in his cure or healing. Alternative medicine seeks to encourage self-healing in both senses of the term.

Sexuality

The dreaded AIDS virus and a reactionary backlash against the sexual permissiveness of the 1970s have recently combined to obscure the fact that a revolution in attitudes to and the understanding of human sexuality has occurred in the last two decades. Although the ideas that sex can be life-enhancing as well as life-creating, a mode of spiritual as well as of physical fulfilment, recreational as well as procreational, an experience of self-discovery and growth as well as of self-gratification or frustration, might have been accorded quite wide assent twenty years ago, a majority of people then were inhibited by a deep-rooted puritanical conditioning which related sex to man's 'lower' nature (the Freudian ID[4], bent upon pleasure) and encumbered its expression with restrictions, and prescriptions as to the right and proper, that more commonly gave rise to feelings of guilt rather than of joy in it. It was not a degenerate permissiveness that subverted this conditioning, but the emergence of new understandings and new orientations in psychology and medical practice, and in society. The FEMINIST[7] critique of male dominance extended beyond the political and economic domains to the sexual (see Kate Millett* on Freud, Henry Miller and D. H. Lawrence), and resulted in female sexuality being exposed, discussed and understood as never before: a development beneficial to men as well as to women. Wilhelm Reich's* evidence that orgasmic potency is fundamental to both psychological and physical health, and his demonstrations of how pathology arises from the body becoming 'armoured' and blocking the flow of sexual energy, not only

gave rise to a number of effective therapies in the context of the HUMAN POTENTIALS MOVEMENT[4] but also contributed to a widespread attitudinal emancipation from censorious puritanism. Likewise, HUMANISTIC PSYCHOLOGY[4], with its orientation towards facilitating human growth and fulfilment rather than ministering to morbid psychic conditions, fostered positive attitudes to sexual experience and relationships. Such developments have filtered down to influence medical practitioners and people engaged in marital guidance and counselling services, and today people in general are more at ease with their sexuality, less constrained by gender-linked sex roles, and better equipped by knowledge to form mutually fulfilling sexual relationships, than they were prior to the sexual revolution of the 1970s. The sex shops, sex shows, pornography and permissiveness of the time may have succumbed to the backlash, or just run their course to reach the ultimate inertia of the superficial, but the changes were profound, widespread and enduring, and probably many of the counter-revolutionaries are their unwitting beneficiaries. [219, 261]

Shiatsu

A Japanese method of massage which is allied to ACUPUNCTURE in that it involves the application of finger or palm-of-the-hand pressure upon specific points on the body. Alternatively known as acupressure, it confers, like the older system from which it derives, the benefit of alleviating organic and

physiological malfunctions remote
from the area where the therapy is
applied, and is said to be particularly effective in treating rheu-
matism and arthritic conditions,
intestinal and stomach ailments,
diabetes, high blood pressure, and
in effecting the elimination of
toxins from the body. Muscle-tone,
the health and complexion of the
skin, and general vitality are also
enhanced by shiatsu massage.

Stress

Stress is generally acknowledged
to be a causative factor in such
conditions as heart disease, high
blood pressure, migraine and
gastro-intestinal disorders, and the
high incidence of these ailments in
modern societies is believed to be
attributable to the fact that the
conditions of modern life are
highly stress-conducive. On the
other hand it is also acknowledged
that a certain amount of stress is
required for optimum physical or
mental functioning, that human
beings respond positively to conditions that challenge and 'stretch'
them. The amount and the kind of
stress that engenders these negative
and positive responses varies
greatly with individuals, and therefore the stress factor in pathology
is not easily quantifiable. An overload or an underload of stimulus
input both tend to jeopardize functioning, but what is an overload
for one person may be an underload for another. Negative stress
occurs when environmental pressures impinge upon a person beyond his capacity to cope with
them, and modern biochemical
and electrophysiological monitor-

ing techniques have enabled its
symptoms to be precisely observed.
BIOFEEDBACK is a method of
stress reduction that employs such
techniques, and they have also
been used to demonstrate the therapeutic benefit of MEDITATION[3]
for the over-stressed. [20, 290]

T'ai chi

A Chinese system of exercise and
meditation designed simultaneously to energize the body and tran-
quillize the mind by facilitating the
natural flow of CH'I[3] energy. T'ai
chi is more like dance than strenuous exercise, the movements that
constitute it are slow, flowing,
unforced, gentle; they do not
expend energy, they create it.
They are basically circular movements, which express the complementary interaction of the forces
of YIN and YANG[3], respectively
represented by the right and left
sides of the body. T'ai chi is the
perfect co-ordination of mind and
body. To become a master in it is
said to take at least ten years, and
to result in the attainment of perfect power and control over the
self – a fact not generally stressed
in the neighbourhood leisure
centres that offer classes in it.
[193]

Tissue salts therapy

A branch of HOMOEOPATHY developed over a century ago by a
German physician, W. H. Schüssler, who maintained that disease
was caused by deficiency or imbalance in the body's content of essential mineral salts. He specified
twelve such salts that the body
needs in right proportions in order

to maintain its health at the fundamental cell and tissue level, and prescribed them as dietary supplements for patients suffering from particular illnesses. Tissue salt preparations are readily available today from pharmacists and health shops, and deficiency diagnosis is generally a part of NATUR-OPATHY as well as homoeopathy. [50]

Visualization

The use of mental imagery to produce physical effects has long been one of the fundamental techniques of MEDITATION[3]. In recent years the recognition that such beneficial effects as the slowing of heart-rate and the lowering of blood pressure, the control of levels of muscle tension in the body, and of hormone concentration in the blood, can be achieved by means of visualization, has led some medical practitioners to employ techniques of guided imagery in their therapies. A sufferer from chronic PAIN, for instance, may be encouraged to visualize his pain as a glowing red ball, to focus attention on its specific location in his body and slowly move it away from there and away from his body altogether, visualizing it projected at a distance. Such techniques work, suggests Dr Larry Dossey*, because they are 'time therapies', i.e.

They ask the patient to step out of a chronic, habitual way of sensing time as an inexorable flowing process into an alternative mode of time perception. They ask the patient to 'stop time'. They invite him into the realm of space-time, although this invitation is never explicit.

[69]

Zone therapy
See REFLEXOLOGY.

7
SOCIETY, ENVIRONMENT AND TECHNOLOGY

Acid rain

Atmospheric pollution is caused by industrial chemical emissions, chiefly from factories and electrical generating plants which burn fossil fuels and vent sulphur and nitrogen oxides into the air, which turn rain into dilute solutions of sulphuric and nitric acid. This acidified rain corrodes buildings, and does incalculable damage to lakes and forests. In the 1960s Swedish scientists identified acid rain as the cause of drastic reductions in fish populations in freshwater lakes, and Sweden introduced legislation to reduce industrial emissions. In the mid 1970s the problem was highlighted by the decline of forest areas in Germany and Central Europe. By this time, however, chemical emissions had actually been reducing for several years, and there were some doubts as to whether they were the chief cause of the deforestation (high ozone concentrations and the European drought of 1976 were possible other causes). Acid rain is a thorny international problem, because often the countries that generate the pollution suffer less drastically from it than do their neighbours, and also because the extent of the damage directly attributable to industrial emissions is uncertain. The emission of nitrogen oxides from vehicle engines must also be taken into account. A group of nations have recently formed a '30 per cent Club', with the objective of reducing industrial sulphur emissions by 30 per cent. Reductions can be achieved by filtration processes, but the filtering medium, pulverized limestone, is required in sub-stantial quantities, and quarrying it can give rise to other environmental problems. [4, 118]

Alternative energy

At present the world's energy demands are met primarily by the exploitation of the non-renewable resources, oil, coal, natural gas and fuel wood, and secondarily by the generation of NUCLEAR POWER. Clearly there will come a time when natural resources are depleted, and although nuclear power could supply the deficiency, particularly if FUSION[2] reactors are developed, governments are at present under pressure to look to alternative energy sources that are not so hazardous environmentally. HYDROPOWER, SOLAR, WIND, GEOTHERMAL and BIOMASS ENERGY are the main such alternatives, and are already contributing in various degrees to meeting energy demands. In the US in 1985 it was estimated that renewable energy sources contributed about 10 per cent to the national energy budget, while nuclear power contributed 5 per cent. [39]

Appropriate technology

The belief that technology is the panacea for all ills, even those that it creates, was widely held in the 1960s, but has been steadily eroded since. Modern industrial technology has been criticized for being uncaringly manipulative and exploitative of both human and natural resources, capital- and energy-intensive, growth- and profit-oriented, ecologically and environmentally irresponsible, politically committed to a capitalist ethos, and incapable of preventing catastrophic accidents resulting from the complexity and sophistication of its mechanisms. Paralleling these criticisms, proposals have been put for the development of alternative technologies which would not have such biases and effects. Common to these proposals is the concept of appropriateness.

Underdeveloped countries that have adopted advanced technology have suffered a number of social and economic ills as a result. The capital needed to acquire, run and service the technology has drained their own reserves and obliged them to seek massive foreign investment and incur dependence; social unrest has become prevalent with the disruption of traditional ways of life and work, with increased unemployment, and with the widening of a gap between a wealthy minority and an impoverished majority. Such consequences underline the inappropriateness of the introduction of advanced technology to the real circumstances of the aspirant country.

Appropriate technologies take into account such circumstances. In underdeveloped countries they seek to be labour-intensive rather than capital-intensive, to minimize energy input, to use local materials, to be compatible with the local culture, to be decentralist, to eschew high specialization, to be long-term rather than short-term functional, and to become established as a steady-state economy rather than a growth- and profit-oriented one. An appropriate technology may be an innovation into a society, a scaled-down version of an advanced technology governed in its organization and operational methods by the above objectives; or it may be an application of scientific and technological knowledge to an indigenous industry with the purpose of increasing productivity and efficiency.

The problems resulting from the adoption and development of high technology have been highlighted in underdeveloped countries but are not confined to them. The criterion of appropriateness is also relevant to the development and deployment of technology in the advanced industrial countries, but although some new enterprises have demonstrated its viability, the fundamental changes in economic and political attitudes and objectives that would have to precede the effective adoption of the criterion are not at the present time in evidence. [67, 287]

Artificial intelligence

Research into how machines can be made to simulate human thinking processes began in the late 1950s, and at that time two scientists, Herbert Simon and Allen Newell, wrote in a technical paper:

There are now in the world machines that think, that learn and that create. Moreover, their ability to do these things is going to increase rapidly until – in the visible future – the range of problems they can handle will be coextensive with the range to which the human mind has been applied.

Depending on your bias, the prediction could be construed optimistically or pessimistically; as foreseeing

Appropriate technology

a triumph for science or a blow to human self-esteem, if the mental faculties that it was largely based upon proved reducible to mechanics. Since the 1950s, research on artificial intelligence has been intense. COMPUTERS have been programmed to perform a range of sophisticated 'mental' or intelligent tasks, such as playing chess, translating texts, holding conversations, making medical diagnoses, recognizing and appropriately responding to human speech, recognizing shapes and patterns, designing complex systems such as electronic circuits, identifying and correcting faults in their own functioning, and developing ways of improving their performance. Considering these and many other functions that computers are capable of, it is undeniable that man has developed 'thinking machines' with powers often equal to and sometimes even superior to his own. Its practical implications aside, AI research has raised some fundamental questions and helped clarify our thinking about the nature of human intelligence.

It has been argued that something that has been programmed cannot be said to think independently and flexibly, and that it is by its very independence and flexibility that human thinking is distinguished. But on the other hand it is arguable that man himself is programmed, genetically, and that his instincts are inherited sub-routines and his acquired skills the product of the kind of programming that we call education or training. On the other hand it is not arguable – although it is often argued – that

computers are inflexible, can only do things that their human programmer has instructed them to do and therefore are necessarily under his control. Chess-playing machines can learn from the experience of their own and their opponents' play, and can compose subprograms for future use independently of their human programmers. To maintain, therefore, that human thought is unique by virtue of its independence and flexibility is insupportable.

But what about CONSCIOUSNESS[4], and what about thought that is informed by feeling? Joseph Weizenbaum* of the MIT developed a program called 'Doctor', modelled on the interviewing techniques of ROGERIAN[4] psychiatrists. He was amazed to find 'that extremely short exposures to a relatively simple computer program could induce powerful delusional thinking in quite normal people'. Many of his subjects had no scruples about attributing consciousness to the computer, and conversing with it 'as if it were a person who could be appropriately and usefully addressed in intimate terms'. Their delusion was that 'Doctor' was patient, understanding and sympathetic. These are all terms that refer to feelings and that presuppose a background of human life experiences, but Weizenbaum's 'Doctor's' words were not chosen by reference to such feelings or such experiences, but were merely verbal formulae elicited by the 'patient's' own words.

There has been a lot of speculation and philosophical hairsplitting over the question of whether machines will ever be endowed with consciousness and feeling, but the main point surely is that they can never be conscious and can never feel in the same way as human beings are and do. Simon and Newell's prediction that 'in the visible future' there will be machines that can handle problems 'coextensive with the range to which the human mind has been applied', prompts such questions as: what about the problem of death? Could a machine ever think like a Kierkegaard or a Schopenhauer? The answer must be 'No.' As Weizenbaum says, there are ideas 'that no machines will ever understand because they relate to objectives that are inappropriate to machines'.

Some enthusiasts of AI foresee the coming of ultra-intelligent machines (known as UIMs) that will eventually supersede man as the most successful and evolved species on earth, and suggest that we should renounce our species partisanship and hail man's creature that will surpass him as an evolutionary advance. The mathematician Alan Turing* even argued that in creating UIMs men would act 'as instruments of God's will providing mansions for the souls He creates'.

Few of us would go along with such stoic enthusiasm. An alternative future scenario might be analogous to the situation in Arthur C. Clarke's* *2001: A Space Odyssey*, where a human being 'murders' a computer that has turned wilfully malevolent, removing one memory block after another from its brain

until it regresses to incoherent babbling and finally falls completely silent. It is a cautionary tale. Isaac Asimov* is more optimistic, and foresees a future in which man and intelligent machine coexist to their mutual benefit and that of the planet as a whole.

AI is with us to stay, and we can expect increasing practical applications of the research. We need to respect it for what it can do, recognize what it can't and what it shouldn't do, and resist deifying or anthropomorphizing it and undervaluing human intelligence, which because it is bound up with human feelings and life experience is generically different from and can never be simulated by a machine. [27, 85, 347]

Balance of nature

A term designating the self-sustaining and self-renewing properties of natural ECOSYSTEMS, generally used with the implication that the balance is complex and highly vulnerable to disturbance by human intervention, deliberate or unwitting.

Beats

The 1950s progenitors of the COUNTERCULTURE of the 1960s and 1970s. The term was ambiguous, signifying on the one hand weariness and despair of the uses and values of a conformist and materialistic society, and on the other an assertion of the spiritual base of their non-conformism (the novelist Jack Kerouac said the word was an abbreviation of 'beatific'). The beats were on principle rootless, scornful of affluence and its rewards and commodities, un-inhibited about sex and in the expression of feelings, spontaneous and undisciplined in creative expression, anti-intellectual, mystical, rhapsodic, enthusiasts for Eastern religions, particularly ZEN[3], for 'cool' modern jazz muzic, for 'mind-blowing' and consciousness-altering experiences induced by drugs. The novelist Kerouac and the poet Allen Ginsberg were their chief spokesmen, and their life-style and orientation are clearly indicated by the titles of these writers' best-known works (Kerouac's *On the Road* and *The Dharma Bums*, and Ginsberg's *Howl* and *Sunflower Sutra*). Youthful and extreme as it was in its subversiveness, outrageousness and antinomianism, the beat movement was not dismissable as a cultural aberration or self-regarding generational fad, for it articulated a genuine and widely felt dissent from and disaffection with the values and purposes of the established culture. [275]

Biomass energy

Biomass is plant or animal matter that can serve as fuel. Wood is the most obvious source of biomass energy, but it is a non-renewable resource. Renewable biomass energy can be derived from grain and other crops by fermentation and distillation into alcohol, which can be used as fuel, and also from sewage, manure and other waste matter by controlled bacterial activity to produce methane gas. Biomass energy technologies are currently employed in many developing countries, but the scope for extension and development is im-mense. Particularly in respect of biogas production, the technology is cheap to develop and run, and there is a bonus in the form of a residue that can be used as a fertilizer, thus reducing the expense and environmental hazards of synthetic chemical fertilizers. [39]

Bionics

A branch of CYBERNETICS which studies the functioning of biological organisms, particularly the principles that govern their methods of information processing and of control, with a view to adapting such principles to accomplish technological innovations.

Biosphere

A term commonly used in the context of ecological and OR-GANICIST[1] views of the planet earth. Its reference is sometimes limited to the surface layer of living organisms on the planet, and sometimes extended to include the elements that support them, the hydrosphere and atmosphere. The question whether planets with biospheres in the more limited sense exist elsewhere in the universe cannot at present be answered with certainty, but it is virtually certain that earth is the only planet in the solar system so endowed. Understanding of the biosphere as an intricately co-ordinated natural system has evolved and spread over recent years, and currency of the term has correspondingly increased, both in scientific literature and in conservationist polemics.

Biotechnology

Applied biology has been one of

the most rapid growth areas in modern science, and has diverged into a number of distinct technologies. Prominent among these is GENETIC ENGINEERING, which is considered in a separate entry.

Biotechnology holds out great possibilities for agriculture. Hybridization has of course long been employed as a technique for increasing crop yield or disease resistance, but the development of RECOMBINANT DNA technology has not only enhanced efficiency and economy in achieving these results but has made it practically possible to accomplish goals that hybridization could never aspire to. In particular, an expected breakthrough of the near future is the transfer of genes governing the nitrogen-fixing process in legumes to other crops such as cereals, which will greatly reduce the use of chemical fertilizers, naturally improve soil fertility, and as a further bonus diminish water pollution.

Micro-organisms such as yeasts can be developed to a high degree of specificity to perform functions such as the conversion of wastes from oil- or sugar-refining plants into protein for animal feed. And methods by which biotechnology can produce alternative sources of energy to those non-renewable sources that the world at present chiefly depends on are already tried and tested and available for larger-scale exploitation (see BIO-MASS ENERGY). [82, 266]

Cloning

The asexual reproduction of an organic entity. The word derives

from a Greek word meaning 'a throng', and a clone may be described as a congregation of identical cells derived from a single parent cell. In 1970 F. C. Steward * published a description of an experiment in which he had taken cells from a carrot root and produced from them a complete new plant. The human clone – an identical individual reproduced from the DNA [2] of a single cell – then became a staple of science fantasy, both in ostensibly true journalistic contexts and in frankly fictional novelistic ones. Biotechnologists have produced clones of cattle and sheep, and some foresee the near possibility of creating human clones, although it must remain highly doubtful whether any acceptable purpose could be proposed for doing so.

Computers

The view of computers as mere 'number crunchers', i.e. nothing but fast mathematical calculators, underestimates not only their versatility but also the power of mathematics as a symbolic language. As research on ARTIFICIAL INTELLIGENCE has shown, semantic meanings can be given to the symbols manipulated by computers, and a wide range of human cognitive and ratiocinative functions can be simulated.

There are two categories, the analogue and the digital computer. The scope of the former is limited, for specific features of the physical problem it deals with have to be set up analogously in its circuitry. Digital computers are infinitely more versatile. They are so called

Counterculture

because their operations are based on binary mathematics (see INFORMATION THEORY), employing 8-digit strings of os and 1s, which are generated at high speed by pulses governing sequential open and shut states of a switching mechanism. Early electrical computers employing valves and vacuum tubes were capable of switching operations at the rate of hundreds per second, but with the development first of the transistor and then the microchip, that rate was increased manyfold, and at the same time the size of computers was correspondingly diminished.

As the brain comprises billions of neurons, each with thousands of branching connections to other neurons, forming pathways along which information is transmitted, so in a computer there are millions of switches, each with numerous connections with other switches and therefore a near-infinite number of potential information-carrying pathways. Programs can be stored in the computer itself, which gives it a capability analogous to that of the brain's memory. In some cases, programming may consist simply in specifying a goal for a computer's operation, and leaving it to select and pursue the stored programs (or 'sub-routines') appropriate to achieving that goal. A capability to learn from experience, to choose between available routes and sub-routines those which have proved effective in the past, is one of the things that makes computer 'thinking' uncannily – and for some alarmists sinisterly – similar to human thinking. [27]

Conservation

The earth supports upwards of 3 million species – some estimates put the total as high as 10 million – of which only about 1.5 million have been recorded. Human encroachments upon, and direct or indirect interference with, the environments that sustain many of these species have had the effect of steadily depleting them, and it has become increasingly clear that a vigorously active global strategy of conservation must be effectively practised to halt the process of depletion. A concern for conservation may formerly have been regarded as a kind of romantic eccentricity, but today it is widely acknowledged to be economically and ethically right and to have potent political implications. It is not just a matter of conserving the world's wildlife and wildlands as an aesthetic or recreational resource for man, or even for their own sake and because we, the dominant species, concede their right to share the planet with us. It is also a matter of more specific economic and self-interest, in that man will need in the future all the wealth and diversity that the wild GENE POOL can bestow to furnish agricultural and medical resources without which he may himself become an endangered species. [4, 39, 338]

Counterculture

The life-styles, dissents and priorities of the BEATS of the 1950s and the Hippies of the 1960s have been construed by some writers, notably Theodore Roszak* (*The Making of a Counter Culture*, 1970), as signifying the emergence of an alternative and challenge to the established and orthodox culture of the Western world. The established culture, in Roszak's analysis, is scientific-rational, utilitarian, secular, in thrall to specialization and expertise, to the values of capitalism, affluence and consumerism. The traditional opposition to this culture has come from the political left in terms of a proletarian radicalism, a championing of the rights of the people, the underprivileged, the poor, the racial minorities, an opposition to war, exploitation and class privilege. The counterculture has affinities with this tradition, but it is transpolitical and more radical, opposed to IDEOLOGY[1] of whatever political complexion. It seeks not piecemeal political change, but change of 'the total cultural context within which our daily politics takes place', not social democratization or a more egalitarian spread of rights, privileges and affluence, but a fundamental change of consciousness, priorities and values.

Countercultural manifestations in the 1960s and 1970s were often bizarre, seemingly frivolous, sometimes morally outrageous in the eyes of the established culture. Hindu mysticism and modes of dress, mantra chanting and cowbell jingling were adopted by the young as emblems of protest. Protest was not angry and earnest, but festive and disarming, with flowers distributed to spectators, with music and dancing, sometimes with mocking rituals, as when an assembly of witches and magicians sought to exorcise and

levitate the Pentagon. There was sexual permissiveness, there were experiments with community lifestyles, with consciousness-altering drugs, there was developed a 'hip' vernacular language and along with it, in the arts, an anti-intellectual, anti-rational aesthetic which valued only spontaneity and rhapsodic exuberance. It was so total but at the same time so incoherent an overturning of the values and priorities of the established culture that it could hardly be taken seriously as a threat or challenge.

But it was fundamentally threatening and challenging. The quest for the sacralization of life, for an injection of spiritual meaning into the workaday; the cultivation of feminine values and modes of being and doing and knowing, of intuition, feeling, caring, mutually helping; the scorn for and repudiation of the consumer society, of utilitarianism, of the mentality of managers, planners and experts: these were the psychic origins and bedrock of the counterculture, and they were not destroyed or discredited with the passing of the 'swinging sixties' and early seventies. Technocratic totalitarianism has taken a tighter hold since then, and it seems that materialism, conformity, a harsh and self-regarding 'realism', a deference to authority, are the psycho-social and cultural determinants of the 1980s. But perhaps the counterculture has become the 'AQUARIAN CONSPIRACY[1]', less flamboyant, fantastical and outrageous, more wary of media exploitation and trivialization, a network of dissenting, radi-

Ecology

cal, unorthodox individuals, groups and agencies less conspicuously working at alternative and transformative developments of themselves, society and culture. [275, 276]

Cybernetics

The word derives from the Greek for 'steersman', and was proposed by Norbert Wiener* 'to express the art and science of control over the whole range of fields in which the notion is applicable'. Central to cybernetics theory is the concept of information FEEDBACK, which enables a system to be self-regulating, by governing and interrelating the processes of input and output. The principle was incorporated in mechanical systems, such as the windmill and the steam engine, long before it was conceptually formulated. The value of Wiener's formulation was that it enabled correspondences to be seen between different types of system and encouraged developments in various areas through transdisciplinary approaches. In this it had much in common with GENERAL SYSTEMS THEORY[1], and indeed today it is widely regarded as a branch of the latter. Although a distinction has to be made between the cybernetics of closed systems and of open systems, and some would maintain that cybernetics proper, as a mathematical science, is restricted to the former, as a conceptual tool for the study of ordered holistic systems, their self-maintenance and evolution, the cybernetical approach has proved fruitful in areas as diverse as neurology and business management. [353]

Earth sciences

The integrated study of sciences concerned with the planet earth has tended in recent years to supplant narrow specialization and constitute a subject in itself. Geography, geology, geophysics, oceanography, meteorology, astronomy, biology and palaeontology are the sciences involved in this coalescence. The shift to such an interdisciplinary approach has coincided with the expansion of ecological awareness, and the two developments are clearly not unconnected.

Ecology

As a science, ecology is the branch of zoology, botany or biology that studies the complex patterns of interrelationship between organisms and their environment. Originally a technical term with this specific meaning, it has over recent years acquired a more general and substantive meaning. In a phrase like 'concern for the ecology', the term refers to an integral and natural environment endowed with self-regulatory processes that ensure its health and survival. It may have a specific referent, the desert or the rain forest for instance, or may be understood in a wider, planetary sense. By extension, an ecologist is now not necessarily a scientist engaged in a particular area of study, but also and more generally a person aware of the conditions necessary to maintain the natural integrity of an environment, and possibly active in protecting those conditions from disruptive encroachment by man. Purists have deplored such shifts in meaning as debased usage of the terms 'ecology' and 'ecologist', but clearly the new significations met a need as people became increasingly aware of the complex interdependence of living systems and their vulnerability to degradation or destruction. [53, 57, 238]

Ecosphere

The planetary totality of ECO-SYSTEMS.

Ecosystem

An integrated congeries of flora, fauna and natural processes in a specific environment. There are different ecosystems, for instance in a tropical forest, a desert, a freshwater lake, the deep ocean, and a coral reef. In any such system the components exist in mutual dependence and generally in co-operation, and even when there is competition between creatures in exploiting the environment, and some prey on others, the overall result is to keep populations in a constant ratio that ensures the integrity and survival of the system. Ecosystems can tolerate natural internal disturbances, and external ones such as freak climatic conditions, but they are highly vulnerable to disruption from without, to the extent that damage done to a part, however small and apparently insignificant, may have amplified repercussions upon the whole.

Energy crisis

Abundant and relatively inexpensive energy is a primary need of modern societies. Most of the energy used by man up to the present time has come from nonrenewable resources. Timber, coal, oil and natural gas are exhaustible commodities. Estimates vary as to how long they will last at present growing rates of consumption, but most projections do not see them lasting more than three or four centuries, and oil is expected to run out during the next century. The energy problem is clearly linked to the world population problem (see OVERPOPULATION), for at prevailing population growth and energy consumption rates energy output has to double about every twenty-five years.

Governments became aware of a possible future energy crisis in the 1950s and 1960s, and their concerted initial response was to look to NUCLEAR POWER for the solution. Environmentalist pressures since have led to ALTERNATIVE ENERGY sources being developed, and at the same time considerable success has been achieved, both by domestic and industrial consumers, in the conservation and more efficient use of energy. The contributions of alternative sources and the effectiveness of conservation policies are factors that pessimistic projections tend to minimize. The extent of the increase in future worldwide energy needs must also be calculated with provisions for the effects of increases upon the THIRD WORLD debt problem and upon the climatic effects of over-developing facilities: considerations which also exert pressure to seek the solution to the energy crisis not merely in terms of technologically increasing production to meet demand, but more in terms of in-

Feedback

creasing energy efficiency in order to stabilize demand. [55]

Environment

The physical habitat of a living organism, comprising a congeries of factors that directly affect the life and survival of the organism. Recently the term 'the environment' has come into use, meaning particularly the human habitat, both rural and urban. So-called environmentalists seek to prevent the degradation of this habitat, for instance by chemical pollution and ill-conceived town-planning and building schemes. Environmental studies in schools and universities focus upon study of relationships between man, his creations and cultures, and nature, the latter comprising other forms of organic and animal life and also the air, water and land that they subsist upon. The development of such studies has stemmed from the recognition that the natural environment, resilient though it is, is not a thing that can indefinitely sustain inconsiderate exploitation and abuse by man, and also that unless the man-made environments of towns and cities serve more than basic living needs they will both suffer and precipitate a process of social degradation. [6, 57, 240, 338]

Fascism

Although Fascism was specifically the name of the Mussolini military dictatorship in Italy (1922-45), the term was widely applied to other contemporary authoritarian regimes, particularly those in Germany and Spain. After the demise of these regimes the term fascist remained a potent one in political rhetoric, designating a congeries of sinister political attitudes and acts. Fascism is illiberal, anti-democratic, nationalist, militarist, authoritarian, ruthless, racist, elitist, regardless of law, intolerant of individualism, and of culture except that which subserves the state or can be so construed. The term has no doubt remained in the political vocabulary because political institutions, of whatever professed persuasion, often tend to manifest some of these characteristics. The technocratic totalitarianism that is one of the futurological scenarios envisaged at the present time has been called a kind of 'friendly fascism'.

Feedback

As a control strategy in mechanical or physical systems, feedback is the governing of a system's input by its output by means of a return process, which may involve energy or information. A system specified for a particular function and requiring an appropriate input to accomplish it efficiently, may be subject to disturbances from without or functional fluctuations within, and in order to adjust its input to compensate for these it requires feedback from its end state. A distinction is made between positive feedback, which increases input, and negative feedback, which decreases it. An efficient feedback loop in a system has the effect of decreasing the system's ENTROPY[2].

See also CYBERNETICS, BIO-FEEDBACK[6]. [337, 353]

Feminism

A broad term which covers a diversity of attitudes to women's rights, roles and endowments and to how they are fulfilled or frustrated in social and domestic institutions. Predominantly, feminism advocates, and with varying degrees of militancy seeks to bring about, women's social, economic and political equality with men. Its first polemic, Mary Wollstonecraft's* *A Vindication of the Rights of Women*, was published in 1792, and the fact that after two centuries it is still active only demonstrates how deeply entrenched in institutions and attitudes male dominance is. There have, however, been some notable triumphs, from the achievement of women's suffrage after the First World War to the passing of the Equal Rights Amendment in the US in 1972 and the Sex Discrimination Act in England in 1975.

The 1960s and 1970s saw a dramatic increase in feminist activism and militancy and the formation of women's liberation movements in many countries. Awareness of the extent to which women had been socially, politically and psychologically oppressed and manipulated was greatly heightened and extended by such books as Betty Friedan's *The Feminine Mystique* (1965), Kate Millett's *Sexual Politics* (1970) and Germaine Greer's *The Female Eunuch* (1971). In their zeal some members of the women's movements went further than the majority of its supporters would have wished in combating male dominance on its own terms and at the cost of compromising

their femininity, and Arianna Stassinopoulos's *The Female Woman* (1974) was an attempt to redress this balance. One might distinguish within feminism two distinct trends, the first predominantly activist and political and the second psychological and consciousness-raising. Both have contributed to making women today more 'liberated' than they were two decades ago. But along with other promising countercultural developments of the 1970s the movement has recently lost its momentum and suffered a backlash from the established order, which is regarded by many feminists today as having made concessions rather than fundamental changes, particularly by co-opting women to positions of power and influence where they are constrained to function more as honorary men than as individuals endowed with different aptitudes, values and priorities. [100, 118, 214, 219, 309]

Food chain

Life feeds on life, and any series of organisms that in turn feed upon each other constitute a food chain. All food chains originate in and are sustained by plants, which by photosynthesis create glucose from solar energy. Herbivores feed on plants and themselves furnish food for carnivores. When the latter die they are fed upon by carrion eaters and insect larvae, and eventually broken down by bacteria into inorganic substances which, returned to the soil, become plant food, and so the cycle goes on. Specific food chains, however, are highly vulnerable, for they are chains of life

Futurology

dependence, and if one component becomes reduced or diseased, populations higher up the food chain are affected. Human activities, for instance the intensive use of chemical fertilizers, have drastically disrupted many natural food chains, resulting in the extinction of some plant and animal species.

Future shock

A term coined by the writer Alvin Toffler* in 1965 to describe 'the shattering stress and disorientation we induce in individuals by subjecting them to too much change in too short a time'. The rate of change in modern societies has so accelerated, Toffler argued, that it has got out of phase with the natural human adaptive response, so that for many people the future seems prematurely to impinge upon their lives, demanding of them adaptive behaviour of which they are incapable. The lag between the pace of environmental change and the pace of human adaptive response gives rise to both personal and social problems which cannot be solved until the future shock syndrome is recognized, and in consequence individual and social efforts are made to increase future-consciousness and promote greater adaptive flexibility. [326]

Futurology

Whether prognosis can ever be scientific is an arguable point, but certainly it can employ scientific methods, and when it does so it is sometimes called futurology. The term was coined by the German historian Ossip Flechtheim*. The

scientific procedure most commonly used is that of computer modelling or simulation, in which a complex system is analysed into a number of component factors, quantitative estimates of the strength of interactions between the factors are fed in, and the computer works out a prognosis of what will happen at a given point in the future if the same interactions continue. Interactive factors in the present global situation are population, natural resources, food supplies, pollution, technological developments, etc. Quantitative increases or decreases in any of these areas will affect the others, and the value of computer simulation is that it can specify these interaction effects fairly precisely. This does not mean, of course, that it can predict the future. It can only model *a* future based on the variables and assessments that are put into it. The introduction of another variable or an alternative estimate may alter the scenario fundamentally. If futurology therefore cannot be a precise predictive science, what it can do is draw attention to outcomes that may be expected if prevailing trends persist, and facilitate the testing of the effects of changes that may be deliberately made to circumvent such outcomes. These effects may be 'counter-intuitive', i.e. quite different from those foreseen when the change was introduced.

Exercises in futurology tend to be pessimistic or cautionary. Probably the best known are the Hudson Institute's *The Year 2000* (Kahn and Wiener, 1967) and the Club of Rome's *The Limits to*

Growth (1972). The latter, the first of a series of Project Reports on 'The Predicament of Mankind', had a profound influence worldwide, drawing attention to the ultimate disastrous consequences of an economic growth ethic and the need to establish and observe limits that would enable the world to attain a steady state of economic and ecological equilibrium. It concluded that the attainment of this would require 'a Copernican revolution of the mind', and other futurological studies have also come to the conclusion that prevailing trends are so intractable that no strategies of change are going to reverse them unless they arise out of a radical change in human consciousness, specifically in values, goals and priorities. [90, 162, 212]

Gaia hypothesis

Gaia was the earth-goddess of ancient Greek religion. In his book *Gaia: a New Look at Life on Earth* (1979), the British chemist James Lovelock* puts forward evidence for the hypothesis that the planet earth has the characteristics of a living system or organism. The hypothesis was informed by, and is a contribution to, GENERAL SYSTEMS THEORY[1]. It also contributed significantly to the spread of ecological awareness.

Lovelock cites many examples of planetary homeostatic processes as evidence for his hypothesis. These are the processes which ensure the stability and constancy of the necessary conditions of life. For instance, the concentration of oxygen in the atmosphere is stabilized at 21 per cent, the planet's surface temperature at between $15°$ and $35\ °C$, and the ozone layer of the upper atmosphere and the ammonia content of the lower atmosphere at the levels necessary for the survival of life. Any significant deviation from these norms would jeopardize or destroy life on earth, and for life to have evolved the levels must have remained constant over aeons. The homeostatic processes involved in this planet-maintenance are so many and so various, and the requirements they serve are so precise and inflexible, that only a 'whole earth' organismic concept can explain the phenomenon − unless you want to invoke a Divinity overseeing his creation. According to this view, the earth is an aggregate of self-modifying sub-systems which collectively constitute, and individually are determined by the needs of, the total planetary system. The earth itself is a living entity, endowed with the resilience, adaptability and self-maintaining capacities of all living things. But these capacities are not infinite or inexhaustible, and it is possible − as again with all living things − for one of its sub-systems to malfunction in such a manner as to subvert the integrity or even jeopardize the continued existence of the whole. It is arguable that some human enterprises, such as the destruction of the equatorial rain forest, constitute such a malfunction. [196]

Gene pool

Every species of plant and animal has a diversity of genetic material that guarantees the production of

Geothermal energy

an immense variety of individual variations. This is the gene pool of the species. A rich gene pool is valuable to a species because it enables it to adapt to different environmental conditions and thus to survive, and because species are interdependent the maintenance of diversity in a particular species will benefit others and the loss of it will likewise disadvantage them. Man has drawn upon natural gene pools to develop many medicines and drugs, to enhance crop yields and disease resistance, and to extend animal and fish farming capacities. Other and greater advantages could accrue in the future from the exploitation of natural gene pools, but with the destruction of habitats and environments such as the equatorial rain forest and the great lakes of Africa, the world's wild gene pools are becoming steadily depleted. [39]

Genetic engineering

Many molecular biologists working in the field deplore the term 'genetic engineering' and are highly sensitive to the accusation that they are 'playing God' when they explore and develop the potentials of RECOMBINANT DNA technology. The synthesis of genetic material designed to perform specific functions may be an achievement that raises the spectre of the 'mad scientist' of fiction sinisterly exploiting a powerful technology, and the ability of science to manipulate life processes at the most fundamental level does raise serious ethical questions, but on the other hand genetic engineering has already to its credit significant

achievements, and is currently embarked upon research that promises others, which are unequivocally beneficial. For medical science it has accomplished the synthesis of insulin, of the human growth hormone, and of interferon – a substance with potential applications to immunology and cancer therapy; and current research looks forward to the development of techniques capable of identifying and correcting genetic defects responsible for such heritable diseases as sickle-cell anaemia. Benefits for agriculture and for industry have also been achieved, and others are in prospect, which promise positive solutions to problems that have long seemed intractable (see BIOTECHNOLOGY). [82, 266]

Geothermal energy

Beneath the earth's surface, temperature increases by about 1 °C every thirty metres on average, and more in volcanically active areas. At present there are some 200 installations worldwide that exploit this energy resource to produce electricity, and many more that draw hot water from subterranean sources. In the Philippines more than 20 per cent of the country's electricity needs are supplied by geothermal generating capacity, and Mexico and Indonesia also derive a significant proportion of their requirements from this source. In the US a large installation in northern California had a 1,300 megawatt output (about 700 million kilowatt hours) in 1985. In the future geothermal energy is expected to make a significant contribution to meeting energy needs in appropriate locations. [39]

Greenhouse effect

Although the earth's atmosphere contains only about 0.03 per cent of carbon dioxide, the gas plays an important part in determining the planet's climate, and a significant increase in it would bring about climatic changes. By absorbing both solar energy and the long-wave energy that the earth itself radiates, carbon dioxide warms the planet's surface. Over the last century the combustion of fossil fuels has increased the proportion of atmospheric carbon dioxide by some 30 per cent, and if prevailing trends continue the present level could double in the next century. The resultant 'greenhouse effect' on the planet's surface would change rainfall patterns to bring fertility to some areas that are desert now, but at the same time drought to currently fertile areas, for instance the North American grain belt. It could also affect sea levels by melting the polar ice sheets, which could result in devastating flooding of the earth's low-lying land areas. However, present trends are not likely to continue, as fossil fuel resources are diminishing and ALTERNATIVE ENERGY sources, including NUCLEAR POWER, will increasingly be exploited. A problem for environmentalists is that they cannot be simultaneously alarmist about the greenhouse effect and about the dangers of nuclear power, for if the effect does threaten to raise the earth's surface temperature significantly, the only way to avert catastrophe will be to increase nuclear energy production. [4]

Greens

A political movement that has gathered impetus and influence throughout the 1980s, campaigning for protection of the environment, a priority shift from growth, to sustainability in social economics, the implementation of alternatives to ecologically damaging industrial and agricultural practices, and responsibility towards future generations. The Green Movement has achieved its most notable successes in Germany, where a system of proportional representation resulted in the election of 28 members to the Bundestag in 1983. Aurelio Peccei* has described the Greens as 'a kind of popular army, with a function comparable to that of the antibodies generated to restore normal conditions in a diseased biological organism'. A distinction is sometimes made between 'light greens' and 'dark greens', the former being gradualists and reformers and the latter radicals and revolutionaries. Although the Green or Ecological parties may not have much chance of exercising direct political power, particularly in countries where non-proportional electoral systems prevail, their policies clearly have an increasing popular appeal which governments have begun to acknowledge as a factor that it would be politically imprudent to discount. [249, 306]

Hardware/software

Terms used in the context of COMPUTER technology to distinguish

Information theory

between the material entity of the machine itself on the one hand, and on the other the instructional programs that it processes. The terms are sometimes used analogically to apply to any system that comprises distinguishable physical and non-physical components, and are useful in specifying different levels of description. Just as a computer operation may be described in terms of what is going on respectively at the hardware and the software level, so a mental operation, for instance, may be described in terms of the neurophysiological activity of the brain or alternatively in terms of the programming and organizing activity of the mind, and a logical distinction between the two entities can be established, although whether the analogy can be extended to afford a basis for maintaining their potential separateness and independence is a moot point.

Hydroponics
A method of producing crops in artificial conditions, using a base of sand instead of soil, and water containing appropriate nutrients. High yields can be achieved by hydroponic cultivation, and the technique may be more widely applied in the future than it is today, when costs tend to be prohibitive except for luxury produce.

Hydropower
About a quarter of the world's electricity is provided by hydropower, which uses falling water to turn turbines. When natural water courses and waterfalls are exploited, hydropower is an ecologically benign resource, but when large dams and reservoirs are constructed a host of potential problems arise. Not only are such facilities hugely capital intensive, but the flooding of large areas of land can create unforeseen geological and ecological disasters. Artificial lakes tend to silt up, and farmland downriver from them becomes impoverished and increasingly reliant on expensive artificial fertilizers, and in the tropics the lakes afford habitats for the profuse breeding of organisms inimical to human health. Despite these problems and dangers, many new large dams are under construction and are being planned throughout the world, a majority of them in THIRD WORLD countries.

Another source of hydropower which could contribute significantly to meeting future energy demands, and that does not have the disadvantages of large dams, is the harnessing of tidal power. This can be done in river estuaries by constructing a barrier which lets incoming tidal water through and holds it until the water behind the barrier is higher than that in front, then uses the ebb tide to release water, which turns turbines as it leaves. It has been estimated that 20 per cent of Britain's energy needs could be met by six such hydropower installations, which would be expensive to construct but subsequently relatively cheap to operate. [4, 39]

Information theory
Information theory is concerned with specifying means of measuring information and the processes

involved in its transmission or communication (it is alternatively known as 'communication theory'). Its principles were developed chiefly by C. E. Shannon* and have since been widely applied in the development of computer technology, and have also proved useful to neurologists and psychologists.

A communication system comprises an output at the transmission end, a channel through which the signal is conveyed, and a means of receiving and reproducing the original output. In some systems, such as TV and telephones, the signal has to reconstruct the output at the receiving end. Less complex systems, however, can work on the principle of encoding and decoding the output, which requires the signal to convey not the output in its entirety but only instructions to select information already stored at the receiving end and available for reproduction. The simplest example of this is the teleprinter, in which the signal serially specifies a selection from the letters of the alphabet. In selective communication systems, the complexity and magnitude of the information output does not matter, provided only that it can be efficiently encoded. The method proposed by Shannon, and employed in modern digital computers, involves the binary scale method of writing numbers, which employs only the digits 0 and 1. If an information bank is divided into two, then into two again, and so on, very few operations are required to specify a particular item. A selective operation in which one out of two possibilities has to be identified is said to have a 'selective information content' of one 'bit' (contraction of 'binary digit'); two 'bits' are required for one out of four, three for one out of eight, etc. The method facilitates rapid and economical specification from a large store of information content, particularly with computers, which have a 'bit rate' of thousands of operations a second.

'Redundancy' is a key concept in information theory. It is the principle of employing more symbols than necessary to guard against the possibility of the corruption of the message by extraneous 'noise' or its misperception by the recipient. For instance, 'nineteen eighty sim' has more redundancy than 198X, and consequently the error can be more easily corrected. The more redundancy there is built into an information system, the more efficient, and tolerant of random error, it will be. It has been suggested that the human brain, which sustains continual cell-loss and -damage without correlated diminution of efficiency, is a supreme example of an information system with a high degree of built-in redundancy. [293, 337]

Interface

The area where two related systems or pieces of equipment are conjoined. Originally used exclusively in the context of electronics, the term has recently been more widely applied, for instance to the areas of communication and interaction between racial or social groups or academic disciplines.

Intermediate technology

In developing countries, the idea of APPROPRIATE TECHNOLOGY is sometimes vehemently rejected. Its critics see condescension in the developed countries' advocacy of it, and suspect a neo-colonial conspiracy to delay their development and prolong their economic dependence. The term 'intermediate technology' is therefore preferred as less loaded and more diplomatic to describe technologies that are small-scale, minimally capital- and energy-intensive but maximally labour-intensive.

Matriarchy

The socio-political ills engendered by PATRIARCHY have become increasingly manifest in the modern world, and some historians and anthropologists have proposed that there existed an antecedent matriarchal order of society. The Swiss anthropologist J. J. Bachofen* developed the idea in the nineteenth century, though in the context of an evolutionary theory which regarded the shift to patriarchy as an advance. Although modified matriarchal societies have been found among present-day primitive peoples, no entirely female-dominated society has been observed, and the historical existence of such is highly doubtful. There is, however, cultural evidence that female values and female influence were stronger and more balanced with their male counterparts in the ancient world. The *Oresteia* of the Greek dramatist Aeschylus has been interpreted as dramatizing a transition to patriarchal dominance, and Robert Graves's study *The White Goddess* demonstrated that the ancient religions of the Western world were less male-oriented than the later Judaeo-Christian and Mohammedan faiths. [264]

Military-industrial complex

A vested-interest cabal, presumed to have powers inaccessible to democratic restriction or control, and concerned on the one hand to maximize the profits of large technological industrial corporations and on the other to maintain high public expenditure on defence budgets. Subsequent US presidents have had reason to regret the coinage, by their predecessor President Eisenhower, of a term so useful to radical polemicists.

Multinationals

Alternatively, Transnationals: large business corporations which operate worldwide and control assets which in some cases exceed those of nations. Their rise to international power has been so rapid that no legislative framework has been developed to govern their activities. They have been able to maximize their profits by minimizing their taxation liabilities through their transnational channels for the movement of funds, and thus have grown to be virtually a law unto themselves, able to influence governments, legislative bodies and the media to their own advantage. Since multinationals are so large that no one may be held accountable for their excesses, and since the maximizing of corporate growth and profit has from their inception been their only purpose, their conduct in the world has tended to be exploitative and irresponsible. In the underdeveloped countries of the world they have exploited natural resources and cheap labour, marketed inappropriate and socially disruptive technologies, manipulated the creation of spurious needs in order to profit by catering to them, and often brought about environmental catastrophes. The need for an external agency to govern the activities of these corporate giants is pressing, but its instrumentation poses formidable problems, particularly since governments are on the whole creatures of the same ilk. [54]

Non-violence
A strategy of resistance to military occupation of a country or political oppression of a minority designed to mobilize opinion and external political pressure against the occupying or oppressive power. Combined with a policy of civil disobedience, it was first effectively practised by Mahatma Gandhi* and his followers against the British occupation of India, which largely as a result of the strategy was terminated in 1947. The Czech resistance to the Russian invasion of their country in 1968 employed the same tactics, but despite global publicity was ultimately ineffective. It has been objected that the strategy constitutes provocation and exacerbates the violent response of the oppressor, but as its purpose is to draw attention to this response the objection is more an ethical cavil than a persuasive argument against it.

Nuclear family
The two-generation family unit comprising husband, wife and children, as distinct from the extended family which embraces three or four generations and a greater breadth of familial involvements and interaction. Many of the social ills of modern industrial societies have been blamed on the nuclear family, among them delinquency, high divorce rates, and neglect of the elderly, and in these respects THIRD WORLD countries are sometimes considered to be exemplary because of the predominance in them of extended family structures.

Nuclear power
In the early 1970s it was anticipated that by the year 2000 half of the world's electricity would be produced by nuclear power. It now looks as if considerably less will be so produced, although some European countries, France, Belgium, Sweden and Finland in particular, already get about half their electricity from it. Nuclear energy programmes have been slowed down or put under moratoria in many countries for several reasons. First, they proved more expensive than anticipated; second, energy demand is proving less than originally projected, largely because industrial and domestic consumers have learnt to conserve energy more efficiently; and third, awareness of the environmental risks involved, particularly after the disaster of Chernobyl in the USSR in 1986, has diminished enthusiasm for the nuclear panacea both with the public and with most

governments. However, even if the problem of the ENERGY CRISIS has been exaggerated, it is doubtful whether ALTERNATIVE ENERGY sources will be adequate to meet future world energy demands, and as resources of fossil fuels are diminishing and anyway their consumption is a major cause of atmospheric pollution (see ACID RAIN, GREENHOUSE EFFECT), in the long term the moratoria will probably have to be lifted, as indeed they have recently been in some countries (Britain and China, for instance, are pressing ahead with expansion programmes). The pros and cons of the issue are complex, but one near-certainty is that nuclear power is with us to stay, even if – as appears likely –. alternative energy technologies prove capable of contributing more substantially to future energy requirements than most present projections allow. It is true that the planet's reserves of FISSION[2] fuels, uranium and thorium, are limited, but current research on developing FUSION[2] reactors, which will be fuelled by sea water, is expected to result in such reactors being operative in the twenty-first century, when the most desirable solution to the energy problem will be to have mixed-energy economies, maximally exploiting local renewable resources and supplementing their yield as minimally as possible with nuclear power. [4, 248]

Nuclear waste

The generation of electricity by NUCLEAR POWER results in the production of waste materials that are radioactive and therefore en-

vironmentally dangerous. There have been incidents in which land and water in the vicinity of nuclear power stations have been contaminated by nuclear wastes as a result of their accidental leakage, and consequently the issue is a highly emotive one. The fact that some wastes remain radioactive for millions of years is widely canvassed by the anti-nuclear power lobby, although scientists point out that the proportions with such longevity are extremely small and argue that after 1,000 years, mixed with other wastes, they will be relatively harmless, and anyway can be safely contained and stored. At present wastes are stored in liquid form, but technologies have been developed to convert liquid wastes to a rock-like substance, called synrock, which will be less susceptible to radioactive leakage. [248]

Overpopulation

The statistics of world population growth are staggering, and have led some futurologists to foresee the 'demographic doom' of mankind in the twenty-first century through consequential famine, competition for dwindling space and resources leading to war, the incidence of epidemic disease in high density populations, and general social breakdown.

The world population tripled, from 1.2 billion to 3.6 billion, between 1870 and 1970. It is estimated that it will reach between 7 and 8 billion by the year 2000, and between 9 and 10 billion by 2020. At present two-thirds of the world's population live in areas already overpopulated and underdeveloped, and the doubling rate of these populations is between 20 and 35 years, whereas the doubling rate in developed countries has slowed down to between 50 and 200 years. Dire predictions seem well founded. Humanitarian aid does not appear to be the answer, for it only temporarily alleviates local conditions, and in the long run even aggravates the situation it was intended to ameliorate. Nor is what has been seriously – and sinisterly – called 'human engineering', i.e. the attempt to abate population growths in Third World countries by implementing 'family planning programmes' which are technologically conceived. The only proven way in which population growth rates decline is as a result of social changes which give existing populations relative affluence and stability. The world could physically support even double its present population, but if an equilibrium state is to be accomplished it must be through the implementation of global policies designed not only to distribute resources and production equitably, but also to tackle the problems of social and economic inequalities, both between nations and within nations, which are the fundamental cause of accelerating population growth. [39, 200]

Ozone layer
In the upper stratosphere there is a thin layer of ozone which serves as a shield from the sun's ultraviolet radiation. Over recent decades this layer has become depleted, particularly over the polar ice caps, and if this process continues it could result in disastrous climatic effects and a significant increase in the occurrence of skin cancers and other ailments. Ozone is dissipated by chlorofluoromethanes, the gases released by aerosols and to a lesser extent by refrigerators and air conditioners. In the US the use of these gases is now banned, and the UN is seeking to extend such legislation worldwide. There is good reason to hope that in this instance an ecological disaster may be averted by a timely galvanizing of public and political awareness. It is also to be hoped that it will establish a precedent. [4, 120]

Patriarchy
The ramifications of male dominance have in recent years come under intense scrutiny and attack, resulting in an increased public awareness of their extent and some modification of their power. It has been widely recognized that male dominance in religion, in social and economic institutions, in philosophical and psychological thinking, has created an imbalance that is not only inequitable but also potentially destructive. Human societies and cultures throughout the world have been patriarchic for at least 3,000 years, and the principles by which they are governed and the ideas with which they are imbued pay scant regard to female modes of being and thinking. Competitiveness, the consolidation of power, the pursuit of status, the assumption of and respect for authority, the exercise of rights conferred by power, hierarchical systems of social organization and con-

Pollution

trol, are characteristics of patriarchal behaviour that have determined the conduct and aims of institutionalized religion, law, business, technology, and even medicine, often with disastrous effects. FEMINISM and the women's movement of recent years have drawn attention to these effects, and in many areas today patriarchy appears to be in decline and an awareness of counterbalancing feminine values and purposes to be ascendant. [109, 264]

Pollution

Arguably the most important area where global strategies and co-operation are needed today is that of control of pollution of the planet's atmosphere, land and waters. The waste- or by-products of industrial processes, the chemicals used agriculturally as pesticides or fertilizers, the organic and inorganic waste produced by dense human populations, constitute the main categories of contaminant that directly affect the environment. Other categories, such as noise and electropollution, are also sometimes considered as matters of urgent concern.

Natural systems generally have an inbuilt tolerance of a certain amount of contamination, and strategies for getting rid of or converting it. But the tolerance levels and conversion capacities of many natural systems have been grossly overloaded in recent decades as a result of human activities. A degree of pollution no doubt has to be accepted as part of the cost of living in a densely populated advanced industrial society, but to

minimize it is both a practical and an ethical imperative which should have priority over motives of profit or convenience, which regrettably for too long it did not have. An example of what can be achieved is the international co-operation on the cleaning up of the Mediterranean, initiated by the Mediterranean Action Plan of 1975, which has averted a major ecological disaster in the world's greatest enclosed sea. There has also been some progress in controlling atmospheric pollution with emissions from industrial plants and motor cars, although the problem of ACID RAIN remains pressing.

Chemical pollution of the land and its products is the most urgent global problem, and in this respect both the developed nations and some of the great MULTINATIONALS are guilty of exploitative conduct towards the THIRD WORLD that is both morally indefensible and short-sighted. Toxic pesticides whose domestic use is banned or severely restricted are commonly exported to undeveloped countries, where they contaminate the cash crops that those countries export back to the developed world. The bioamplification of such pollutants, whereby they become increasingly concentrated as they pass up the FOOD CHAIN, is a danger that has only recently been realized.

At present the harmful effects of electropollution are not widely recognized or actively mitigated, but evidence is accumulating that exposure to high electromagnetic frequencies increases susceptibility to leukaemia, cancer, headaches and fatigue, and that low frequencies affect brain-waves and behaviour and induce depression. [47, 240, 338]

Post-industrialism

The industrial revolutions of the nineteenth century created social structures and institutions, and were supported by rationales and value-systems, that in the late twentieth century are becoming obsolete or inappropriate. Observers who have inferred from this fact that we are witnessing in our time a transition to a post-industrial society tend to have widely divergent views of the principles that will govern the change and the new order. The sociologist Daniel Bell*, who coined the term, foresaw a change from a goods-producing to a service economy, a dominance of technology in many aspects of life, culture and decision-making, and the rise to pre-eminence of a professional intellectual technocracy. Other writers have foreseen that the obsolescence of the social structures and the ethos of industrialism will afford an opportunity for the emergence of a less materialistic and economic-growth-oriented, more spiritual, environmentally and globally aware consciousness and work- and culture-orientation. There are observable trends towards both of these alternative post-industrial social scenarios, though which will prevail remains a contentious question of FUTUROLOGY. [18, 276]

Rain forest

Extending about 10° each side of the equator, a band of dense forest stretches around the earth, most of which receives heavy rainfall and is therefore known as the tropical rain forest. This forest is a precious planetary resource, both as a GENE POOL that harbours at least 40 per cent of the earth's plant and animal species, and as a global climate regulator. Today it is being steadily destroyed for the commercial exploitation of its timber, leaving low-grade scrub land where it formerly flourished, and if such exploitation continues unabated mankind will not only lose a genetic resource of incalculable potential value, but will also suffer the consequences of disastrous climatic disruption.

Recombinant DNA

Techniques employing enzymes were developed by molecular biologists in the late 1970s and early 1980s to enable them to slice the DNA^2 molecule in order to isolate specific genetic components. When further techniques were perfected that enabled these genes to be implanted in bacterial cells, and biological molecules with specific characteristics to be synthesized, what became known as recombinant DNA technology was born. Initial fears that science had acquired a sinister ability to produce, whether deliberately or involuntarily, the monster mutants or virulent viruses of science fiction, were no doubt exaggerated, but the potentials of the new technology are certainly as awesome as they are exciting.

See also GENETIC ENGINEERING, BIOTECHNOLOGY. [82, 266]

Recycling

The re-use of spent or degraded material is a prominent feature in the efficient functioning of natural ECOSYSTEMS, but human activities, particularly in areas of dense population, produce a steady and substantial output of detritus of once-used material that ends up as waste. Much of this waste derives from non-renewable planetary resources, and the realization that these resources are finite and that so prodigal an exploitation of them is both irresponsible and unnecessary, has led in recent years to the development of methods of reclaiming and recycling some of them, in particular paper, glass, iron and aluminium. The processes can be, and no doubt eventually will have to be, more widely and efficiently operated, and it is to be expected that in the future BIO-TECHNOLOGY will contribute new methods for recycling organic waste.

Science fiction

The term embraces a range of fictive subjects, conventions and strategies which depart from present-world realism and constitute a sub-genre of fantasy fiction. Though SF writers often appropriate or make play with scientific ideas (e.g. Samuel R. Delany, *The Einstein Intersection*), or extrapolate speculative future scenarios from scientific or technological developments (Aldous Huxley, *Brave New World*; Ursula LeGuin *The Left Hand of Darkness*), or employ, seriously or satirically, scientific rationales or devices to lend credence to a fantasy (H. G. Wells,

The Time Machine; Kurt Vonnegut, *The Sirens of Titan*), neither these strategies nor any ostensible scientific content constitutes qualifying conditions of the genre. Utopian and dystopian fictions, which use fictive models of human societies, or of a postulated human nature, as teaching or testing devices (Anthony Burgess, *The Wanting Seed*; B. F. Skinner, *Walden Two*; Aldous Huxley, *Island*), are generally categorized as science fiction. So are philosophical fables (Olaf Stapledon, *Star Maker*), theological romances (C. S. Lewis, the '*Narnia*' books), and philosophico-anthropological analogies (Ian Watson, *The Embedding*). Contemporary science fiction is a sophisticated literature which blends with post-realist and post-modern literature in employing fictive strategies of 'defamiliarization' to render novel perspectives upon the world and its potentials.

Sexism

A discriminative attitude towards others which discounts any considerations of intrinsic worth or character and judges capabilities or assigns roles solely on a basis of gender. It is primarily an attitude manifested by the male sex towards the female, and based upon assumptions of superiority that are generally unconscious or at least unconfessed. FEMINIST critiques of sexism have been so successful that today few males would have the temerity to flaunt the attitude publicly, although it clearly continues to flourish in domestic circumstances as well as in many institutions and professions.

Solar energy

The diffuse energy that radiates from the sun on to the earth's surface has been estimated as equivalent to the output of 173 million large power stations. Clearly, the planet's energy problems could be solved once and for all if efficient technologies could be developed to exploit this benign resource. And they do exist, though as yet in fairly primitive forms. The solar cell, which produces electricity from sunlight, has been used to power calculators and instruments on spacecraft, and solar panels have been installed on buildings to contribute to their energy requirements. The construction of solar power stations presents formidable engineering problems, but with appropriate investment in research and development they could become a reality in the next century. An interesting alternative has been proposed in the form of satellite islands that would convert solar energy in space and beam it down to earth in microwaves which a receiving station could in turn convert to electrical power. [39]

Spaceship Earth

A term coined by R. Buckminster Fuller* to convey his vision of global unity and the challenges its realization poses at the present time. 'Humans are swiftly coming to understand', he wrote in *Earth, Inc.*, 'that they must now consciously begin to operate their space vehicle Earth with total planetary co-operation, competence and integrity.' To operate 'space vehicle Earth' in this way requires technological skills at least as sophisticated as those deployed in the US and Russian space programmes: skills based upon an understanding of the interrelatedness and interdependence of the many sub-systems that make up the larger system of the planet. Our awareness of our environment, Fuller maintained, should be such that we are continually reminded of the fact that 'all of us are, always have been, and so long as we exist always will be, nothing but astronauts ... aboard a space vehicle that is not going to get any new equipment yet could be operated successfully for all'. [101]

Syndicalism

A form of extreme revolutionary socialism which developed in France in the late nineteenth century. It sought the destruction of capitalism, but rejected political means of bringing it about, preferring policies of sabotage and violence. It rejected, too, the very concept of the state, and advocated a near-anarchist idea of a loose federation of autonomous co-operative units. It had a following in Europe and the US up to the First World War, but little influence thereafter except briefly in Spain in the 1930s.

Technology transfer

The transfer of technological capability from developed to developing countries is necessary and inevitable, but it is fraught with problems, chiefly because MULTINATIONALS are responsible for something like 90 per cent of the business. So long as the sale or lease of technology is governed by the multinationals' profit-orientation, and is hedged with restrictive conditions designed to maximize their profits, and pays scant regard to the appropriateness of the technology to the economic and social conditions of the country acquiring it, technology transfer will remain an issue that focuses the ethical ambivalence of relations between the developed and the developing world. The UN has drawn up a Code of Conduct for technology transfer, but the prospects of its being effectively implemented and enforced are not at present encouraging. [54]

Third World

A collective term for the undeveloped and developing countries of the world that are not directly affiliated to either the Communist or the capitalist 'blocs'. Most Third World countries were formerly colonies, and hold their former colonizers responsible for their present status. Poverty and rapid population expansion are intractable problems in some Third World countries, and famine and epidemic disease intermittently reach crisis proportions. Some Third World countries are more developed and richer in natural resources than others, and the ones that are not so endowed and have little potential for endogenous development are sometimes said to constitute a 'Fourth World'.

Utopianism

The imaginative projection of, or belief in, or attempt practically to establish, an ideal human society.

The word (from the Greek, meaning 'no-place') was coined by Sir Thomas More*, whose *Utopia* (1516) described what today we would call an ideal socialist republic, with common ownership of property, full but not onerous employment, garden cities, a population policy, proper education, and harmonious social relations. More was a man of the HUMAN-IST[1] Renaissance. The following century, the seventeenth, was the beginning of the scientific era, and its utopian literature, such as Francis Bacon's* *New Atlantis* and Tommaso Campanella's* *City of the Sun*, shows an enthusiasm for the contribution that science might make to the establishment of the ideal society.

In the nineteenth century utopianism became more than a speculative literary genre. In the wake of the Enlightenment belief in the perfectibility of man and society influenced social theory and practice. Early socialism was thoroughly utopian. The Scottish industrialist Robert Owen* set up at New Lanark a secular socialist utopian society for his workers. But the so-called New Harmony society foundered after two years, partly because Owen himself was in the US most of the time lecturing on utopianism. Contemporaneously, the French social theorist Charles Fourier* developed ostensibly scientific ideas about a 'natural' order that could pertain in human societies, ensuring social harmony and optimum individual life-satisfaction. His recommendation was for social units, which he called 'phalanxes', of 1,620 individuals, each 'phalanx' occupying 5,000 acres of land. Fourier's principles were put into practice, as were many other utopian communitarian schemes, in the US and Europe in the nineteenth century, but the experiments were short-lived.

In the present century, utopian idealists have been less energetic in seeking to establish the visionary commonwealth. Utopian literature has continued to flourish (H. G. Wells's *A Modern Utopia*, B. F. Skinner's *Walden Two*, Aldous Huxley's *Island*), but a new literary genre of 'dystopian' fiction (Y. Zamyatin's *We*, Huxley's *Brave New World*, George Orwell's *1984*) has expressed the disillusion and despair of writers who have witnessed a world fashioned not to the heart's desire but by the realities of unregenerate human nature and the exigencies of brutal political and economic life. [214, 228]

Voluntary simplicity
An alternative life-style to that pursued in the majority culture, consisting in a repudiation of the pursuit of affluence and of a high level of economic consumption. In the late 1970s in the US it was estimated that some five million people had embraced the principle of voluntary simplicity in their life-style and twice as many again had incorporated some elements of it. It is of course easy to mock as a species of Rousseauist idealism, and in the light of the subsequent cultural trend in which even greed has become an admissible motive

and comes close to being sanctioned as a public virtue because it fuels the production-consumption momentum of the economy, voluntary simplicity is widely regarded either with dumb incomprehension or as an ineffectual and irrelevant countercultural fad. However, the questions whether present trends will secure long-term benefits for mankind, and whether even in the short term they endow the individual life with really profound satisfactions, are debatable, and the life-style of voluntary simplicity, with its values of frugality of consumption, global and ecological awareness, and concern with personal spiritual growth and fulfilment, remains arguably at once a more socially responsible as well as a more personally satisfying alternative. [78]

Wind power
An ALTERNATIVE ENERGY resource which can be effectively exploited in appropriate locations. In 1985 in California there were several thousand commercial wind generators on 'wind farms', which produced enough electricity for more than 50,000 homes. Wind farms, however, are large and unsightly installations, and since for optimum functioning they need to be located on exposed high land, the benefit they yield as a renewable energy resource has to be balanced against a kind of environmental encroachment that would be unacceptable on a large scale. [40]

Bibliography

* Cited places and dates of publication refer to editions available to the author. In many cases other editions will also be available.

1 Adams, R. and Murray, F., *Megavitamin Therapy* (New York, 1975)

2 Adler, Alfred, *The Practice and Theory of Individual Psychology* (London and New York, 1924)

3 Alexander, F. M., *Alexander Technique: Essential Writings of F. M. Alexander* (London, 1974)

4 Allaby, Michael, *Ecology Facts* (London, 1986)

5 Arrhenius, Svente, *Worlds in the Making* (London, 1908)

6 Ashby, E., *Reconciling Man with the Environment* (Oxford, 1978)

7 Assagioli, Roberto, *Psychosynthesis* (New York, 1965)

8 Assagioli, Roberto, 'The New Dimensions of Psychology' in *Human Dimensions*, vol. 3 (New York, 1974)

9 Ayer, A. J., *Language, Truth and Logic* (London, 1936)

10 Ayer, A. J., *The Origins of Pragmatism* (London, 1968)

11 Bach, Edward, *Heal Thyself* (London, 1931)

12 Bailey, Alice, *A Treatise on Cosmic Fire* (New York, 1930)

13 Barker, J. C., 'Premonitions of the Aberfan Disaster' in *Journal of the Society for Psychical Research* (London, 1977)

14 Barlow, W., *The Alexander Principle* (London, 1973)

15 Bates, William, *Better Eyesight Without Glasses* (New York, 1971)

16 Bateson, Gregory, *Steps to an Ecology of Mind* (New York, 1972)

17 Bateson, William, *Mendel's Principles of Heredity* (Cambridge, 1902)

18 Bell, Daniel, *The Coming of Post-Industrialism* (New York, 1974)

19 Bender, Hans, 'Modern Poltergeist Research' in Beloff (ed.) *New Directions in Parapsychology* (London, 1975)

20 Benson, Herbert, 'The Relaxation Response' in White and Fadiman, *Relax* (New York, 1976)

21 Bergson, A. and Tuchak, V., *Zone Therapy* (New York, 1975)

22 Bernal, J. D., *The Origin of Life* (London, 1965)

23 Berne, Eric, *Games People Play* (London, 1970)

24 Berne, Eric, *Sex in Human Loving* (New York, 1970)

25 Berne, Eric, *Transactional Analysis in Psychology* (London, 1975)

26 Bertalanffy, Ludwig von, *General Systems Theory* (New York, 1968)

27 Bertram, Raphael, *The Thinking Computer* (San Francisco, 1976)

28 Besant, Annie, *The Ancient Wisdom* (London, 1910)

29 Binswanger, Ludwig, *Being in the World* (New York, 1963)

30 Black, S., *Mind and Body* (London, 1969)

31 Blackie, Margery G., *The Patient, Not the Cure: The Challenge of Homoeopathy* (London, 1975)

32 Blavatsky, Helena, *The Secret Doctrine* (Los Angeles, 1947)

33 Blavatsky, Helena, *Isis Unveiled* (Pasadena, California, 1972)

34 Bohm, David, *Wholeness and the Implicate Order* (London, 1980)

35 Bohr, Niels, *Atomic Physics and Human Knowledge* (New York, 1958)

36 De Bono, Edward, *Lateral Thinking* (London and New York, 1970)

37 Brazier, Mary, *A History of the Electrical Activity of the Brain* (London, 1961)

38 Brown, Barbara, *New Mind, New Body* (New York, 1963)

39 Brown, Lester R., *State of the World, 1985* (New York, 1985)

40 Brown, Phil, *Radical Psychology* (London, 1973)

41 Bucke, R. M., *Cosmic Consciousness* (New York, 1901)

42 Burr, Harold Saxton, *Blueprint for Immortality* (London, 1972)

43 Campbell, K., *Mind and Body* (London, 1970)

44 Capra, Fritjof, *The Tao of Physics* (Berkeley, California, 1975)

45 Capra, Fritjof, *The Turning Point* (London, 1982)

46 Carlson, R. J. (ed.), *Frontiers of Science and Medicine* (London, 1975)

47 Carson, Rachel, *Silent Spring* (London, 1965)

48 Chancellor, P., *Handbook of the Bach Flower Remedies* (London, 1971)

49 Chapman, George, *Extraordinary Encounters* (Aylesbury, 1973)

50 Chapman, J. B., *Dr Schüssler's Biochemistry* (Wellingborough, 1973)

51 De Chardin, Teilhard, *The Phenomenon of Man* (London, 1959)

52 Chew, Geoffrey, '"Bootstrap": A Scientific Idea?' in *Science*, 23.5.68

53 Chisholm, A., *Philosophers of the Earth* (London, 1972)

54 Clarke, Robin, *Science and Technology in World Development* (Oxford and New York, 1985)

55 Clarke, Robin (ed.), *More than Enough: An Optimistic Assessment of World Energy* (Paris, 1982)

56 Cohn, Norman, *The Pursuit of the Millennium* (New York, 1961)

57 Commoner, Barry, *The Closing Circle: Confronting the Environmental Crisis* (London and New York, 1972)

58 Conway, David, *The Magic of Herbs* (New York, 1977)

59 Crick, Francis, *Life Itself* (London, 1981)

60 Crookall, Robert, *The Supreme Adventure* (Edinburgh, 1961)

61 Darwin, Charles, *The Origin of Species* (London, 1859)

62 Darwin, Charles, *The Descent of Man* (London, 1871)

63 Davies, Paul, *God and the New Physics* (London and New York, 1982)

64 Davies, Paul, *Superforce* (London and New York, 1984)

65 Dawkins, Richard, *The Selfish Gene* (Oxford and New York, 1976)

66 Dawkins, Richard, *The Blind Watchmaker* (London and New York, 1986)

67 Dickson, David, *Alternative Technology* (London, 1974)

68 Dinterfass, J., *Chiropractic: A Modern Way to Health* (New York, 1970)

69 Dossey, Larry, *Space, Time and Medicine* (Boulder, Colorado, 1982)

70 Doyle, Arthur Conan, *A History of Spiritualism* (London, 1926)

71 Driesch, H., *History and Theory of Vitalism* (London, 1914)

72 Dubrov, Alexander P., 'Biogravitation and Psychotronics' in *Impact of Science on Society*, vol. XXIV, no. 4 (Paris, 1974)

73 Dychtwald, Ken, *Bodymind* (New York, 1977; London, 1978)

74 Eagle, Robert, *Alternative Medicine* (London, 1975)

75 Eccles, John and Popper, Karl, *The Self and Its Brain* (Berlin, 1977)

76 Edmunds, S., *Hypnotism and Psychic Phenomena* (Los Angeles, 1961)

77 Einstein, Albert, *et al.*, *The Principle of Relativity* (New York, 1923)

78 Elgin, Duane, *Voluntary Simplicity* (New York, 1981)

79 Eliade, Mircea, *Myths, Dreams and Mysteries* (London, 1960)

80 Eliade, Mircea, *Shamanism* (Princeton, 1964)

81 Eliade, Mircea, *Yoga, Immortality and Freedom* (Princeton, 1970)

82 Esbjornson, R. (ed.), *The Manipulation of Life* (San Francisco, 1984)

83 Evan-Wentz, W. Y., *The Tibetan Book of the Dead* (New York, 1973)

84 Evans, Christopher, *Cults of Un-reason* (London and New York, 1973)

85 Evans, Christopher, 'Computers and Artificial Intelligence' in George, F. (ed.) *Science Fact* (London, 1977)

86 Fast, Julius, *Body Language* (New York, 1976)

87 Feinberg, Gerald, 'Precognition, A Memory of Things Future' in *Quantum Physics and Parapsychology* (New York, 1975)

88 Ferguson, Marilyn, *The Aquarian Conspiracy* (Los Angeles, 1980)

89 Festinger, L., *A Theory of Cognitive Dissonance* (New York, 1962)

90 Flechtheim, Ossip, *History and Futurology* (London and New York, 1967)

91 Fortune, Dion, *The Mystical Qabalah* (London, 1970)

92 Foucault, Michel, *Madness and Civilization* (New York, 1965)

93 Frankl, Victor, *Man's Search for Meaning: An Introduction to Logotherapy* (New York, 1974)

94 Freud, Sigmund, *The Interpretation of Dreams* (1900), standard edn, vols 4 & 5 (London, 1953)

95 Freud, Sigmund, *The Psychopathology of Everyday Life* (1904), standard edn, vol. 6 (London, 1960)

96 Freud, Sigmund, *Beyond the Pleasure Principle* (1922), standard edn, vol. 18 (London, 1955)

97 Freud, Sigmund, *The Ego and the Id* (1923), standard edn, vol. 19 (London, 1961)

98 Freud, Sigmund, *Civilization and*

its Discontents (1930), standard edn, vol. 21 (London, 1961)

99 Freud, Sigmund, *New Introductory Lectures on Psychoanalysis* (1933), standard edn, vol. 22 (London, 1964)

100 Friedan, Betty, *The Feminine Mystique* (New York, 1963; London, 1965)

101 Fuller, R. Buckminster, *Earth, Inc.* (New York, 1947)

102 Fung, Yu-Lan, *A Short History of Chinese Philosophy* (London and New York, 1958)

103 Gallwey, Timothy, *The Inner Game of Tennis* (London, 1975)

104 Gamow, George, *Thirty Years that Shook Physics* (New York, 1966)

105 Garrison, Omar, *Tantra: The Yoga of Sex* (New York, 1974)

106 Gauquelin, Michel, *Cosmic Influences on Human Behaviour* (London, 1966)

107 Gauquelin, Michel, *The Cosmic Clocks* (Chicago, 1967; London, 1973)

108 Gazzaniga, Michael, 'The Split Brain in Man' in Ornstein (ed.) *The Nature of Human Consciousness* (San Francisco, 1973)

109 Goldberg, Steven, *Male Dominance* (New York, 1973)

110 Goleman, Daniel, *The Varieties of Meditative Experience* (New York, 1977)

111 Gould, Stephen Jay, 'Punctuated Equilibrium – A Different Way of Seeing' in *New Scientist*, 15.4.82

112 Grad, Bernard, 'Healing by the Laying on of Hands' in Sobel (ed.) *Ways to Health* (New York, 1979)

113 Green, Celia, *Out-of-the-Body Experiences* (London, 1968)

114 Green, Celia, *Lucid Dreams* (London, 1968)

115 Green, Elmer and Alyce, *Beyond Biofeedback* (New York, 1977)

116 Greenberg, Ira, *Psychodrama Theory and Therapy* (New York, 1974)

117 Greenhouse, Herbert, *The Astral Journey* (New York, 1975)

118 Greer, Germaine, *The Female Eunuch* (London and New York, 1971)

119 Grey Walter, W., *Observations of Man, His Frame, His Duty and His Expectations* (Cambridge, 1969)

120 Gribbin, John (ed.), *The Breathing Planet* (Oxford, 1986)

121 Grof, Stanislav, *Realms of the Human Unconscious* (New York, 1976)

122 Grossman, Richard, *Planet Medicine* (Boulder, Colorado and London, 1982)

123 Hall, Calvin, *The Meaning of Dreams* (New York, 1953)

124 Harrington, Michael, *The Twilight of Capitalism* (New York, 1976)

125 Heidegger, Martin, *Being and Time* (London and New York, 1962)

126 Heisenberg, Werner, *Physics and Philosophy* (New York, 1962)

127 Henry, S. M., *Symbiosis* (New York, 1966)

128 Herrigel, E., *Zen and the Art of Archery* (New York, 1971)

129 Heuvelmans, Bernard, *On the*

Track of Unknown Animals (London, 1958)

130 Hilbert, D. and Cohn-Vossen, S., *Geometry and the Imagination* (New York, 1971)

131 Hilgard, E. R., *Hypnotic Susceptibility* (New York, 1965)

132 Hilgard, E. R., *The Experience of Hypnosis* (London and New York, 1968)

133 Hitching, Francis, *Pendulum* (London, 1977)

134 Hoag, J. M., *Osteopathic Medicine* (New York, 1969)

135 Hoffmann, Banesh, *The Strange Story of the Quantum* (New York, 1959)

136 Hoyle, Fred, *The Intelligent Universe* (London, 1982)

137 Hoyle, Fred and Wickramasinghe, C., *Lifecloud* (London, 1978)

138 Hubbard, L. Ron, *Scientology* (Los Angeles, 1967)

139 Hulke, M. (ed.), *The Encyclopaedia of Alternative Medicine and Self-Help* (London, 1978)

140 Hulme, T. E., *Speculations* (London, 1922)

141 Husserl, Edmund, *Ideas: General Introduction to Pure Phenomenology* (London, 1931)

142 Huxley, Aldous, *The Art of Seeing* (London, 1943)

143 Huxley, Aldous, *The Perennial Philosophy* (New York, 1970)

144 Illich, Ivan, *Medical Nemesis* (London and New York, 1975)

145 Inglis, Brian and West, Ruth, *The Alternative Health Guide* (London, 1983)

146 Inyushin, Victor, 'Bioplasma, The Fifth State of Matter?' in White and Krippner (eds)

Future Science (New York, 1977)

147 Irwin, Yukiko, *Shiatzu* (London, 1977)

148 Isherwood, Christopher (ed.), *Vedanta for the Western World* (London, 1948)

149 James, William, *The Varieties of Religious Experience* (London and New York, 1902)

150 James, William, *Pragmatism* (New York, 1907)

151 Janov, Arthur, *The Primal Scream, Primal Therapy* (New York, 1970)

152 Jantsch, Erich, *The Self-Organizing Universe* (New York, 1980)

153 Jeans, James, *The Mysterious Universe* (London and New York, 1930)

154 Jensen, B., *The Science and Practice of Iridology* (Essondido, California, 1974)

155 Jonas, Hans, *The Gnostic Religion* (Boston, 1958)

156 Jung, Carl Gustav, *Psychological Types* (Collected Works, vol. 6, 1921)

157 Jung, Carl Gustav, *The Structure and Dynamics of the Psyche* (Collected Works, vol. 8, 1927)

158 Jung, Carl Gustav, *Psychology and Alchemy* (Collected Works, vol. 12, 1944)

159 Jung, Carl Gustav, *Flying Saucers* (Collected Works, vol. 10, 1958)

160 Jung, Carl Gustav, *Memories, Dreams, Reflections* (Collected Works, vol. 16, 1967)

161 Jung, Carl Gustav and Pauli, W., *Synchronicity: An Acausal Connecting Principle* (Collected Works, vol. 8, 1952)

162 Kahn, H. and Wiener, A. J.,

Bibliography

The Year 2000 (New York, 1967; London, 1969)

163 Karlins, M. and Andrews, L., *Biofeedback* (New York, 1972; London, 1975)

164 Kierkegaard, Søren, *Concluding Unscientific Postscript* (Princeton, 1968)

165 Kilner, Walter, *The Human Atmosphere* (London, 1911; New York, 1974)

166 King, Francis, *The Cosmic Influence* (London, 1976)

167 Koestler, Arthur, *The Case of the Midwife Toad* (London, 1971)

168 Koestler, Arthur, *The Roots of Coincidence* (London, 1972)

169 Koestler, Arthur, *Janus: A Summing Up* (London, 1978)

170 Koestler, Arthur and Smythies, J. R. (eds), *Beyond Reductionism* (London, 1969)

171 Korzybski, Alfred, *Science and Sanity* (Lakeville, Connecticut, 1933)

172 Kriege, Theodor, *Fundamental Basis of Iris Diagnosis* (London, 1969)

173 Krippner, S. and Rubin, D., *Galaxies of Life* (New York, 1973)

174 Krishna, Gopi, *Kundalini: Evolutionary Energy in Man* (Berkeley, 1971)

175 Krishna, Gopi, 'Prana, The Traditional and the Modern View' in White and Krippner, *Future Science* (New York, 1977)

176 Kübler-Ross, Elisabeth, *On Death and Dying* (New York, 1969)

177 Kübler-Ross, Elisabeth, *Death: The Final Stage of Growth* (Englewood Cliffs, N.J., 1975)

178 Kuhn, Thomas S., *The Structure of Scientific Revolutions* (Chicago, 1962 and 1970)

179 Laing, Ronald, *The Divided Self* (London, 1960)

180 Lao-Tzu (tr. Feng and English), *Tao Te Ching* (New York, 1972)

181 Laszlo, Irvin, *Introduction to Systems Philosophy* (New York, 1968)

182 Latner, Joel, *The Gestalt Therapy Book* (New York, 1973)

183 Laurence, R. and Upton, C., *Psionic Medicine* (London, 1974)

184 Leadbeater, C. W., *The Hidden Side of Things* (Madras, 1923)

185 Leadbeater, C. W., *The Chakras* (Wheaton, Illinois, 1972)

186 Lee, S. G. M. and Mayes, A. R., *Dreams and Dreaming* (London, 1973)

187 Leftwich, Robert H., *Dowsing* (Wellingborough, 1976)

188 LeShan, Lawrence, *The Medium, the Mystic and the Physicist* (New York, 1974)

189 LeShan, Lawrence, *How to Meditate* (New York, 1974)

190 Lilly, John, *The Center of the Cyclone* (New York, 1972)

191 Lilly, John, *The Deep Self*.

192 De Liso, Oscar, *Padre Pio* (New York, 1960)

193 Liu, Da., *Tai Chi and I Ching* (London, 1975)

194 Lorenz, Konrad, *On Aggression* (London, 1966; New York, 1969)

195 Lovelock, James, *Gaia: A New Look at Life on Earth* (London and New York, 1979)

196 Lowen, Alexander, *Bioenergetics* (New York, 1975)

197 Luce, Gay Gaer, *Body Time* (London, 1972)

198 Macbeth, N., *Darwin Retried* (London and New York, 1971)

199 Macquarrie, J., *The Scope of Demythologising* (London, 1960; New York, 1961)

200 McGraw, E., *Population Today* (London, 1979)

201 Maltz, Maxwell, *Psychocybernetics* (New York, 1967)

202 Mann, Edward, *Orgone, Reich and Eros* (New York, 1973)

203 Mann, Felix, *Acupuncture: Ancient Art of Chinese Healing* (London, 1971)

204 Marmet, Abbé, *Principles and Practice of Radiesthesia* (London, 1959 and 1975)

205 Maslow, Abraham, *Religions, Values and Peak Experiences* (New York, 1964)

206 Maslow, Abraham, *Toward a Psychology of Being* (Princeton, 1969)

207 Maslow, Abraham, *The Farthest Reaches of Human Nature* (New York, 1970)

208 Masters, R. and Houston, J., *The Varieties of Psychedelic Experience* (New York, 1966)

209 Mathers, Macgregor, *The Kabbalah Unveiled* (London, 1951)

210 Maury, Marguerite, *The Secret of Life and Youth* (London, 1964)

211 Mead, G. S., *Fragments of a Faith Forgotten* (New York, 1960)

212 Meadows, D. H., *et al.*, *The Limits to Growth* (New York, 1972)

213 Melzack, Ronald, *The Puzzle of Pain* (London, 1973)

214 Merchant, Carolyn, *The Death of Nature: Women, Ecology and the Scientific Revolution* (New York, 1980; London, 1982)

215 Merleau-Ponty, Maurice, *The Phenomenology of Perception* (London and New York, 1962)

216 Messegué, Maurice, *Health Secrets of Plants and Herbs* (London, 1981)

217 Metzner, Ralph, *Maps of Consciousness* (New York, 1972)

218 Michell, John, *A View Over Atlantis* (London, 1969)

219 Millett, Kate, *Sexual Politics* (New York, 1970; London, 1971)

220 Mishlove, Jeff, *The Roots of Consciousness* (New York, 1975)

221 Mishra, R., *Yoga Sutras: The Textbook of Yoga Psychology* (New York, 1973)

222 Miura, I. and Fuller-Sasaki, R., *The Zen Koan* (New York, 1965)

223 Monroe, Robert, *Journeys Out of the Body* (London, 1972)

224 Moreno, Jacob L., *Psychodrama* (New York, 1959)

225 Morris, Desmond, *The Naked Ape* (London, 1967)

226 Morris, Desmond, *Manwatching* (London, 1977)

227 Moss, Thelma, *The Possibility of the Impossible* (Los Angeles, 1974)

228 Mumford, Lewis, *The Story and Utopias* (New York, 1922)

229 Murphy, Gardner, *The Challenge of Psychical Research* (New York, 1961)

230 Murphy, Gardner, *Human Potentialities* (New York, 1958 and 1975)

231 Murray, Margaret, *The God*

of the Witches (New York, 1960)

232 Myers, F. W. H., *Human Personality and Its Survival of Bodily Death* (London, 1903)

233 Nagel, E. and Newman, J. R., *Gödel's Proof* (New York, 1958; London, 1959)

234 Needleman, Jacob, *The New Religions* (New York, 1970)

235 Needleman, Jacob, *The Heart of Philosophy* (New York, 1982; London, 1983)

236 Neumann, John von and Morgenstern, O., *The Theory of Games & Economic Behavior* (New York, 1944)

237 Newman Turner, R., *Naturopathic Medicine* (Wellingborough, 1984)

238 Odun, E. P., *Fundamentals of Ecology* (Philadelphia, 1971)

239 Oparin, A. I., *The Origin of Life on Earth* (Edinburgh, 1957)

240 O'Riordan, T., *Environmentalism* (London, 1976)

241 Ornstein, R., *The Psychology of Consciousness* (New York, 1973)

242 Ornstein, R. (ed.), *The Nature of Human Consciousness* (San Francisco, 1973)

243 Osis, Karlis, *Deathbed Observations of Doctors and Nurses* (New York, 1961)

244 Ouspensky, P. D., *In Search of the Miraculous* (New York, 1949)

245 Owen, Iris and Sparrow, M., *Conjuring up Philip – An Adventure in Psychokinesis* (New York, 1976)

246 Panati, Charles, *The Geller Papers* (New York, 1976)

247 Parker, Adrian, *States of Mind* (London, 1975)

248 Patterson, W., *Nuclear Power* (London, 1976)

249 Peccei, Aurelio, *100 Pages for the Future* (London, 1982)

250 Pelletier, K. and Garfield, C., *Consciousness East and West* (New York, 1976)

251 Perls, Fritz, *Gestalt Therapy Verbatim* (New York, 1971)

252 Playfair, Guy Lyon, *The Flying Cow* (London, 1975)

253 Poncé, Charles, *The Game of the Wizards* (London, 1975)

254 Popper, Karl, *The Logic of Scientific Discovery* (London, 1959; New York, 1965)

255 Prigogine, Ilya and Stengers, Isabelle, *Order out of Chaos* (London and New York, 1984)

256 Puthoff, H. and Targ, R., *Mind-Reach* (New York, 1977)

257 Puthoff, H. and Targ, R., 'Information Transfer under Conditions of Sensory Shielding' in *Nature*, 1974

258 Rank, Otto, *Will Therapy, Truth and Reality* (New York, 1945)

259 Regush, Nicholas, *The Human Aura* (New York, 1974)

260 Reich, Wilhelm, *Character Analysis* (London, 1958)

261 Reich, Wilhelm, *The Function of the Orgasm* (New York, 1961; London, 1966)

262 Rhine, J. B., *Extra-Sensory Perception* (rev. edn, Boston, 1964)

263 Rhine, Louisa, *Psychokinesis* (New York, 1972)

264 Rich, Adrienne, *Of Woman Born* (New York, 1977)

265 Rifkin, Jeremy, *Entropy* (New York, 1980)

266 Rifkin, Jeremy, *Algeny* (New York, 1983; London, 1984)

267 Roberts, Jane, *Seth Speaks* (Englewood Cliffs, N.J., 1972)

268 Roberts, Jane, *The Seth Material* (New York, 1976)

269 Rogers, Carl, *Client-Centered Therapy* (New York, 1951; London, 1965)

270 Rogers, Carl, *On Becoming a Person* (London, 1974)

271 Rolf, Ida, *Structural Integration* (New York, 1977)

272 Rose, Steven, *The Chemistry of Life* (London, 1970)

273 Rose, Steven, *et al.*, *Not in Our Genes* (London and New York, 1984)

274 Ross, Shirley, *Fasting* (London, 1978)

275 Roszak, Theodore, *The Making of a Counter Culture* (New York, 1968; London, 1970)

276 Roszak, Theodore, *Where the Wasteland Ends* (New York, 1972; London, 1973)

277 Roszak, Theodore, *Unfinished Animal* (New York, 1975; London, 1976)

278 Russell, Edward W., *Design for Destiny* (London, 1975)

279 Sagan, Carl and Page (eds), *UFOs: A Scientific Debate* (New York, 1974)

280 Sagan, Carl and Shklovsky, J., *Intelligent Life in the Universe* (New York, 1976; London, 1977)

281 Salter, W. H., *Evidence for Survival from Cross-Correspondences* (London, 1938)

282 Sans, C., *About Macrobiotics* (Wellingborough, 1972)

283 Sartre, Jean-Paul, *Being and Nothingness* (New York, 1956)

284 Sartre, Jean-Paul, *Existentialism and Humanism* (London, 1958)

285 Schrödinger, Erwin, *What is Life?* (Cambridge, 1944; New York, 1945)

286 Schultz, J. and Luthe, W., *Autogenic Training* (New York, 1959)

287 Schultz, Wm C., *Elements of Encounter* (New York, 1975)

288 Schumacher, E. F., *Small is Beautiful* (New York and London, 1974)

289 Scofield, A. G., *Chiropractic* (Wellingborough, 1968)

290 Seyle, Hans, *Stress Without Distress* (New York, 1974; London, 1975)

291 Shah, Idries, *The Sufis* (London, 1964; New York, 1971)

292 Shah, Idries, *The Way of the Sufi* (London, 1974)

293 Shannon, C. E. and Weaver, W., *The Mathematical Theory of Communication* (Urbana, Illinois, 1949)

294 Sheldrake, Rupert, *A New Science of Life* (London and Los Angeles, 1982)

295 Shirley, Ralph, *The Mystery of the Human Double* (London and New York, 1972)

296 Silberer, H., *Hidden Symbolism of Alchemy and the Occult Arts* (New York, 1971)

297 Simonton, Carl, *Getting Well Again* (Los Angeles, 1978)

298 Simonton, Carl, *The Role of Mind in Cancer Therapy* in Carlson (ed.) No. 46

299 Sinnett, A. P., *Esoteric Buddhism* (Madras, 1898)

Bibliography

300 Skinner, B. F., *Science and Human Behavior* (New York, 1953)

301 Skinner, B. F., *Walden Two* (New York, 1962)

302 Skinner, B. F., *Beyond Freedom and Dignity* (New York, 1975)

303 Skinner, Stephen, *The Living Earth Manual of Feng-Shui* (London, 1982)

304 Smith, Justa, *Bioenergetics in Healing* in Carlson (ed.) No. 46

305 Smuts, Jan, *Holism and Evolution* (London, 1926)

306 Spretnak, C. and Capra, F., *Green Politics* (London, 1984)

307 Stanford, Rex, 'Clairvoyance' in Mitchell (ed.) *Psychic Exploration* (New York, 1974)

308 Stapp, H. P., 'Quantum Theory and Bell's Theorem' in *Foundations of Physics*, Feb. 1979

309 Stassinopoulos, A., *The Female Woman* (London, 1974)

310 Steiner, Rudolf, *The Evolution of Consciousness* (London, 1966)

311 Steiner, Rudolf, *Occult Science* (London, 1969)

312 Stevenson, Ian, *Twenty Cases Suggestive of Reincarnation* (Charlottesville, Virginia, 1974)

313 Szasz, Thomas, *The Myth of Mental Illness* (New York, 1961)

314 Szent-Gyorgi, A., 'Syntropy' in *Synthesis*, spring 1974

315 Tansley, David, *Radionics and the Subtle Anatomy of Man* (London, 1972)

316 Tart, Charles T., *Psi: Scientific Studies of the Psychic Realm* (New York, 1977)

317 Tart, Charles T., 'States of Consciousness and State-Specific Sciences' in Ornstein (ed.) No. 220

318 Tart, Charles T., 'Out-of-the-Body Experiences' in Mitchell (ed.) *Psychic Exploration* (New York, 1974)

319 Tart, Charles T. (ed.), *Altered States of Consciousness* (New York, 1969)

320 Tart, Charles T., 'Physiological Correlates of Psi Transmission' in *International Journal of Parapsychology*, no. 5, 1963

321 Taylor, John, *Black Holes* (London, 1973)

322 Thommen, George, *Is This Your Day?* (New York, 1973)

323 Tiger, L. and Fox, R., *The Imperial Animal* (New York, 1971; London, 1972)

324 Tisserand, R., *The Art of Aromatherapy* (London, 1977)

325 Toben, Bob, *Space-Time and Beyond* (New York, 1975)

326 Toffler, Alvin, *Future Shock* (New York, 1971)

327 Toguchi, Masaru, *The Complete Guide to Acupuncture* (Wellingborough, 1974)

328 Trefil, James, *From Atoms to Quarks* (New York, 1980)

329 Ullman, M., Krippner, S. and Vaughan, A., *Dream Telepathy* (New York, 1973)

330 Underhill, Evelyn, *Mysticism* (New York, 1961)

331 Underwood, Guy, *The Pattern of the Past* (London, 1969)

332 Vallée, Jacques, *UFOs: The Psychic Solution* (New York, 1975; London, 1977)

333 Vaughan, Alan, *Patterns of Prophecy* (London, 1974)

334 Velikovsky, Immanuel, *Worlds*

in Collision (London and New York, 1950)

335 Velikovsky, Immanuel, *Ages in Chaos* (London and New York, 1953)

336 Velikovsky, Immanuel, *Earth in Upheaval* (London and New York, 1955)

337 Waddington, C. H., *Tools for Thought* (London, 1977)

338 Ward, B. and Dubos, R., *Only One Earth* (London and New York, 1972)

339 Watkins, Alfred, *The Old Straight Track* (London, 1925)

340 Watson, James, *The Double Helix* (London, 1972)

341 Watson, J. B., *Behavior* (New York, 1914)

342 Watson, J. B., *Behaviorism* (New York, 1970)

343 Watson, Lyall, *Supernature* (London, 1973)

344 Watson, Lyall, 'Is Primitive Medicine Really Primitive?' in Carlson, No. 46

345 Watts, A. W., *The Way of Zen* (New York, 1957)

346 Weinberg, Stephen, *The First Three Minutes* (New York and London, 1977)

347 Weizenbaum, J., *Computer Power and Human Reason* (San Francisco, 1976)

348 Westbrook, A. and Ratti, O., *Aikido and the Dynamic Sphere* (New York, 1970)

349 Wheeler, John A., *Geometrodynamics* (New York, 1962)

350 Whitehead, A. N., *Science and the Modern World* (London and New York, 1926)

351 Whitehead, A. N., *Process and Reality* (London and New York, 1929)

352 Whyte, L. L., *The Unconscious Before Freud* (New York, 1960; London, 1962)

353 Wiener, Norbert, *Cybernetics* (New York, 1948)

354 Wilber, K. (ed.), *The Holographic Paradigm* (Boulder, Colorado and London, 1982)

355 Wilhelm, Richard (tr.), *The I Ching* (New York, 1950; London, 1951)

356 Williams, Charles, *Witchcraft* (New York, 1975; London, 1976)

357 Wilson, Colin, *The Occult* (London and New York, 1971)

358 Wilson, Colin, *Poltergeist* (London, 1982)

359 Wilson, Colin, *The Psychic Detectives* (London, 1984)

360 Wilson, E. O., *Sociobiology: The New Synthesis* (Cambridge, Mass., 1975)

361 Wittgenstein, L., *Philosophical Investigations* (Oxford, 1953)

362 Zaner, R. and Ihde, D., *Phenomenology and Existentialism* (New York, 1973)

Index of Names

With over 150 titles currently in print, Arkana is the leading name in quality new-age books for mind, body and spirit. Arkana encompasses the spirituality of both East and West, ancient and new, in fiction and non-fiction. A vast range of interests are covered, including Psychology and Transformation, Health, Science and Mysticism, Women's Spirituality and Astrology.

If you would like a catalogue of Arkana books, please write to:

Arkana Marketing Department
Penguin Books Ltd
27 Wright's Lane
London W8 5TZ

ARKANA – NEW-AGE BOOKS FOR MIND, BODY AND SPIRIT

A selection of titles already published or in preparation

The I Ching and You Diana ffarington Hook

A clear, accessible, step-by-step guide to the *I Ching* – the classic book of Chinese wisdom. Ideal for the reader seeking a quick guide to its fundamental principles, and the often highly subtle shades of meaning of its eight trigrams and sixty-four hexagrams.

A History of Yoga Vivian Worthington

The first of its kind, *A History of Yoga* chronicles the uplifting teachings of this ancient art in its many guises: at its most simple a beneficial exercise; at its purest an all-embracing quest for the union of body and mind.

Tao Te Ching The Richard Wilhelm Edition

Encompassing philosophical speculation and mystical reflection, the *Tao Te Ching* has been translated more often than any other book except the Bible, and more analysed than any other Chinese classic. Richard Wilhelm's acclaimed 1910 translation is here made available in English.

The Book of the Dead E. A. Wallis Budge

Intended to give the deceased immortality, the Ancient Egyptian *Book of the Dead* was a vital piece of 'luggage' on the soul's journey to the other world, providing for every need: victory over enemies, the procurement of friendship and – ultimately – entry into the kingdom of Osiris.

Yoga: Immortality and Freedom Mircea Eliade

Eliade's excellent volume explores the tradition of yoga with exceptional directness and detail.

'One of the most important and exhaustive single-volume studies of the major ascetic techniques of India and their history yet to appear in English' – *San Francisco Chronicle*

ARKANA – NEW-AGE BOOKS FOR MIND, BODY AND SPIRIT

A selection of titles already published or in preparation

Weavers of Wisdom: Women Mystics of the Twentieth Century Anne Bancroft

Throughout history women have sought answers to eternal questions about existence and beyond – yet most gurus, philosophers and religious leaders have been men. Through exploring the teachings of fifteen women mystics – each with her own approach to what she calls 'the truth that goes beyond the ordinary' – Anne Bancroft gives a rare, cohesive and fascinating insight into the diversity of female approaches to mysticism.

Dynamics of the Unconscious: Seminars in Psychological Astrology Volume II Liz Greene and Howard Sasportas

The authors of *The Development of the Personality* team up again to show how the dynamics of depth psychology interact with your birth chart. They shed new light on the psychology and astrology of aggression and depression – the darker elements of the adult personality that we must confront if we are to grow to find the wisdom within.

The Myth of Eternal Return: Cosmos and History Mircea Eliade

'A luminous, profound, and extremely stimulating work . . . Eliade's thesis is that ancient man envisaged events not as constituting a linear, progressive history, but simply as so many creative repetitions of primordial archetypes . . . This is an essay which everyone interested in the history of religion and in the mentality of ancient man will have to read. It is difficult to speak too highly of it' – Theodore H. Gaster in *Review of Religion*.

Karma and Destiny in the I Ching Guy Damian-Knight

This entirely original approach to the *I Ching*, achieved through mathematical rearrangement of the hexagrams, offers a new, more precise tool for self-understanding. Simple to use and yet profound, it gives the ancient Chinese classic a thoroughly contemporary relevance.

ARKANA – NEW-AGE BOOKS FOR MIND, BODY AND SPIRIT

A selection of titles already published or in preparation

A Course in Miracles: The Course, Workbook for Students and Manual for Teachers

Hailed as 'one of the most remarkable systems of spiritual truth available today', *A Course in Miracles* is a self-study course designed to shift our perceptions, heal our minds and change our behaviour, teaching us to experience miracles – 'natural expressions of love' – rather than problems generated by fear in our lives.

Medicine Woman: A Novel Lynn Andrews

The intriguing story of a white woman's journey of self-discovery among the Heyoka Indians – from the comforts of civilisation to the wilds of Canada. Apprenticed to a medicine woman, she learns tribal wisdom and mysticism – and above all the power of her own womanhood.

Arthur and the Sovereignty of Britain: Goddess and Tradition in the Mabinogion Caitlín Matthews

Rich in legend and the primitive magic of the Celtic Otherworld, the stories of the *Mabinogion* heralded the first flowering of European literature and became the source of Arthurian legend. Caitlín Matthews illuminates these stories, shedding light on Sovereignty, the Goddess of the Land and the spiritual principle of the Feminine.

Shamanism: Archaic Techniques of Ecstasy Mircea Eliade

Throughout Siberia and Central Asia, religious life traditionally centres around the figure of the shaman: magician and medicine man, healer and miracle-doer, priest and poet.

'Has become the standard work on the subject and justifies its claim to be the first book to study the phenomenon over a wide field and in a properly religious context' – *The Times Literary Supplement*

ARKANA – NEW-AGE BOOKS FOR MIND, BODY AND SPIRIT

A selection of titles already published or in preparation

Head Off Stress: Beyond the Bottom Line D. E. Harding

Learning to head off stress takes no time at all and is impossible to forget – all it requires is that we dare take a fresh look at ourselves. This infallible and revolutionary guide from the author of *On Having No Head* – whose work C. S. Lewis described as 'highest genius' – shows how.

Shiatzu: Japanese Finger Pressure for Energy, Sexual Vitality and Relief from Tension and Pain
Yukiko Irwin with James Wagenvoord

The product of 4000 years of Oriental medicine and philosophy, Shiatzu is a Japanese variant of the Chinese practice of acupuncture. Fingers, thumbs and palms are applied to the 657 pressure points that the Chinese penetrate with gold and silver needles, aiming to maintain health, increase vitality and promote well-being.

The Magus of Strovolos: The Extraordinary World of a Spiritual Healer Kyriacos C. Markides

This vivid account introduces us to the rich and intricate world of Daskalos, the Magus of Strovolos – a true healer who draws upon a seemingly limitless mixture of esoteric teachings, psychology, reincarnation, demonology, cosmology and mysticism, from both East and West.

'This is a really marvellous book . . . one of the most extraordinary accounts of a "magical" personality since Ouspensky's account of Gurdjieff' – Colin Wilson

Meetings With Remarkable Men G. I. Gurdjieff

All that we know of the early life of Gurdjieff – one of the great spiritual masters of this century – is contained within these colourful and profound tales of adventure. The men who influenced his formative years had no claim to fame in the conventional sense; what made them remarkable was the consuming desire they all shared to understand the deepest mysteries of life.

ARKANA – NEW-AGE BOOKS FOR MIND, BODY AND SPIRIT

A selection of titles already published or in preparation

The TM Technique Peter Russell

Through a process precisely opposite to that by which the body accumulates stress and tension, transcendental meditation works to produce a state of profound rest, with positive benefits for health, clarity of mind, creativity and personal stability. Peter Russell's book has become the key work for everyone requiring a complete mastery of TM.

The Development of the Personality: Seminars in Psychological Astrology Volume I Liz Greene and Howard Sasportas

Taking as a starting point their groundbreaking work on the cross-fertilization between astrology and psychology, Liz Greene and Howard Sasportas show how depth psychology works with the natal chart to illuminate the experiences and problems all of us encounter throughout the development of our individual identity, from childhood onwards.

Homage to the Sun: The Wisdom of the Magus of Strovolos
Kyriacos C. Markides

Homage to the Sun continues the adventure into the mysterious and extraordinary world of the spiritual teacher and healer Daskalos, the 'Magus of Strovolos'. The logical foundations of Daskalos' world of other dimensions are revealed to us – invisible masters, past-life memories and guardian angels, all explained by the Magus with great lucidity and scientific precision.

The Year I: Global Process Work Arnold Mindell

As we approach the end of the 20th century, we are on the verge of planetary extinction. Solving the planet's problems is literally a matter of life and death. Arnold Mindell shows how his famous and groundbreaking process-orientated psychology can be extended so that our own sense of global awareness can be developed and we – the whole community of earth's inhabitants – can comprehend the problems and work together towards solving them.

ARKANA – NEW-AGE BOOKS FOR MIND, BODY AND SPIRIT

A selection of titles already published or in preparation

Encyclopedia of the Unexplained
Edited by Richard Cavendish   Consultant: J. B. Rhine

'Will probably be the definitive work of its kind for a long time to come' – *Prediction*

The ultimate guide to the unknown, the esoteric and the unproven: richly illustrated, with almost 450 clear and lively entries from Alchemy, the Black Box and Crowley to faculty X, Yoga and the Zodiac.

Buddhist Civilization in Tibet   Tulku Thondup Rinpoche

Unique among works in English, *Buddhist Civilization in Tibet* provides an astonishing wealth of information on the various strands of Tibetan religion and literature in a single compact volume, focusing predominantly on the four major schools of Buddhism: Nyingma, Kagyud, Sakya and Gelug.

The Living Earth Manual of Feng-Shui   Stephen Skinner

The ancient Chinese art of Feng-Shui – tracking the hidden energy flow which runs through the earth in order to derive maximum benefit from being in the right place at the right time – can be applied equally to the siting and layout of cities, houses, tombs and even flats and bedsits; and can be practised as successfully in the West as in the East with the aid of this accessible manual.

In Search of the Miraculous: Fragments of an Unknown Teaching   P. D. Ouspensky

Ouspensky's renowned, vivid and characteristically honest account of his work with Gurdjieff from 1915–18.

'Undoubtedly a *tour de force*. To put entirely new and very complex cosmology and psychology into fewer than 400 pages, and to do this with a simplicity and vividness that makes the book accessible to any educated reader, is in itself something of an achievement' – *The Times Literary Supplement*